PERCEPTION OF LANGUAGE

MERRILL'S
INTERNATIONAL PSYCHOLOGY
SERIES

Under the Editorship of

DONALD B. LINDSLEY
University of California at Los Angeles

and

ARTHUR W. MELTON
University of Michigan

PERCEPTION
OF
LANGUAGE

Conference Chairman
PAUL M. KJELDERGAARD
University of Pittsburgh

Edited by
DAVID L. HORTON
University of Maryland
and
JAMES J. JENKINS
University of Minnesota

Proceedings of a Symposium of the
LEARNING RESEARCH AND DEVELOPMENT CENTER
University of Pittsburgh

CHARLES E. MERRILL PUBLISHING COMPANY
Columbus, Ohio   *A Bell & Howell Company*

International Standard Book Number: 0-675-09250-7

Library of Congress Catalogue Card Number: 75-139963

1 2 3 4 5 6 7 8 9 10—75 74 73 72 71

PRINTED IN THE UNITED STATES OF AMERICA

74   916

To Maxine, Eric, and Mark

Paul M. Kjeldergaard
1931-1968

This book is dedicated to the memory of Paul Myron Kjelder-gaard who arranged the conference reported here and served as its chairman. His premature death cut short a productive and promising career and deprived us of a warm, thoughtful and affectionate friend.

Paul Kjeldergaard was born in St. Paul, Minnesota. All of his higher education was at the University of Minnesota where I first knew him as an undergraduate major in psychology. His interests, at first, were in applied psychology and together we decided that he should pursue a career in that field. Accordingly, after his Bachelor's degree (*cum laude*), he concentrated on the applied aspects of psychology for his Master's degree and worked part-time both in the counseling bureau and in a survey research firm. His work during this period (exemplified by his unique study of the semantic image of a newscaster[1]) led him to increased concern with fundamental issues in the psychology of language. He decided to go on for his Doctorate with a concentration on experimental psychology and verbal behavior.

From 1957 to 1959, Paul and David Horton were both part-time instructors at Minnesota. The three of us formed, and were the sole participants in, a singularly intense and serious seminar. Once each week we met for four hours to work through some portion of the scholarly literature related to verbal behavior. I remember those sessions as models of intense and careful analyses of experiments. Out of the seminar came their Ph.D. theses and their joint Psychological Monograph[2] which I regard as a fundamental contribution to the experimental study of verbal mediation.

In 1959, Paul went off to the Harvard Graduate School of Education to teach and to work with John B. Carroll as a research asso-

---

[1]Attitudes towards newscasters as measured by the semantic differential: a descriptive case. *J. appl. Psychol.*, 1961, **45**, 35-40.

[2]With D. L. Horton. An experimental analysis of associative factors in mediated generalization. *Psychol. Monographs*, 1961, **75**, Whole No. 515.

ciate. His interests roamed broadly over a set of related areas as he reviewed work in the psychology of language and second language learning.[3] He and Carroll launched a set of studies of free and constrained word association behavior.[4] He turned his attention to a reanalysis of the data of the semantic atlas and with his students teased out the interrelations between various measures of word meaning and meaningfulness.[5]

In the fall of 1964, Robert Glaser invited Paul to join him at the Learning Research and Development Center at the University of Pittsburgh. At the Center, Paul turned again to problems in applied psychology, such as the teaching of reading, but also continued his work in theoretically interesting issues. In the spring of 1965, he reviewed the work on mediation for the conference that Dixon and Horton had planned at the University of Kentucky[6] and, in the summer of 1966, he returned to Minnesota for a special summer session on higher mental processes. As things turned out, conferences became our usual way of keeping in touch. Under Glaser's gentle guidance, someone was rounding up an interesting conference at Pittsburgh every year and we usually managed to meet there or at a similar conference, give our respective papers and then try to catch up on one another's affairs until the next time. During such visits I learned of Paul's development of a set of unusual materials for teaching reading,[7] of his computer simulation of word association behavior,[8] and of his growing interest in the broad problem of the perception of language in all its forms.

Almost two years before the date of the conference reported here, Paul began conferring with people in a variety of fields as to the important contribution being made in the perception of language.

---

[3]The psychology of language. *Rev. of ed. Res.*, April, 1961, **31**, 119-29.

[4]With J. B. Carroll & A. S. Carton. Number of opposites versus number of primaries as a response measure in free-association tests. *J. verb. Learn. and verb. Behav.*, 1962, **1**, 22-30.

With J. B. Carroll. Two measures of free-association response and their relation to scores on selected personality and verbal ability tests. *Psychol. Reps.*, 1962, **12**, 667-70.

[5]With M. Higa. Degree of polarization and the recognition value of words selected from the semantic atlas. *Psychol. Reps.*, 1962, **11**, 619-20.

[6]Transfer and mediation in verbal learning. In T. Dixon and D. Horton (Eds.), Verbal learning theory and general S-R theory. Englewood Cliffs, N. J.: Prentice-Hall, 1968.

[7]With R. Frankenstein and R. Glaser. *Stepping Stones to Reading.* 12 vol. New York: Appleton-Century-Crofts, 1970 (in press).

[8]Simulation of cognition and learning: The role of individual differences. In R. Gagne (Ed.), *Learning and individual differences.* Columbus, Ohio: Charles E. Merrill Publishing Company, 1966. Pp. 346-63.

He was intrigued by the differences so apparent in the perception of language by the eye and by the ear. He was impressed with the vast areas of ignorance in the domain. He was interested in the possibilities of making progress by bringing together personnel from diverse areas and letting them interact within the confines of the conference format. At Glaser's urging and with the help of many people (particularly Franklin Cooper and Alvin Liberman of Haskins Laboratories), Paul put the conference together and took care of the host of things that go into making a conference a reality.

The conference was a notable success. The participants found it productive and stimulating. We learned a lot and felt that we had achieved some new understandings. Many of us were still phrasing our "thank you" letters when we learned that Paul was in the hospital. We scarcely had time to reflect on the surprise before we heard the unbelievable news of his death.

The book that follows is dedicated to him by his friends. David Horton has done most of the editorial work, Robert Glaser has supplied the resources and made available the skilled personnel who prepared the manuscript. I have helped in some small ways. It is not as good a book as it would have been in Paul's hands, but it is our hope that it will extend to readers the challenge and stimulation that the participants felt and that it will have the long-range productive effect that Paul intended it to have.

James J. Jenkins
April, 1970

FOREWORD BY THE CHAIRMAN

This report describes the proceedings of a conference held at the University of Pittsburgh on January 11-12, 1968. The conference brought together twenty psychologists and psycholinguists to present their particular research interests and to attempt to find communalities of thinking through discussion of "The Perception of Language." The following statement, prepared prior to the conference, represents the approach of the chairman in organizing the conference:

The past decade has produced evidence that has forced psychologists to re-evaluate the traditional views of the psychology of language, from those of the 1920s when J. B. Watson declared thinking to be "merely subvocal speech" to those of the mid-1950s when several psychologists including Mowrer, Osgood, and Skinner each attempted to fit language and language related phenomena into the traditional explanatory molds which served for the simpler behaviors investigated by the conditioning theorists. Conditioning theories are alike in that they assume that complex behavior is made up of a linear sequence of simple acts that evolve in a predetermined order. It has been shown both mathematically, and, to an extent, empirically, that language is not learned, generated, nor understood in this fashion. At the base of all languages is a simple set of recursive rules that permit speakers to understand and to generate an infinite set of sentences, most of which they have never heard nor said before.

The evidence that leads one to this position comes from many sources such as from child development, which has shown that young children develop a grammar prior to and independent of the adult grammar, a grammar which slowly evolves into the adult grammar. As the child approaches the adult form, he learns the grammatical rules, not in a simple trial and error, piece-meal fashion as the conditioning theories would lead us to expect, but rather he acquires them in a systematic fashion. Typically, a whole grammatical rule emerges at one time, relatively intact. For example, consider the ordinary pattern of a child mastering the past tense of the irregular verbs: first he uses the forms correctly due to specific learning; he then goes through a period where he produces incorrect forms as he learns and generalizes the grammatical rule governing the regular past tense; finally, he goes back to the appropriate specific forms as he learns that the irregular verbs are exceptions to the grammatical rule. One aspect of this behavior, difficult for the reinforcement theorists to account for, is that the inappropriate behavior that follows the "learning" of the grammatical rule is often highly resistant to extinction. This behavior occurs in spite of the fact that the child has never heard the incorrect response nor has he been reinforced for responding incorrectly; whereas, he had been reinforced for the earlier appropriate behavior.

Equally devastating to the traditional view of language is recent evidence from the field of experimental phonology. For example, two different phonemes / d / and / g / are physically (acoustically) more similar to each other when followed by the same vowel, say / e /, than the same phoneme, i.e., / d / and / d /, when it is followed by two different vowels. In spite of this, adults and very young children alike have no trouble producing or understanding either of these phonemes regardless of their vowel environments. To say that we learn as specifics all possible vowel-consonant or consonant-vowel combinations is non-parsimonious and difficult to accept. Furthermore, the principle of generalization gradients as worked out in the conditioning laboratories indicates that such fine discriminations would be difficult if not impossible to establish and maintain.

It has been demonstrated that the addition of blank pieces of recording tape spliced into otherwise normally recorded experiments can significantly alter the perception of what is being said. The blank may be perceived as an added phoneme (voiceless stop) or as stress (emphasis). Although the former might have been anticipated, the latter was not. In both instances the critical length of blank tape that must be inserted to affect the perception is very specific, not like the gradients that one might expect generalizing from the work in physical perception experiments.

One of the newest, most dramatic, and enigmatic phenomena to challenge the traditional viewpoint, is the work being done on micromuscular movement and speech synchronism. Armed with a slow motion camera, researchers have demonstrated that speech and the gestures of both the speakers *and the listener* are highly coordinated and synchronous. Gestures, eyeblinks, and other bodily movements begin and end on the phoneme boundaries. These findings hold cross culturally for very diverse language groups and also chronologically from infancy through adulthood. Since this phenomenon is not even observable without a slow motion camera, since the specific motions appear to be independent of the speech content, and since this finding appears to be a language universal, it appears unlikely that any extension of the traditional approaches to language will provide a useful account of this phenomenon.

This, then, is just a sampling of the evidence that indicates that an explanation of language demands a new, more powerful theory to explain the many facts that have been and are continuing to accumulate. The complexities of explanation that will be required may even require a new form of theory. Unfortunately, due to the newness and the complexity of these discoveries, no new theories have yet been offered as alternatives to the traditional approach. Those who are most involved have devoted their energies to proving the inadequacy of the available theories.

Paul M. Kjeldergaard
October, 1967

ACKNOWLEDGMENTS

The conference "The Perception of Language" was sponsored by the Learning Research and Development Center at the University of Pittsburgh with support from the Office of Naval Research. An expression of appreciation is offered to those of ONR and LRDC who made this conference possible.

A special expression of appreciation is extended to Robert Glaser whose initial discussions with Paul Kjeldergaard served as a springboard for organizing the conference and whose assistance after the conference assured that the proceedings got into print.

Gratitude is also expressed to Gayle Murrel who made the conference arrangements and assisted in transcribing the conference discussions. Barbara Howe, the typist of the manuscript, is thanked for her extensive effort. The editors are especially grateful to Mary Lou Marino who shouldered many of the difficult chores of organizing the entire manuscript effort and who managed to keep the efforts of all of us coordinated in spite of considerable separations of distance and time.

TABLE OF CONTENTS

Contents

1

LISTENING, READING AND GRAMMATICAL STRUCTURE[1]

HARRY LEVIN and ELEANOR L. KAPLAN[2]

Cornell University

Current linguistic and psycholinguistic theories emphasize that understanding language involves the recovery of the underlying functional relations among sentence components from the superficial linguistic input. However, the fact that these relations are not necessarily represented directly in the superficial structure, the left-to-right ordering of sentences, poses a particular problem for psychologists. It is thus essential to study the relationship between the temporal ordering of the input and these underlying functional relations in order to explain how a listener understands what he hears.

While it is obvious that sentences are not understood word-by-word from left-to-right, it is also obvious that listeners begin to understand sentences long before they are completed. That is,

[1]This research program was supported by the Bureau of Research, U. S. Office of Education.
[2]Now at Stanford University.

1

whole sentences are not fully examined from beginning to end and then understood. Instead, both listeners and readers alike, appear to decode sentences not only by interpreting as they hear or read, but also by anticipating what is likely to come next. A dramatic illustration of this point is provided by the Garden Path sentences first used by Quantz in 1897. The end of these sentences is discrepant with the interpretation suggested by the first part of the sentence. The fact that listeners and readers are amused by the sentences or do not understand them indicates that the interpretation given to the first part of the sentence led them to expect a specific and different ending. There are two important implications arising from the fact that listeners and readers alike, are able to decode or understand as they hear or read: (1) there must be some information in the input, i.e., some particularly informative aspect of sentence structure which extends more-or-less from left-to-right, "signalling" important sentential relations and (2) decoders can, in fact, utilize this structure to interpret or understand what they hear or read. It is important, then, to question the kind of structural properties in the input which mark these relations. In addition, it is interesting to speculate about a model for the process; that is, a model of how grammatical structure is actually used by decoders to facilitate language processing.

Two studies have examined the effects of particular linguistic patterns — the distribution of constraints among major sentence components — upon the decoding process. Consequently, sentences for which the pattern, or distribution of constraints, could be obtained were selected for study. The first study involved a comparison between active and passive sentences, while the second study compared the processing of left-embedded (or self-embedded) with right-embedded sentences. Since each sentence type was known to be constrained differently, systematic differences in processing were expected.

Our initial investigation involved a technique, the Eye-Voice Span, which taps the processing of orally read material. In reading aloud, the EVS is the distance, usually measured in words, that the eye is ahead of the voice. Although there is a substantial history behind the use of this technique, only a small portion of the literature is relevant to our investigations. Lawson (1961) and Morton (1964 a, b) demonstrated that the EVS increased with more structured or constrained materials; the more redundant the material, the larger the EVS. Schlesinger (1966) found that the size of the EVS varied with the phrase structure of the material. In addition, there have been consistent observations that the size of the EVS is directly related to the level of education, age, and reading rate of readers. These findings recommend EVS as a useful tool for studying the effects of structural constraints upon language processing.

There are two general procedures used to study the EVS, the first of which was used in our early studies. In this method, the subject is instructed to read aloud, and the text is then removed from his view at some predetermined point. The subject is instructed to report text that he has seen but not yet read aloud. The number of words the subject gives is his EVS. The procedure used in the first two studies simply consisted of rear projecting the material to be read on a small ground glass screen positioned directly in front of the subject. When the subject reached the appropriate point in the text, the shutter mounted on the projector was closed, removing the text from his view. In the third study the reading material was displayed inside a "light-box" behind a one-way mirror. When the light inside the box was illuminated, the text could be read; the text could be removed from view simply by turning off the light. We also administered a recognition test following this report as a check on "guessing" as well as to gauge any tendency for subjects to be conservative in their reports.

The second technique involves recording eye movements while the person is reading aloud. This technique as well as the one involving recording the eye movements during silent reading, was used in a more recent study. Only the small portion of the eye movement data that has been analyzed can be reported in this paper.

In spite of the volume of research on EVS, it is fair to say that we do not understand the details of the behaviors which result in longer or shorter spans. Input, processing, and performance are implicated a d the final behavior is likely a complex amalgamation of all three. Short-term memory plays a part. We are certain that the reader uot picking up the span peripherally as he focuses on the word he reading aloud. Rather, as he reads aloud he actively scans the succeeding text and this active process determines the length and nature of the span. We are also convinced that the span is not simply a guess about what is likely to be the text given the materials he has read. For one thing, the correct guessing of a string of words is highly improbable. For another, when we used the recognition task to measure the EVS, the probability of choosing a word that was not actually present in the text was less than one in a thousand.

STUDY 1. THE EYE-VOICE SPAN FOR ACTIVE AND PASSIVE SENTENCES

For this study two types of sentences — active and passive — within which the constraints were known to be differently distributed were selected for study. Clark (1965) had found that the pattern of contingencies between major sentence parts was quite different for active and passive sentences. His subjects generated sentences from active or passive sentence frames from which two or three of the major sentence parts, the actor, verb, or object, had been deleted. An uncertainty analysis of the results yielded a measure of the diversity of each sentence part and the extent to which the sentence parts co-varied. The uncertainties associated with the actors, verbs, and objects, and the patterns of constraint between them were found to be different within the two forms. The important finding here is that the latter part of the passive sentence, the verb and the actor, is highly constrained by the former part, the object; this was not true for the corresponding parts of active sentences. The latter part of the active sentence, the verb and object, is relatively independent of the former part, the actor. In addition, Clark (1966) and Roberts (1966) later demonstrated that recall for different sentence parts could be predicted from these uncertainties and contingencies.

We hypothesized, therefore, that if the EVS is sensitive to constraints within sentences it should increase toward the middle of the passive form but not increase toward the middle of the active form. More specifically, the EVS should increase when the reader reaches information which specifies that the sentence is a passive. This information is directly signalled by the form of the main verb phrase; and the subsequent *by phrase* offers additional confirmation of the passive form. There is no reason to believe that there is unequivocal information for this decision prior to either of these points.

Eighteen college students attending Cornell University served as subjects. The combination of two different phrase lengths with two different sentence types comprised the four sentence types used:

Active sentences composed of 4-word phrases
Passive sentences composed of 4-word phrases
Active sentences composed of 5-word phrases
Passive sentences composed of 5-word phrases

The 4-word-phrase sentences contained 19 words, broken up into five phrases or constituents: 4 words, 4 words, 3 words, 4 words, 4 words. The 5-word-phrase sentences contained 18 words divided into four phrases or constituents: 5 words, 5 words, 3 words, 5 words. The short 3-word phrase represented the *by phrase* in the 4- and 5-word-phrase active sentences. The sentences were constructed so that the first half of both the active and passive sentences were structurally identical. For example:

Passive: The cute chubby boy was slowly being wheeled by the maid along the pebbled lane to the quaint store.

Active: The brash tall man was certainly being loud at the rally of the new group on the main campus.

Differences in the size of the EVS could be attributed then to the presence or absence of the passive form. Each sentence was embedded in a separate paragraph of either four or five sentences. The sentences within each paragraph were not related in order to prevent inflation of the EVS by the subject's ability to guess succeeding words on the basis of context. Since exploratory data indicated that the subjects seemed to scan the first line before beginning to read aloud, the experimental or target sentence was never first. Target sentences were positioned so that there were at least three words preceding the critical word on the same line and at least eleven succeeding it for the 4-word-phrase sentences, eight for the 5-word-phrase sentences. Few subjects extended their EVS to the last word in the sentence.

In addition, 10 paragraphs made up entirely of lists of unrelated words were included in order to ascertain the relative contribution of syntactic structure to the variation in EVS. Finally, an additional 20 paragraphs were included as fillers. The first sentence in these paragraphs was treated as the target sentence in order to encourage the subject's equal attention to all sentences. These sentences were not included in the data analysis. There was a total of 142 paragraphs. Subjects were assigned to 1 of 6 different random presentation orders.

In order to satisfactorily examine differences in the processing strategies which occur as a consequence of differential linguistic constraints, we systematically measured the EVS at numerous places *(critical positions)*, within the set of experimental sentences. EVS scores were obtained at various points after the third word and after every succeeding word up to the *by phrase* in the passive sentences and the corresponding point in the active sentences, a prepositional phrase.

The paragraphs were exposed on a small ground glass rear projection screen directly in front of the subject, who was positioned so that he could scan the lines with minimal head movement. The size of the letters when projected on the screen was approximately equivalent to that found in texts. A fixation point, indicating where the beginning of each paragraph would appear, eliminated the need for the subject to search the screen each time a new paragraph was exposed. The contrast between the letters and the background was low enough to eliminate any after images.

As soon as the paragraph appeared on the screen, the subject began to read aloud at his normal reading rate. When the subject reached the predetermined place in the target sentence, the projector shutter closed, removing the material from view. The subject then reported all material he had seen but not yet read aloud. The number of correct words reported was considered his recall EVS for that sentence.

A recognition test was administered immediately after this report as a check on "guessing" and the subject's tendency to give conservative reports. The test consisted of recognition lists, one for each target sentence. All content words occurring after the critical word were included on the list. Function words were omitted since these words occurred more than once in a given target sentence, making it difficult to know which function word was referred to. In order to discourage guessing, the lists were constructed so that only 50 percent of the words actually appeared in the target sentence, while the other 50 percent were words that were visually and semantically similar to those that had appeared in the sentence. The first three or four letters of these words were identical to those that had actually appeared, and they could be readily substituted for the words that had appeared in the text. After reporting all words seen but not yet read aloud (recall EVS), the subject searched through the list of words, circling any additional words that he recognized as having appeared in that sentence. This second score was taken as a measure of the subject's recognition EVS. The subject was informed that only half of the words on the list had actually appeared in the sentence.

The results of this study can be seen most clearly in Figures 1 and 2. Each point on the curves is the mean recall EVS after the shutter was closed. In the 4-word-phrase sentences, active and passive sentences do not differ for positions 1 through 4, but they

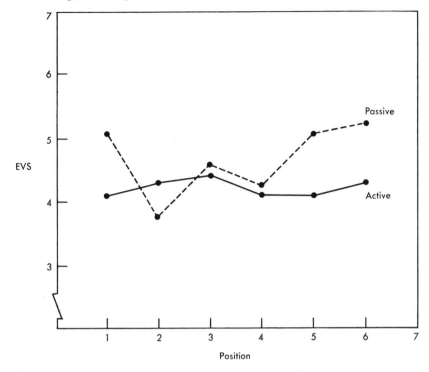

FIGURE 1. Mean recall EVS for various critical positions: four word phrase active and passive sentences.

do vary for critical positions 5 and 6. Within the active sentences, there are no differences among the critical positions. Among the passive sentences, however, positions 1 through 4 differ significantly from positions 5 and 6. The results for five word phrase sentences are comparable.

The findings, then, are (1) in sentences composed of 4- and 5-word phrases, the EVS is longer for the passive at the two terminal critical positions than for the active sentence; (2) within the active sentences, the position at which the shutter was closed had no effect on the EVS; and (3) in the passive sentences, the EVS at the two final positions was larger than at critical positions earlier in the sentence. These findings support the major hypothesis that the EVS varies in accordance with intra-sentence contingencies. The results show that the EVS is longer for passive sentences at that point where the active and passive forms begin to be differently constrained (Clark, 1965). Since the first portions of both

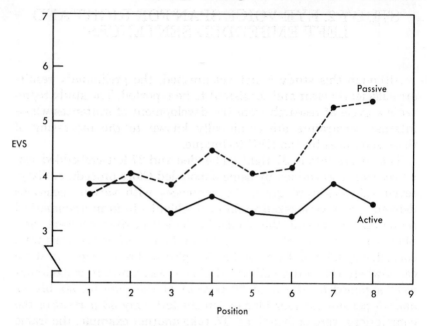

FIGURE 2. Mean recall EVS for various critical positions: five word phrase active and passive sentences.

active and passive sentences were identical and the short three-word phrase in the active sentence was a prepositional phrase in which the intra-phrase contingencies would not be expected to differ from those within the passive *by phrase* (Aborn *et al.*, 1959; Treisman, 1965; Fillenbaum *et al.*, 1964), these differences must be attributed to the structure of the sentence as a whole.

Two additional findings further support the view that these data represent differences in decoding which are dependent upon differential linguistic constraints. First, and indeed an important point, is the low false alarm rate for the recognition test. The ratio of correct to incorrect word choices on the recognition test was well over 1000:1. Considering the way in which these lists were constructed, it seems most improbable that the EVS represents guessing ability. Rather, it is more likely that the reader utilized the structure present in the written material. A second finding that the EVS was constant at all positions in the strings of unrelated nouns and verbs, further supports this.

STUDY 2. EYE-VOICE SPAN FOR RIGHT AND LEFT EMBEDDED SENTENCES[3]

Although this study is not yet finished, the preliminary results are sufficiently clear and consistent to be reported. The study represents a cycle of research from the development of sentences whose internal constraints are empirically known to the processing of these sentences by the EVS technique.

The constraints in 37 right-embedded and 27 left-embedded sentences were ascertained by using a modified Cloze procedure. Sixty-seven subjects were given the sentences with various positions deleted. They were asked to fill in the blanks to form grammatical sentences. In general, the blanks to the left of the verb were completed by a variety of forms while the blanks after the verb were consistently filled in by an embedded phrase. For example, in those cases where the entire embedded phrase was omitted, embeddings were supplied on the right 70 percent of the time for six blanks and 78 percent for four blanks. On the left, only 33 percent of the completions were embeddings. To take another example, the frame in which all of the sentences except the initial noun phrase and the final prepositional phrase were deleted could be completed as either a right- or left-embedded sentence. In fact, embeddings occurred 34 percent of the time, of which 77 percent were right embeddings and 23 percent were left. From these findings, we conclude that embedding is more often expected after the main verb than before it, and the form this type of structure takes is more restricted on the right.

The sentences used in the EVS section of this study were similar to those in which the constraints were earlier ascertained. We, of course, expected that the EVS would be longest when embedding after the main verb. However, this form of embedding occurs farther into the sentence than left-embedding, which means that the longer EVS may be due to position in the sentence. To control the position of embedding, left-embedded sentences were formed with a 3-word adverbial phrase, making the beginning of the critical phrase the sixth word in both types of sentences. To examine the possibility that the initial "filler" phrase affected the EVS, a second set of right-embedded sentences with an initial adverbial phrase

---

[3]Jean Grossman and Raymond Yang are co-authors of this study.

was added. Twenty sentences of each of these three types were placed in paragraphs, as in the earlier studies. The subjects were nine undergraduate students. The procedure followed in this study was identical to that used in the previous one.

Even with these few subjects, the results are clear. First, neither the initial adverbial phrase nor the number of words the subjects are into the sentence affects the length of the EVS. The important effects are due to the position of the embedding in relation to the main verb. An embedded phrase before the main verb produces a markedly lower EVS than an embedded phrase after the main verb. The scores differ by two words, which is a substantial amount.

The subsequent study includes a denser sampling of critical positions particularly at the end of the initial NP. Together with the earlier studies, these findings indicate that the size of chunk in reading is related to the grammatical constraints within the sentence.

STUDY 3. THE EYE-VOICE SPAN FOR SIMPLE ACTIVE SENTENCES[4]

The previous two studies indicate that readers both detect and use the structural information, the quasi-temporally arrayed constraints, which relates various sentence components or phrases to one another. This third study focuses on the effects of constraints which operate within phrases as opposed to those which operate across phrases. Schlesinger (1966) had demonstrated earlier this effect for Hebrew readers, and we undertook to corroborate his findings with English readers under more carefully controlled conditions. Since there is reason to believe that the ability to employ efficient strategies for sampling texts is more available to sophisticated language users (Hochberg, Levin, and Frail, unpublished manuscript), the problem was explored developmentally. In keeping with Schlesinger's results, we expected that the EVS of mature readers should be particularly sensitive to the structure within phrases. The increased size of the EVS expected for sophisticated readers should be directly related to phrase size, i.e., it should vary in accordance with the location of phrase boundaries.

Ten subjects at each of six grade levels were studied: second, fourth, sixth, eighth, tenth, and adults. Four types of sentences

---

[4]Ann Turner is co-author of this study.

were used, three of which will be treated here: (1) active sentences made up of *two word* phrases entirely; (2) active sentences of *three word* phrases; and (3) active sentences of *four word* phrases. There were enough sentences within each of the types to permit the light to be turned off at all possible between-word points in the first two phrases.

A different sentence content was used for each of the light-out positions. Thus, there was a total of eight two-word phrase sentences, 12 three-word active sentences, and 16 four-word phrase active sentences. In addition, there were eight structureless word lists. Sentences were constructed with enough phrase units to always have at least ten words in the sentences beyond the light out position. Starting with the sixth grade subjects, each of the critical sentences was embedded in a paragraph of four sentences. The critical sentence occurred an equal number of times in the first, second, third and fourth sentence position. For the second and fourth graders, the paragraphs contained two sentences and the critical sentence occurred in either the first or second position. Two similar sets of sentences were used. One set was made up with the vocabulary of a second grade reader and was used with second and fourth grades; another set was made up with the vocabulary of a sixth grader and was used with the sixth grade and all older subjects.

The paragraphs were exposed in a box with a one-way mirror in the lid which allowed subjects to see the text when the light was on. At predetermined points, the experimenter turned out the light and the subject was asked to report all the words he had seen beyond the word he was reading when the light went out.

A comparison was made between the mean length of the EVS on the unstructured word lists (mean span = 2.19 words) and the mean length on all of the sentences (3.91 words). This difference is highly significant. The results can be generally summarized as follows:

1. Older subjects had longer EVS's than younger ones.
2. There was a tendency for the EVS to be longest on the three word phrase sentences.
3. Faster readers had larger EVS's than slower readers.

We were able in this study to replicate Schlesinger's findings (1966) that the EVS tended to extend to a phrase boundary. This tendency was not related to the age of the reader nor to the phrase sizes except in the case of the second graders. Also, when readers inserted words which were not really in the text, these insertions usually completed phrases.

The results of this study support the hypothesis that subjects read in phrase units, i.e., they utilize the within phrase constraints to pick up semantic-syntactic units larger than the word. There was no difference in the number of times subjects read to the phrase boundaries on the different types of sentences; thus, this finding cannot be a function of the facilitative effect of a particular phrase length. The fact that older subjects read to the phrase boundaries more times than the second grade subjects suggests that beginning readers tend to read more word by word than older subjects who use the inter-word constraints occurring within phrases.

Fast or good readers read to the end of phrase boundaries more frequently than slower or poorer readers. Thus, good readers seem to process more in terms of larger units or phrases which is reflected by the adaptability of their EVS to the structure or content of the reading material. The slow readers, like the beginning readers, may be reading more in terms of what Anderson and Swanson (1937) call "perceptual" factors, i.e., they tend to read every word individually, not taking advantage of the contextual constraints.

Another finding which confirms previous research is the significantly shorter EVS for unstructured or word list material than for structured sentences. The fact that this difference exists suggests that all readers, both slow and fast, must take some advantage of the contextual constraints of the material they are reading.

DISCUSSION

An explanatory model must account for these observations: (1) There is some information given by the superficial structure of sentences relating sequentially arranged phrases to each other. There is an equivalent type of structuring within phrases as well. (2) Readers seem to use these constraints to facilitate language processing, i.e., to understand the meaning of what they have read. (3) The ability to take advantage of these constraints depends upon the proficiency of the reader. That is, the more experienced reader can make more efficient use of the structure or redundancy of language.

How do these constraints affect language processing? Constraints allow the decoder (listener or reader) to anticipate, predict, or formulate hypotheses about what comes next. These hypotheses not only permit the reader to limit the range of possible alternatives, but also provide him with a set of tentative interpretations for what he has read and what is likely to appear next.

The important point is that the constraints facilitate processing only insofar as they lead to the formation of successful anticipations. The reader then can test his hypothesis for himself. If it is confirmed, the previously assigned interpretation is accepted and the material can be easily and efficiently processed. If he cannot confirm his previously assigned interpretation, he must backtrack and reassign interpretations, which seems easier to do in reading than in listening. To elaborate, successful hypothesis generation depends upon the ability to formulate or assign some tentative interpretation to what has been read or heard. These tentative interpretations may be revised depending upon the confirmation or lack of confirmation provided by what is subsequently read or heard. The extent to which these revisions become necessary should have a pronounced effect on the ease of processing. There are, then, at least two ways in which hypotheses affect processing: (1) they provide the decoder with some strategy for sampling the material and the more constrained the material, the more efficient the sampling strategy, and (2) they force the decoder to provide tentative interpretations for incoming material. The degree to which the decoder can commit himself to a particular interpretation determines the form in which he must hold the "reading" in memory. The greater the commitment, i.e., the more sure he is of a particular reading or interpretation, the further he can process that segment. If revision is necessary, the degree to which the material has been processed determines the extent to which revision can be easily accomplished. In summary, the process of hypothesis testing influences efficient sampling strategies and governs the extent to which previously received material can be processed.

A recent study (Wanat and Levin, 1967) using normal passives and agent deleted passives is easily interpreted in terms of successive predictions of grammatical structure and their subsequent confirmation or lack of confirmation. The sentences were like the following: "John was hit by the stick," "John was hit by the park." We assume that to English speakers the first form is the more usual; that is, given a passive verb form, the reader expects *by + agent*.

He is surprised when he reads, or hears, *by* + *locative adverb*. In fact, the EVS is longer on the first than on the second form. Also, on the basis of preliminary eye movement data, the fixations on and regressions to "park" are longer than on "stick."

We are saying that language processors form and confirm or do not confirm successive guesses about what is coming next. Confirmation permits efficient processing; lack of confirmation involves backtracking and reassigning interpretations. This implies a two step process: confirmation/lack of confirmation and then the processing of the input. We might expect that with confirmation the implicated text may be sampled more loosely and hence the longer EVS. Lack of confirmation results in rereading or denser sampling of the text.

There is a third possibility: delayed confirmation. For example, an active, affirmative self-embedded sentence such as, "The man that I like brought the package," illustrates an instance in which the status of the initial noun phrase is delayed by the intervening modifying phrase. If the interpretation assigned to a portion of the message cannot be confirmed more or less immediately, it must be held in some readily accessible form until confirmation is possible. Therefore, the greater amount of material intervening between the proposed hypothesis and its fate, the greater the burden on memory and the more difficult processing will be. The EVS for left branching and right branching sentences supports this interpretation.

We have used the term "constraints" rather loosely and should be more specific about what we mean by the bases of hypothesis formation. Some of the more obvious constraints result from the direct realization of formal linguistic rules. For example, the verb form is an especially informative point since it signals differences between sentence types and the words which may follow. For example, *NP* follows *the,* an adjective signals a *noun* or *noun phrase;* and words such as *that* and *by,* depending on the context, signal the occurrence of specific constructions. A recent study by Fodor and Garrett (1967) well illustrates the importance of these syntactic markers for understanding sentences. Their subjects were presented with simple, self-embedded sentences in which the relative clause was introduced either with a relative pronoun, e.g., "that," or without a relative pronoun. Sentences in which the embedded phrases were introduced by the relative pronoun were more easily paraphrased, and the reaction time needed for the paraphrase was shorter.

Another order of constraints is more difficult to describe, but it still obviously follows from the expectations of the readers and speakers of a language. These constraints relate the subject and predicate of a sentence. That is, given the subject, the predicate must follow, and vice versa. In turn, the language user employs the syntactic markers to formulate hypotheses about which is the main noun phrase and verb phrase.

In summary, we have suggested that the reader, or listener continually assigns tentative intepretations to a text or message and checks these interpretations. As the material is grammatically or semantically constrained, he is able to formulate correct hypotheses about what will follow. When the prediction is confirmed, the material covered by that prediction can be more easily processed and understood. This model of reading is, in its important aspects, applicable also to the understanding of spoken language.

REFERENCES

Aborn, M., Rubenstein, H., & Sterling, T. Sources of contextual constraint upon words in sentences. *Journal of Experimental Psychology,* 1959, **57,** 171-80.

Anderson, I. H., & Swanson, D. E. Common factors in eye-movements in silent and oral reading. *Psychological Monographs,* 1937, **48,** 61-69.

Clark, H. H. Some structural properties of simple active and passive sentences. *Journal of Verbal Learning and Verbal Behavior,* 1965, **4,** 365-70.

Clark, H. H. The prediction of recall patterns in simple active sentences. *Journal of Verbal Learning and Verbal Behavior,* 1966, **5,** 99-106.

Fillenbaum, S., Jones, L. V., & Rappoport, A. The predictability of words and their grammatical class as a function of rate of deletion from a speech transcript. *Journal of Verbal Learning and Verbal Behavior,* 1964, **2,** 186-94.

Fodor, J. A., & Garrett, M. Some syntactic determinants of sentential complexity. *Perception and Psychophysics,* 1967, **7,** 289-96.

Lawson, Everdina. A note on the influence of different orders of approximation to the English language upon eye-voice span. *Quarterly Journal of Experimental Psychology,* 1961, **13,** 53-55.

Morton, J. The effects of context upon speed of reading, eye-movements and eye-voice span. *Quarterly Journal of Experimental Psychology,* 1964, **16,** 340-51. (a)

Morton, J. A model for continuous language behavior. *Language and Speech*, 1964, **7**, 40-70. (b)

Quantz, J. O. Problems in the psychology of reading. *Psychological Monographs*, 1897.

Roberts, K. The interaction of normative associations and grammatical factors in sentence retention. Paper presented at the Midwestern Psychological Association, Chicago, 1966.

Schlesinger, I. M. *Sentence structure and the reading process*. In press, 1966.

Treisman, Anne. Verbal responses and contextual constraints in language. *Journal of Verbal Learning and Verbal Behavior*, 1965, 4, 118-28.

Wanat, S., & Levin, H. Reading efficiency and syntactic predictability. Mimeo, 1967.

EYE-VOICE SPAN OR RESPONSE BIAS?[1]

PAUL A. KOLERS[2]

Research Laboratory of Electronics
Massachusetts Institute of Technology

The remarks that follow are directed to the version of the paper Levin and Kaplan presented. In that paper they made several assumptions, three of which I shall discuss. They are: (1) the eye-voice span (EVS) is a direct measure of the visual processing of a text; (2) the acquisition of skill in reading is expressed as a change in the linear extent of the array of letters or words processed; and (3) vocalized reading is a direct index of the processes characterizing silent reading. In this present version of their paper they have dropped the assertion of equivalence between the two kinds of reading, altered the argument about change in unit size, and qualified their notions of what EVS is measuring. I applaud their decision on all three issues. Because the initial assertions seem to be held by a number of other students of reading, however, I have left my remarks substantially as they were.

Levin and Kaplan describe some data and propose a model of reading. The model is reasonable and consistent with the notions held by other investigators of reading who also have been influenced by "psycholinguistics." It is so reasonable and so general

[1]This work was supported principally by the National Institutes of Health (Grants 1 PO1 GM-14940-01 and 1 PO1 GM-15006-01) and in part by the Joint Services Electronics Program (Contract DA 28-043-AMC-02536(E)).

[2]Present address: Dept. of Psychology, University of Toronto, Ontario, Canada.

that one cannot have a serious quarrel with it; at least I have none. I do not see, however, that it emerges from the data on the eye-voice span that we have had presented. I shall direct my remarks to an understanding of that phenomenon, therefore, rather than to the model.

As I understand Levin and Kaplan, their description of the eye-voice span presupposes that it is an index of perceptual processing of the printed text, i.e., an index of what the reader has seen. They conclude that the reader scans the printed array in "units" that are syntactic segments. In implying this, they have confused at least two aspects of reading.

The idea that the EVS measures visual input assumes that eyes deposit in memory a faithful representation of what they have looked at, which the mouth then speaks. Levin and Kaplan interpret the clustering of responses around syntactic boundaries as showing that the eye has seen and deposited in memory the same clumps of words that are found in the response. There is no reason to believe that what comes out of the mouth stands in faithful relation to what goes into the eyes; rather, the idea that the reader is "processing" his inputs implies just the contrary. Some of the characteristics of processing are selecting, organizing, coding, and ordering. Many such activities occur between the look and the lip. Because they do, we must regard the EVS as a response, the *result* of coding, rather than as an index of the stimulus. Two related observations will support this assertion.

Students of memory speak of an "echo-box," short-term memory, or buffer storage to describe a stage of information processing that occurs between the appearance of the physical signal and the deposit in memory of some recorded version of it (e.g. Waugh and Norman, 1965). We know that the physical signal itself is not stored in memory nor are all events that are perceived stored. "Short-term remembering" defines a process that is thought to operate on the input side of information-processing. There seems to be a complementary process on the output side. I call it "short-term intention," a buffer-storage intervening between, say, our formulating a thought and our expressing it in words. Our description of a picture that was presented briefly or our struggle when we are talking to specify precisely what we mean are instances drawn from phenomenology that support the idea that some stage intervenes between the mind and the mouth, between the "idea" and its words. Many of us "hear" an internal representation of what we are going to say or are trying to say before we actually say it; indeed, Karl Lashley (1951) wrote that Titchener found lecturing very easy: he merely relayed the results of the work performed by his internal speech generators which, apparently, produced only well-formed sentences arranged in neat paragraphs. Titchener claimed that he didn't have to think when he lectured, he had only to listen! Most of us are not so fortunate in the talent our internal generators possess; neverthless we do have them. Their existence makes implausible the idea that EVS is a direct index of visual input.

A second aspect of linguistic processing relevant to understanding the source of EVS is the grammatical constructing that we engage in when we read. My own view of the matter falls within the confines of a "generative theory;" I believe that we construct a representation (model) of the environment in some way. We do not merely detect it or discriminate aspects of its objects. The constructing is performed according to well learned rules, stratagems, and procedures. Our grammars provide us with a set of rules for ordering verbal items; a grammar that has been well-inculcated is a powerful ordering instrument if not for mind itself, at least for verbal production. Furthermore, much of our linguistic processing involves jargon, familiar phrases, cliches, and other readily anticipated sequences. If I say to you, "The National Anthem of the United States is 'The Star-Spangled . . .'" you will hear "Banner" even though I do not say it. Clearly, what you hear, then, is something you have produced yourself, anticipating what you expect to hear. If I am reading a paper aloud in which I discuss some idea I am trying to support, and say "A recent paper by Jones and Smith . . ." you really have only two options open in your constructing: the paper either supported or rejected a particular assumption, and you, the listener, do not have to do much processing of the stimulus in order to learn which option is supported.

Are EVS data that show responses clustering around syntactic boundaries really any more than a demonstration of linguistically-biased *response* coding? What if the subject were reading a report discussing the difference between formal and informal prose and found the sentence, "Compared to informal prose, second-graders found . . .," in which the grammatically induced expectation is "formal prose" rather than "second graders?" What if, indeed, sentences were presented in scrambled word-order, such as "Floor dirty the cleaned she" rather than its normal "She cleaned the dirty floor." Would not the reader's response reflect his unfamiliarity with the order of words rather than only some attribute of perceptual processing? In my own experiments (Kolers, in press), which I assume Harry Levin knows about, I have found that it takes skilled readers more time just to mouth unfamiliar sequences that are created by scrambling the order of words in a sentence. The reader normally wants to speak *sequences* of words—not merely sounds or isolated words. His propensity is to form these sequences as best he can. I think Levin and Kaplan have failed to distinguish between constructional activities in producing responses and the way in which the visual system scans printed arrays of words. The EVS cannot be taken as a direct indicator of perceptual scanning.

I wish to emphasize that I do not dispute that the reader's eyes scan ahead and that his mouth lags his eyes when he is reading aloud. What I do dispute is the idea that what he says after you have obscured the text is a faithful representation of what his visual system has seen. Too many other kinds of processing are going on, and too many biases are present on the response side, for us to believe that we have such a reliable index of visual processing.

A few remarks on the change in unit in reading and the difference between silent and vocalized reading will conclude my comments. Many students of reading seem to assume that the acquisition of reading skill is associated with an increase in the size of the unit processed perceptually. The novice is thought to work on a letter-by-letter sequence which increases with skill to syllabic units, words, and then phrases. His performance is thought to improve along a single dimension, the linear extent of the visual input. I doubt the validity of this assertion. I know of no evidence that suggests that the visual span of a person who reads at 2,000 words per minute is twice as great as the visual span of a person who reads 1,000 words per minute, or twenty times the size of a person who reads 100 words per minute. It may be that the novice spends more time with the purely visual aspects of the text than the skilled reader does, but the skilled reader's performance cannot be understood only as an ability to process larger quantities of material in a single fixation. The skilled reader, I believe, is doing something other than inputting larger amounts of material; he does more constructing, more guessing, more anticipating, more filling in. He is predicting what he will find on the page (Huey, 1908; 1968). Let me illustrate this with the eye-movement tracks taken from a very rapid

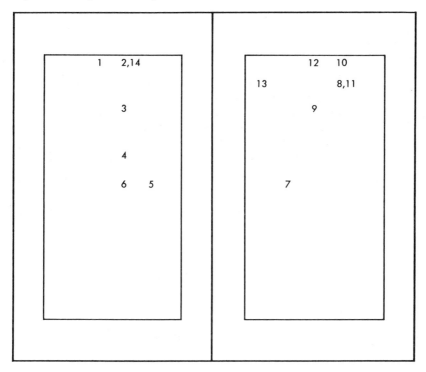

FIGURE 1. Sequence of fixations of a rapid reader (10,000 wpm)
on two pages of text.

reader (Llewellyn-Thomas, 1962). The dean of a college main-
tained that she read the book Llewellyn-Thomas gave her as
she reads normally. The frequency of her eye-movements was
in the normal range, about three or four per second. Her rate
of reading, however, was in excess of 10,000 words per minute.
In Figure 1, I have plotted the sequence of her fixations on two
pages of a book. Notice that she goes down the middle of the
left-hand page and up the middle of the right-hand page; but
surely she is not "taking in" 100 words in each fixation. If she
were, she would have an incomprehensible jumble of words in mind
as she followed the upward scan of the right-hand page. In my
opinion, she must be looking for particular items of information
to fill out the story she is telling herself. Such constructive, antici-
patory activities probably characterize all skilled readers; their performance cannot be understood sensibly if it is assumed to vary

only on the single dimension of the linear extent of visual material processed.

The performance of highly skilled readers sets off sharply a distinction between silent and vocalized reading. Vocalized reading by its very nature demands that output follow faithfully the sequence of words on the page. Silent reading does not necessarily follow that sequence. Even skilled readers' eyes regress in silent reading, and often dart about the page rather than follow along from line to line. Silent and vocalized reading involve substantially different processes, although they surely have some overlap; the EVS obviously can characterize only vocalized reading. I look forward to the day when our technology will permit us to measure an eye-mind span in silent reading. It will be interesting to find how similar the two spans are.

REFERENCES

Huey, E. B. *The psychology and pedagogy of reading.* New York: Macmillan, 1908. Reprinted, Cambridge, Mass.: M.I.T. Press, 1968.

Kolers, P. A. Three stages of reading. In H. Levin and J. Williams (eds.), *Basic studies on reading.* New York: Harper and Row, in press.

Lashley, K. The problem of serial order in behavior. Reprinted in F. A. Beach *et al.* (eds.), *The neuropsychology of Lashley.* New York: McGraw-Hill, 1960.

Llewellyn-Thomas, E. Eye movements in speed reading. In R. G. Stauffer (ed.), *Speed reading: practices and procedures.* Reading study center, 1962, **10**, 104-14. Newark: University of Delaware.

Waugh, N. C., & Norman, D. A. Primary memory. *Psychological Review,* 1965, **72**, 89-104.

2

AGE CHANGES IN THE SELECTIVE PERCEPTION OF VERBAL MATERIALS

ELEANOR E. MACCOBY

Stanford University

The work reported here deals with the perception of words or groups of words, when the listener is exposed to two messages, spoken in different voices, which arrive at approximately the same time. In some instances, the listener is asked to respond to one voice and ignore the other; in other instances, he is asked to divide his attention and take in both messages. The work has concerned the changes in performance that occur through childhood and old age on these tasks. The studies begin with the widely-noted fact that the amount of information available to the individual at any given moment is often greater than he can process at that moment (cf. Broadbent, 1958; Sperling, 1960). The perceiver must, therefore, select certain portions of the stimulus input to organize, code, "recognize", store, or respond to. There is currently a large volume of research on signal detection and information processing among adults, much of it involving verbal material. Relatively little has been done, however, to trace the development of selective, or "attentional" processes in childhood and the change in these processes that occurs during senescence. It is the purpose of the studies reported here to fill this gap, in the expectation that information on developmental change may throw light upon the nature of the selective processes themselves.

The studies deal with the perception of *speech* in only a very limited sense. That is, the stimuli used are brief snatches of speech. The technique of measurement involved asking the subject to wait till the stimulus voices finished speaking, and then repeat the messages spoken by the desired voice. This method was preferred to shadowing on the grounds that shadowing would be difficult for the youngest children with whom we worked. The method has its advantages, but it does mean that the stimuli used must be within (or not greatly in excess of) the memory span of the subjects. This places a severe limitation on the length of any stimulus unit. While the sequential probability of the phrases has been varied in a number of the studies, the complex organization of a continuing stream of speech is not involved in the materials the subjects hear. This simplifies the experiments, but it also means that the studies do not bear on the issue of grammatical structure and its relation to speech perception.

It will come as no surprise to anyone to learn that the perception of verbal phrases becomes more accurate with age. This would be predictable on the basis of the fact that familiar words are more easily perceived. With increasing age, the child acquires an ever larger vocabulary and presumably becomes more familiar with the words in most common use, so that recognition of words should occur progressively more rapidly and with fewer errors. What may not be as obvious is that there is a concurrent growth in the ability to exclude simultaneous unwanted messages. When verbal stimuli are so familiar that, with one voice speaking alone, even the youngest subject can repeat them almost without error, the introduction of a second voice which is to be ignored interferes with perfomance, and it interferes more for younger children than it does for older ones. Data from a recent study with children ranging from first grade to the seventh grade will illustrate this point (Maccoby and Leifer, 1968).

The subjects in this study were 48 children from each of four school grades: first, third, fifth, and seventh. The children listened to two voices, a man's and a woman's, and were asked to repeat what one of the voices said. The voices came over external speakers, set about 18 inches apart on a table in front of the subject, so that he could use spatial localization cues in separating the two voices. The voices did not speak exactly simultaneously, but alternated; each voice spoke in the pauses between the words spoken by the other voice. If one voice said, "hole in the" and the other voice said "some more to" the words would reach the listener in the following order: "hole some in more the to." The listener was told in advance which voice he would be asked to report. The phrases used were either three, four, or five words long, some of which were in proper English order ("sequential" phrases), while others were in scrambled order ("non-sequential" phrases).

In one experimental condition, the subjects listened to one voice only. The volume for the second voice was turned down to zero. The speech of the voice speaking alone sounded quite slow, since there were pauses between the words where the other voice could speak. In a second experimental condition, called the "select" condition, the listener heard both voices, and was asked to report only one of them. In a third condition, he was asked to listen to both voices and report both, in specified order.

The responses of the subjects were written down by the experimenter and were later scored according to the number of words spoken by the target voice and correctly reported by the subject. The subject received two points for a correct word, one point for a word which was correct except for a change of a single phoneme. The subject also received points for correct order. Inspection of the distribution of scores for the different age groups revealed considerable differences in variance. In some instances, the older subjects approached the ceiling on the task, and hence the variance of their scores was lower than that for younger children. In order to provide distributions which were comparable in variance, the scores were subjected to a transformation, (arcsin, square root or log, depending on the distributions), and the analysis was carried out with these transformed scores.

In choosing stimulus materials, we had attempted to use phrases which would be easily understood and repeated by all age groups when one voice was speaking alone. As may be seen from Table 1, all age groups performed near the ceiling on the "Alone" task, but, nevertheless, the older subjects did hear and report somewhat more accurately under this condition.

The effect of the introduction of the second voice which was to be ignored can probably be most clearly evaluated by examin-

TABLE 1
MEAN RAW SCORES, CORRECT RESPONSES, BY GRADE, FOR ALONE, SELECT, AND BOTH VOICE LISTENING CONDITIONS.

Mean Raw Scores	Grade			
(maximum possible: 171)	First	Third	Fifth	Seventh
Alone	164.0	168.1	169.4	169.8
Select	118.4	147.8	159.6	164.8
Alone minus Select*	42.7	18.9	8.4	3.1
Both: first voice	86.3	105.1	120.3	127.8
Both: second voice	40.5	69.2	88.4	88.3
Select minus both: first voice*	22.9	33.2	32.0	32.8

*In this study, the male voice was somewhat less easily understood than the female voice. In deriving difference scores, if a subject had listened for the male voice under one condition and the female voice under the other, a correction was made for voice difference before determining the difference score. This correction accounts for the fact that the mean of difference scores is not identical with the difference between mean scores.

ing the difference between performance under the "Alone" and "Select" conditions. The difference score tells how much deterioration in the baseline performance resulted from the introduction of a distracting voice. It is clear that the performance of younger children was more disrupted by the introduction of the second voice than was the performance of the older children. The F value for grades for the difference score is 29.7, $p < .001$.[1]

Another indication of the disruptive effect of the second voice may be found in the number of intrusion errors. Scores were given representing the number of words the subject reported that had been spoken by the wrong voice—the voice the subject had been instructed to ignore. Scoring of these errors was also based upon a 2-point system, two points for the intrusion of a whole word, 1 point for the intrusion of a word changed by a single phoneme. Order was not considered for these scores. As may be seen in Table 2, the number of intrusion errors was considerably greater among the younger subjects ($F = 31.4$, $p < .001$).[2]

---

[1]The analyses of variance for "correct" scores were done on arcsin transformed scores.
[2]Analyses of variance for intrusion errors were done with log transformed scores.

TABLE 2

MEAN INTRUSIVE ERRORS, BY GRADE, FOR SELECT AND
BOTH VOICE CONDITIONS, ALTERNATING VOICES STUDY.

Mean Raw Scores, Intrusive Errors	Grade			
(maximum possible: 114)	First	Third	Fifth	Seventh
Select	13.0	8.8	3.9	1.3
Both (intrusions of second voice upon first voice)	18.7	17.7	13.4	10.9

We see, then, that young subjects have difficulty in selecting a wanted from an unwanted message. This is true despite the fact that they can easily distinguish a male from a female voice— the attribute they are asked to use for selection.

Children in all the grade levels tested have more difficulty in dividing their attention than in selecting one voice. That is, when asked to listen for both voices and report both in a specified order, they reported the first voice requested less accurately than they reported the same voice when it was the only one to be reported. Younger children do less well on this task than older children ($F = 27.0$, $p < .001$). Improvement with age on the "both voice" task is slower than the improvement in simple selection. The increasing difference between *Select* and *Both* (*first voice*) scores with grade level (see Table 1) documents this fact.

Attempts to remember both voices result in increased intrusion errors (compared with the *Select* condition) for children of all ages tested. That is, when a subject is reporting the first voice and attempting to hold the second-voice message for a later report, the elements from the second-voice message intrude upon the first more frequently than when the subject only attempts to remember the first message. Again, under the *Both* condition, it is the youngest subjects who make the largest number of intrusion errors. However, in an absolute sense, the rate of intrusion errors is rather low for all age groups.

What accounts for the younger children's poorer performance on the *Select* and *Both Voice* conditions? A first hypothesis is that their performance is limited by a shorter memory span. A more general way of conceptualizing this deficit would be to postulate that they have a more limited capacity for processing information. The tasks we have used differ in the amount of information processing they require. Under the *Both Voice* condition, when, for example, each voice speaks a four-word phrase, the subject must remember eight words, after sorting them on the basis of the sex of the speaker's voice; with five-word phrases, he must remember ten words. It seems likely that portions of this task exceed the memory span of at least some of the subjects. Whether the *Select* task would impose a similar burden upon the information-processing capacity depends upon how the selection process is accomplished. If, in selecting one voice, the listener must hear both, understand what both of them are saying, and then report one but not the other voice, selecting one voice would involve nearly as much processing as reporting both voices. If, however, the listener functions with a first-level screening or filtering process, in which he first identifies the sex of the voices, and then perceives and remembers the content of only the message spoken by the target voice, the information-processing demands are less than those for the *Both Voice*, but more than those for the *Alone* condition. The fact that *Both* is more difficult than *Select* for all our subjects, and *Select* more difficult than *Alone*, suggests that a two-step process is involved in selection.

If the source of the younger children's difficulty is a limitation in their information-processing capacity, then they ought to do more poorly than older children on the tasks that have the heaviest requirements for information processing. As we have seen, the three experimental conditions (*Alone, Select, Both Voices*) involve increasing information-processing requirements. Within experimental conditions, the stimuli also vary in the amount of information (in the technical sense of the word) that must be dealt with. The stimuli included three-, four-, and five-word sequential phrases, and three- and four-word non-sequential phrases. In the case of sequential phrases, it is not clear that increasing the length of the message automatically increases the amount of information to be dealt with. It was found previously, for example (Maccoby and Konrad, 1966), that two-syllable words are easier to hear than one-syllable words, presumably because longer words provide more redundancy. There is no simple way, however, to measure how much redundancy compensates for the added memory load in remembering an additional word. It *is* clear that sequential phrases should involve less memory load than non-sequential phrases of the same length, since sequential phrases permit the subject to "chunk" the information to a great extent. Also,

TABLE 3

MEAN ARCSIN SCORE, NUMBER CORRECT, BY PHRASE
LENGTH AND SEQUENTIALITY, BY LISTENING
CONDITION AND GRADE.
INTERWOVEN VOICES STUDY.

	Grade			
	First	Third	Fifth	Seventh
"Alone" condition				
(hear one voice)				
3-word sequential	140.8	151.6	154.6	155.0
4-word sequential	147.7	150.7	155.4	156.5
5-word sequential	143.6	154.9	155.4	153.3
3-word non-sequential	146.0	148.4	155.8	155.4
4-word non-sequential	121.2	138.3	139.3	149.3
"Select" condition (hear two				
voices, report one)				
3-word sequential	102.9	123.4	140.3	147.2
4-word sequential	109.3	129.0	144.1	148.3
5-word sequential	91.9	120.6	139.4	142.7
3-word non-sequential	90.0	120.3	130.9	139.7
4-word non-sequential	58.1	95.3	115.1	133.4
"Both"—first voice				
3-word sequential	72.0	88.7	114.2	114.4
4-word sequential	61.5	88.4	100.5	110.7
5-word sequential	53.1	74.3	81.3	90.3
3-word non-sequential	55.3	74.3	84.9	92.7
4-word non-sequential	41.6	44.8	57.1	67.3
"Both"—second voice				
3-word sequential	39.0	61.4	90.5	93.3
4-word sequential	31.7	55.7	73.6	76.4
5-word sequential	25.3	41.4	55.6	54.9
3-word non-sequential	20.4	45.1	53.1	61.1
4-word non-sequential	11.7	18.8	27.4	24.2

shorter, non-sequential phrases should involve less memory load
than longer ones. We wished to determine whether young children
are at greater disadvantage than older children, on those tasks
and stimulus materials that involve the greatest memory load.

Table 3 presents the relevant data. A number of facts may be
seen: first, under *Alone* conditions, all stimuli were approximately

as easy with the exception of four-word non-sequential phrases. This is the only class of stimuli that appeared to tax information-processing capacity in any degree and it did so more for younger than older children. Under the *Select* condition, four-word non-sequential phrases are more difficult than three-word ones, and again the difference is greater for the younger subjects (F for grades$=15.9$, $p<.001$). Furthermore, under this condition, non-sequential phrases are more difficult than sequential ones of the same length, and the difference is greatest for the younger subjects (F for grades, 15.0, $p<.001$).

It would appear that limitation of memory (or information-processing) capacity does constitute at least a partial explanation of the poorer performance that characterizes young children on the *Select* task. This conclusion follows from the fact that they show a greater deficit on those stimulus materials which make the greatest demands upon memory.

When the task involves listening for two voices, however, the situation is not as clear. Here, it is true that non-sequential phrases are more difficult than sequential phrases, and that among non-sequential phrases, the longer ones are more difficult. This, however, is true for all age groups—there is no age interaction. Hence the difficulty that younger children have with the *Both* condition cannot be traced directly to limitations in memory span; at least, there appears to be another source of difficulty in this task, which depresses the performance of younger subjects by a constant amount, regardless of the amount of information they must deal with in the stimulus.

In the three-word, four-word and five-word sequential phrases, there are some curious findings, about which we can only speculate at the moment. Under the *Alone* condition, these phrases do not differ in difficulty. Under the *Select* condition, the *four*-word phrases are easiest, the three-word phrases next most difficult, and the five-word phrases the most difficult.[3] Under *Both Voice* conditions, difficulty is a simple linear function of length, with the three-word phrases easiest, four-word phrases next, and five-word phrases hardest. In listening for both voices, the number of words to be reported becomes particularly important. Could this be true because the *Both Voice* condition involves sub-vocal rehearsal of

---

[3]The superiority of four-word phrases over three-word phrases has a p value of $<.07$. Both three- and four-word phrases are significantly easier than five, $p < .01$.

the second voice? Rehearsal involves saying each word, and it is plausible that the disruptive effect of rehearsal depends more upon the number of things rehearsed than upon the possibilities of grouping that a sequential string of words provide.

It is instructive to contrast these findings with those from an earlier series of studies in which the listening conditions were somewhat different. In the earlier studies, subjects listened to two voices that spoke simultaneously—the words spoken by the two voices arrived at the subject's ears at the same moment in time, instead of being alternated. Under these conditions, each voice provided a degree of masking noise for the other. The words were more difficult to hear than they were under the alternative words condition. In some instances, single-word stimuli were used, and these words varied in their familiarity and number of syllables; in other instances, the stimuli were two-word phrases, which varied in their sequential probability. The results of these studies have been previously published (Maccoby and Konrad, 1967; Maccoby, 1967; Maccoby and Konrad, 1966), and will not be repeated in detail here. Some of the major findings may be summarized as follows:

1. Skill in selective listening to one of two simultaneous voices increases with age through the range 5 to 12.
2. The content of the message spoken by the target voice is more important in determining the accuracy of listening than the content spoken by the voice to be shut out. Nevertheless, the content of the unwanted message does affect performance. In the case of word familiarity, there is a contrast effect: if the target voice is speaking a *familiar* word, it is more easily heard if the word spoken by the masking voice is *unfamiliar;* however, if the target voice speaks an *unfamiliar* word, the unwanted voice is easier to shut out (interferes less with performance) if it is speaking a *familiar word.* A similar situation prevails, though not so strongly, in the sequential probability of two-word phrases: when the target voice speaks a low-probability sequence, performance is better if the unwanted voice speaks a high-probability sequence. High sequential probability spoken by either the target voice or the masking voice seems to reduce intrusion errors.
3. The deficit in the performance of the younger children cannot be directly traced to difficulty in using a prepara-

tory set. In several studies, subjects were tested under two experimental conditions: (1) when they were signalled in advance which voice was to be listened to, and (2) when the voice signal came *after* the two voices had spoken. Younger children were as able as older ones to use the preparatory signal—their performance improved to an equal degree when this signal was available. In fact, there was some indication (of borderline significance, statistically) that the younger children were *more* helped by a preparatory signal.

4. Sequential probability is more helpful to older subjects than younger subjects. That is, the improvement in performance that results when stimuli are sequential is greater for older than younger subjects.

There appears to be a contradiction, then, between the findings of selective listening when the voices are simultaneous and the findings when the voices are alternate. Using alternating voices, the youngest children show the greatest improvement in performance when stimulus phrases are made sequential. Using simultaneous voices, older subjects derive the greatest benefit from this experimental condition. This discrepancy might be explained by the fact that in the simultaneous voice studies, stimuli were brief (each voice speaking either a single word or a two-word phrase), so that limitations in the memory span did not affect performance, or did so only minimally. Sequentiality in the stimuli may have helped performance, not by permitting "chunking" as an aid to memory, but by providing clues as to what a masked syllable or word might have been. In the simultaneous voice situation, the quality of the stimuli is reduced as it would be by the addition of any form of noise. The listener must fill in the gaps on the signal that are produced by the masking effect of one voice on the other. Older children presumably have a greater familiarity with the regularities of the language than younger children, so that they can more easily guess the masked segments on the basis of the probabilities derived from the clear portions of the message. In using alternating voices, the problem of masking does not arise. However, in the studies using alternating voices, longer strings of words were used—long enough to tax the memory span, at least for certain classes of stimuli. Younger children evidently were able to use the sequential probabilities in the language well enough to use them for "chunking" the sequential phrases as an aid to memory, but were considerably handicapped in their efforts to remember the non-sequential phrases. Older children, while able to take advantage of sequentiality (perhaps even more than younger children), were more skillful in remembering phrases in which the words could not be grouped easily. Their greater skill in this task may only be partially a function of greater memory span; perhaps older children have developed devices for organizing relatively unrelated strings of items in order to reduce the memory load they impose.

The central fact emerging from these studies done with children is that younger children do less well than older ones in repeating one message while ignoring another available message which may be distinguished from the first on the basis of an easily discriminated cue. When the messages are long, limitation in memory span appears to be a factor in the difficulty younger children have with the task. But even when the stimuli are sufficiently brief or sequential, so that the younger children's memory spans are adequate to the task, their performances still show a deficit. It is unlikely that this deficit may be traced to their difficulty in organizing and producing the response, since the response called for under *Select* conditions is identical to the response required under *Alone* conditions, and yet performance is much better under the *Alone* condition. The introduction of the unwanted voice interferes with performance even though there is no change in the nature of the response requested, and the interference is particularly great for the younger subjects, resulting in their higher rate of intrusion errors. These facts support the view that the younger children find exclusion difficult. They may not be able to take from the unwanted voice only the small bit of information they need to know (i.e., whether it is a man's or a woman's voice). Instead they take in too much information, probably up to the point of identifying the words spoken by the unwanted voice. Yet the fact that young children can make as much use of a preparatory signal as older children indicates that they can and do "filter" successfully, at least to a degree. Available data do not permit a good assessment of the extent to which young children are characterized by a filtering deficit.

Let us now turn to the studies of changes in selective listening in old age. A number of issues concerning the perceptual and cognitive functioning of aging people arise. It is a common observation that elderly people are disturbed by noise. Does this mean that they are especially distractable—that they have difficulty in shutting out unwanted information? It has also been reported that older people suffer from deficiencies of immediate memory. Will this affect their listening performance? Specifically, does it mean that they will have great difficulty in retaining two messages long enough to select one of them *after* the messages have been received? Will they, therefore, rely on a preparatory signal more than younger people do? And finally, there is the possibility that the high-frequency hearing losses that occur in old age are especially important in the selective listening situation—that they magnify the masking effects of one voice upon another.

The first of series of studies in selective listening in old age dealt with the effect of preparatory signals. (For a more detailed description of these studies and their findings, see Maccoby Jones, and Konrad, 1967). In this study, a man and woman spoke simultaneously, each speaking two-word phrases. The two voices came over a single speaker. There were 40 subjects, ranging in age from 59 to 81 years. The performance of these subjects was contrasted with the performance of 20 children attending a summer school session who had just completed either the third or fourth grade.

When asked to listen to one voice and ignore the other, the elderly subjects performed very poorly. The accuracy of their reports was only about two-thirds as great as that of the children. Judging from other studies from which data are available for children over a wider range of ages, the performance of the elderly subjects was approximately comparable to the performance of a group of five or six year old children. Within the aged group, performance was related to chronological age. The subjects in their late seventies and eighties performed poorly compared with subjects in their sixties. (The correlation of chronological age with mean number of correct responses, within the aged sample was −.57). The effect of a preparatory signal, howevre, did not vary with age. Following the procedure described earlier, on some trials the subjects were signalled in advance which voice to report, while on other trials they received the signal only after both voices had spoken. Performance was better for both elderly people and the children with whom they were compared when the preparatory signal was given, but the degree of improvement was the same for both groups. Within the elderly sample, the advantage provided by a preparatory signal was only slightly and insignificantly related to age ($r = .20$). Hence, the decline in skill that occurs in old age in listening to one or two simultaneous voices cannot be attributed to an inability to maintain a brief selective set nor to any decline in the ability to do without a set. At least, this is true for the brief stimuli which do not tax memory capacity.

Is the poor performance of elderly subjects due to hearing loss, or does it reflect a difficulty in shutting out an unwanted message? In pretesting the simulus materials, it was determined that elderly subjects could report with almost perfect accuracy when one voice spoke along. This would suggest that a hearing loss was not the problem. Yet a hearing loss might affect the kind and degree of masking effects that occur when the subject attempts to listen in noise. It is well known that in later life, the ear loses its sensitivity to high frequencies. What is not as well known is that before a given high frequency becomes inaudible, it is converted into an a-tonal buzz, so that for the older ear, sounds which previously helped in the discrimination of sound patterns become, for a time, noise in the system. In addition, older people suffer from "recruitment"—that is, a given increase in the objective volume of a sound produces a larger increase in subjective loudness for the older ear than for the younger one. There is literally, then, a buzzing and booming in the aged ear, and this may exaggerate the masking effects when two voices speak simultaneously, making it more difficult to discriminate between the elements of a complex stimulus.

The next experiment was designed to rule out masking one voice by another, and to determine whether or not, when this was done, older people would still perform poorly in a selective listening situation. For this experiment, the alternating word technique, described above, was used. In this experiment, also, the phrases varied in length and sequentiality. The two voices came from two separated speakers, and there were three experimental conditions. On one series of phrases, the subjects heard and reported only one voice; on another, they heard both voices but were asked to listen to, and report, only one. On still another series, they were asked to report what both voices said, in specified order.[4] Under the "alone" condition, where the volume of the second voice was turned down to zero, the voice that was heard spoke quite slowly, as noted earlier. On each series of trials, the subject knew in advance which voice or voices he was supposed to be listening for—there were no "after" signals, and for any given experimental condition, the same voice was to be

---

[4]The order of these conditions was counterbalanced across subjects.

reported throughout, so there were fewer changes of sets than in the previous experiment.

For this experiment, there were two groups of subjects. The 30 older subjects ranged in age from 54 to 81, with a median age of 71. The 30 younger subjects were in the ninth grade. The scores for the two age groups may be seen in Table 4. Both groups performed at high levels under the "alone" condition, although the elderly subjects did have a significantly lower mean score. With the introduction of the second voice that was to be ignored (the *Select* condition), the performance of the two groups was essentially identical. Starting from a slightly higher base line, the younger group actually showed a greater loss in performance with the introduction of the irrelevant voice than the elderly group. Under these experimental conditions, then, the aging subjects could easily select a wanted message and filter out an unwanted message. Furthermore, while it was somewhat easier for both age groups to select sequential phrases rather than non-sequential phrases, the elderly subjects did as well as the younger ones on both classes of stimuli. The fact that their selective

TABLE 4

SELECTIVE LISTENING FOR ALTERNATING VOICES, UNDER ALONE, SELECT, AND BOTH VOICE CONDITIONS, FOR ELDERLY VERSUS YOUNG SUBJECTS.

Experimental Condition	9th Grade Children (N=30)	Elderly Subjects (N=30)	P
Listen for one voice, speaking *alone*:			
Mean score, correct responses	142.0	137.8	.001
Select one voice, two speaking			
Mean score, correct responses	135.0	135.4	n. s.
Mean, intrusive errors	3.2	1.6	.05
Report *both* voices, in specified order			
First voice, mean correct	102.3	114.7	.05
First voice, mean intrusive errors	11.9	6.5	.01
Second voice, mean correct	61.8	39.9	.001
Second voice, mean intrusive errors	7.0	2.2	.001
Total both voices, correct	164.1	154.7	n. s.
Total both voices, intrusive errors	18.9	8.7	.001

processes were efficient is indicated by their lower rate of intrusion errors. A futher indication that performance on this task is not related to age is that fact that, within the elderly sample, there was no decline in selective skill with increasing age; the correlation of chronological age with correct responses under the *Select* condition was only −.11, and with intrusive errors −.05. The success of the older subjects on this selection task suggests that their poor performance on the earlier experiment may have been due to hearing loss. Another possibility, however, is that elderly people dealt more successfully with the alternating-voice condition because the wanted message was delivered more slowly.

There are some interesting contrasts between the performances of the two groups when they were asked to listen to, and report, both voices. The elderly people were more accurate in their report of the first voice asked for, and considerably less accurate in their report of the second voice. The total amount recalled, when scores for first and second voice are added, is not significantly different for the two age groups, but the successes are differently distributed between the two voices. The older subjects do not appear to divide their attention as successfully as the younger subjects, but concentrate on one message to the exclusion of the other. This interpretation is supported by the fact that, on the *Both voices* task as well as the *Select* task, older subjects made fewer intrusion errors.

Our results are partially consistent, and partially inconsistent, with the findings of James Inglis (1965), in his studies of age changes in dichotic listening. He found deterioration with increasing age (comparing young and middle-aged adults with elderly subjects) on the second set of digits reported, when one set of digits had been presented to one ear and another to the other ear. He did not find any age changes, however, in the first set of digits recalled. He interpreted his data to mean that among elderly subjects there is rapid decay of material held in short-term store. This would be consistent with our findings on the poor performance of the older subjects on the second voice reported. But, our findings that elderly subjects do better on the first voice points to something more than a memory defect; a greater focusing of attention on a single voice, to the exclusion of the other, would seem to be implied.

When asked to report both voices, a number of the elderly subjects reported that they had heard and understood both of them initially, but that the process of reporting the first voice seemed to erase the memory of the second one. There is some experimental work which suggests that elderly subjects are particularly susceptible to the interfering effects of intervening tasks (see Cameron, 1943; Broadbent and Heron, 1962). In a recent experiment Tom Jones (1968) wished to determine whether the poor performance of aged subjects on the second voice in the two-voice alternating-word tasks could be attributed to greater response interference (or "destructive readout") effects among older subjects than young subjects.

In the Jones experiment, the two-voice alternating words technique was again used. Stimuli were three- and four-word sequential phrases, and three-word nonsequential phrases. In the experiment, the subject was told only after the voices had spoken which voice to report. In one experimental condition, the subject received a signal to report only one voice, and the signal came as soon as the voices had finished speaking. This is called the *Immediate* condition. In another condition, the subject was signalled to report both voices, in a specified order, and again the signal came as soon as the voices had finished. In a third condition, the signal to select one voice came after a brief delay. The delay was timed to be approximately the same duration as the time taken to report Voice 1 in the *Both* voices condition. Thus, under the delay condition, the subject reported a single selected voice at the same time that Voice 2 was reported under the *Both* condition. The design was intended to show whether the poor performance on the second voice in the *Both* condition was due to the delay in being reported—after the message had died out of short-term store—or whether it was due to the interfering effects of reporting an intervening message. Assuming interference effects were shown, the next question would be whether or not they were greater for older subjects than younger subjects. In this experiment, there were two groups of subjects, an older group ranging from 61 to 82 in age, (mean 73), and a middle-aged group ranging from 24 to 59, with a mean of 48.

Table 5 shows the initial findings.[5] The older group performed less well than the middle-aged group under all conditions, (these differences are all significant by *t*-test). Comparing the *Delay* condition with the report of the second voice under the *Both* condition, it may be seen that the second voice is reported with considerably less accuracy. Furthermore, performance under the *Delay* condition was only slightly worse than that under the

---

[5]At the time of writing, the analysis of the data had not been completed.

Immediate condition, (the difference was not significant for either age group). These facts suggest that it is having reported the first voice, rather than simply having waited a few moments, that makes it especially difficult for subjects to recall the second voice. However, the interference effect attributable to having reported the first voice is no greater for elderly subjects than middle-aged subjects. These effects do not explain the poorer performance of the older subjects on the second voice in the previous study.

TABLE 5

MEAN SCORE CORRECT, AND MEAN INTRUSIVE ERRORS, BY EXPERIMENTAL CONDITIONS AND AGE GROUPS, ALTERNATING VOICES. (JONES, 1968)

| | Age Groups | |
Experimental Condition	Elderly	Middle Aged
Immediate, report one voice		
Mean correct (maximum = 104)	65.4	80.8
Intrusion errors (maximum = 104)	12.3	6.4
Delay, report one voice		
Mean correct	57.9	78.8
Intrusive errors	12.7	8.3
Report both voices:		
first voice:		
Mean correct	62.4	75.2
Intrusive errors	12.3	9.8
second voice:		
Mean correct	43.5	59.2
Intrusive errors	5.8	5.3

Perhaps the most interesting finding of the Jones study, in terms of relevance to the process of selective listening in old age, is the fact that the elderly subjects performed obviously less well under all the experimental conditions than middle-aged subjects. In order to put this fact in perspective, it may be useful to contrast it with the findings of the two previous studies. Using brief stimuli (two-word phrases), presented simultaneously, when the subject was asked to select one voice out of two, the accuracy of report increased during childhood and declined during old age.

With longer phrases (3-, 4- and 5-word phrases) delivered so that the voices alternated, performance improved during childhood but did *not* decline in old age. The situation is represented schematically in Figure 1. These findings suggested that it was the simultaneity of the stimuli in the first study that produced the old-age deficit—that the problem was one of masking, perhaps

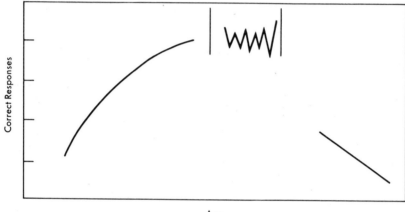

Age
SELECTIVE LISTENING WITH
SIMULTANEOUS INPUT

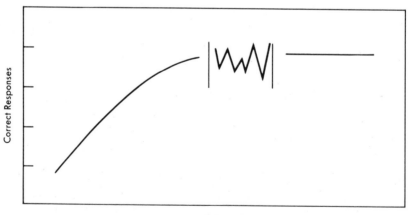

Age
SELECTIVE LISTENING WITH
ALTERNATING INPUTS

FIGURE 1. Comparison of selective listening under conditions of simultaneous vs. alternating presentation.

related to hearing loss with aging. In the Jones study, however, there is again a loss in performance among elderly subjects, and this occurs in a situation in which the voices speak their words alternately, so that masking is eliminated.

The interpretation of the Jones study presents problems in some respects. Inspection of the data suggests that, while the older subjects as a group performed poorly on the tasks, there were no correlations with chronological age within the aged sample. One crucial difference between the Jones study and the previous study with alternative voices is that, in the Jones study, the subjects performed exclusively with an after signal. Under all the experimental conditions, the two stimulus voices were first presented, and then the subjects received a signal indicating which voice to report. It would apear that elderly subjects were especially handicapped by the after-signal condition, in comparison with the situation in the previous study in which they knew before the test which voice would be asked for. The Jones finding is consistent with the previous finding that older subjects were especially poor at reporting the second voice in the *Both voice* condition, and strengthens the case for the view that division of attention is especially difficult for elderly people.

It will be recalled that in the study with simultaneous two-word phrases (the study in which the effects of before signals and after signals were compared), the elderly subjects did not show any greater reliance on a preparatory signal than the young subjects. This was probably true because the stimuli were too brief to tax memory capacity. In a study of Konrad (described in Maccoby, 1967) it was shown that the amount of advantage provided by a preparatory signal was a function of the length of the stimulus set to be selected. In the Jones study, phrases were long enough so that, with an after signal procedure in which the subject must remember what both voices said, there would be a considerable memory load. It might be expected that elderly subjects, suffering as they do from a deficit in short-term memory, would be at a particular disadvantage in such a procedure.

The best interpretation of the series of studies of selective listening among aging subjects would appear to be as follows:

1. For elderly people, the masking effects of one voice upon another simultaneous voice are greater than for younger people. It is as though the clarity of the signal for the voice being listened for is more reduced by noise for the older ear than the younger one.
2. Elderly people are as able as younger ones to select one

signal and shut out another. Their "filtering" processes appear to be unimpaired.

3. Elderly people do show a deficit in the division of attention. When they are required to take in more than one signal at a time, their performance suffers. If they are required to report both messages, and know in advance which voice will be asked for first, they tend to concentrate on the first message to the detriment of the second. When they do not know, at the time of listening, which voice will be asked for, the recall of both voices is impaired.

REFERENCES

Broadbent, D. E. *Perception and communication.* New York: Pergamon Press, 1958.

Broadbent, D. E., & Heron, A. Effects of a subsidiary task on performance involving immediate memory by younger and older men. *British-Journal of Psychology,* 1962, **53**, 189-98.

Cameron, D. E. Impairment of the retention phase of remembering. *Psychiatric Quarte*rly, 1943, **17**, 395-404.

Inglis, J. Immediate memory, age, and brain function. In A. T. Welford and J. E. Birren (eds.), *Behavior, aging and the nervous system.* Springfield, Ill.: Charles C. Thomas, 1965.

Jones, T. M. Divided attention on an auditory task in old age: the response interference hypothesis. Manuscript in preparation, Stanford University, 1968.

Maccoby, E. E. Selective auditory attention in children. In L. P. Lipsitt and C. C. Spiker (eds.), *Advances in child development and behavior,* Vol. III. New York: Academic Press, 1967.

Maccoby, E. E., & Konrad, K. W. Age trends in selective listening. *Journal of Experimental Child Psychology,* 1966, **3**, 113-22.

Maccoby, E. E., & Konrad, K. W. The effect of preparatory set on selective listening: developmental trends. *Monograph of the Society for Research in Child Development,* 1967, **32** (Whole No. 4).

Maccoby, E. E., Jones, T. M., & Konrad, K. W. Selective listening in later life. In K. Riegel (ed.), *Interdisciplinary topics in gerontology,* Vol. I. New York: S. Karger, 1967.

Sperling, G. The information available in brief visual presentation. *Psychological Monographs,* 1960, **74** (Whole No. 11).

DIVISION OR ORDER?

DAVID MCNEILL[1]

Harvard University

Dr. Maccoby has given us a fine discussion of a fascinating problem. It is also a complex problem, touching on many issues in development. For my assignment as her discussant, I will undertake a consideration of just one of these, leaving many matters untouched.

To begin, I must recast slightly, but I think significantly, Dr. Maccoby's interpretation of the developmental changes she has so nicely demonstrated. Doing so will not violate the spirit of her interpretation, but it reveals a general pattern that is otherwise obscured.

Dr. Maccoby reports that younger children do not differ much from older children in repeating 3-, 4-, and 5-word phrases, but differ markedly in repeating these same phrases when they are heard interwoven with others. This is true, even when a child is told in advance which voice (male or female) to repeat; the difference here is the one between the *Alone* and *Select* conditions. Dr. Maccoby argues that these differences arise when attention must be divided and an unwanted message rejected, because younger children have a smaller capacity to process information.

It is probably true that children's capacity for processing information increases between 6 and 12 years. In support of this assumption is the fact that improvement in the *Alone* condition is larger for longer phrases. It is also probably true that the ability to separate messages is also increasing during this time. However, I would

---

[1]Now at the University of Chicago.

suggest that there is also a qualitative change between early and late childhood, and that Dr. Maccoby's sample of children falls in the middle of this transition. Dr. Maccoby suggests that selection of a wanted message takes place in two steps. A child first identifies the sex of the voices, and then stores in memory the voice he wants. The order of events in this case is *Select-Remember.* Dr. Maccoby believes that younger children are deficient on both steps, but particularly on the first. Their problem is one of division. She also considers but rejects another possibility — that a child perceives and remembers both voices and then selects and reports only one. This also is a two-step process, although Dr. Maccoby describes it as one, which differs from the first in the order of events. In this second case, the order is *Remember-Select.* Dr. Maccoby rejects it as a possibility because performance in the *Both* and *Select* conditions is different at all ages.

However, the difference between the *Both* and *Select* conditions is smaller for younger than for older children. It is conceivable that the younger children were in transition — sometimes remembering both voices in the *Select* condition and selecting one for report, and sometimes selecting one voice and remembering only it for report. Let me refer to the first of these approaches as *post-selection* and the second as *pre-selection,* and suggest that post-selection is characteristic of young children, and pre-selection is characteristic of older children and adults. Paradoxically, the children least able to remember anything try to remember the most. Their problem is one of order.

One point in favor of this interpretation is the absence of an interaction with age in the *Both* condition, about which Dr. Maccoby expresses puzzlement. In the *Both* condition all subjects, regardless of age, must remember all words. Pre-selection cannot reduce the load. Thus, when older children must remember sequential and nonsequential strings of words they differ from younger children only in the total amount they can hold in short-term memory. Apparently this difference is not large. But when pre-selection can reduce the load on memory, as in the *Select* condition, older children not only are able to remember slightly more but they have to remember considerably less. Hence there is an interaction with age in the *Select* but not in the *Both* condition.

The assumption that younger children post-select whereas older children pre-select also helps explain why — with the simultaneous presentation of two messages — telling the subjects in advance to listen for a particular voice helps younger children as much as older children. In a sense the *Select* condition with simultaneous voices is the opposite of the *Both* condition with interwoven voices. The *Both* condition forces older children to remember as much as younger children remember; simultaneous presentation of two messages forces younger children to pre-select as finely as older children pre-select. There is no possibility of changing the order of selecting and remembering in simultaneous presentation because everyone must select before remembering (Savin, 1967). A preliminary set can therefore benefit everyone alike. It would be interesting to know if telling children after presentation which of two interwoven voices to report causes younger and older children to become more alike. There should be such an effect if the major advantage for older children is pre-selection.

If younger children must post-select and older children can pre-select, elderly people seem to follow the rule of obligatory pre-selection. Compared with older children, elderly people suffer in the *Both* condition when they report the second voice. As Dr. Maccoby points out, such a difference between older children and elderly adults cannot be the result of a deterioration of memory — for old people do better than children in reporting the first voice. We can fit the results of Inglis' study into this picture. He also found deterioration on a second-reported group of digits, but (unlike Maccoby) found no superiority on a first-reported group of digits. Inglis' "old" subjects were middle-aged, as against the really old subjects used by Maccoby. There is, therefore, a continuum running from obligatory post-selection in young children through optional pre-selection in older children and younger adults to increasingly obligatory pre-selection in older adults. There is no regression in old age; there is continuing development.

The obligatory post-selection of young children can be viewed as a special case of a more general phenomenon — namely, young children record information before they operate on it. Pre-selection, whether obligatory or optional, can be regarded as a special case of operating on information before recording it. Recording information before operating on it has special advantages to young children. It allows information to get into the system *before* it is distorted by the very operations it is to change. On the other hand, operating on information before recording it has special advantages to more mature persons in whom operations are well-established, since the problem for them is efficient processing, not efficient development.

As an example of the importance of the order of functions let me mention two so-called "training situations" in the acquisition of syntax — imitation and expansion. An expansion is an imitation of a child by an adult, expanded to be fully grammatical. The ages involved are 2 and 3 years, younger than Maccoby's youngest subjects, and an age at which children should be most extreme on postoperation. The facts, very briefly, are that children strongly tend to include in imitation only what they already include in spontaneous speech, so imitations are not grammatically progressive, but expansions accelerate acquisition. There is some difference of opinion about the effectiveness of expansions but I believe the relevant evidence shows them to help.

Now, if young children record first and operate second, just this difference in effectiveness between expansion and imitation would arise. An imitation of adult speech is assimilated to a child's own grammar, since in order to imitate a child must operate on what he has recorded. A child may record *that's a dog*, but he operates on it to get, *that dog;* the imitation therefore makes no contribution to linguistic progress. An expansion, in contrast, is not affected by a child's own grammar if he records first and operates second — for in expansion a child only records, he does not operate. *That's a dog* gets into the system and produces whatever effects it can.

Were children to follow the mature order of operating first and recording second, neither expansion nor imitation could assist language acquisition. In both, assimilation to a child's own grammar would occur before the example of adult speech could be recorded. The difference between imitation and expansion illustrates the utility of the record-then-operate order of events for young children. It is the lingering effects of this order that appear in Dr. Maccoby's experiments on selective listening.

REFERENCES

Savin, H. B. On the successive perception of simultaneous stimuli. *Perception and Psychophysics*, 1967, **2**, 479-82.

3

SOME ACOUSTIC AND GRAMMATICAL FEATURES OF SPONTANEOUS SPEECH[1]

JAMES G. MARTIN[2]

Chico State College

In the title of this paper the term *acoustic features* means pauses in speech, and *grammatical* means constituent boundaries. We will discuss when and how much these features are related. We began our experimental program by wondering how a thought becomes translated into speech sounds, which led us to the question of how the speech sounds become transformed back into thoughts again, and then to the question of how real speech differs from what is described by linguistic theory. I mention these questions more to indicate the motivation behind the experiments than to suggest that we have made a great deal of progress toward an answer to any of them. As always, the choice was whether to first explore a small corner of the program in detail or to reconnoiter a larger

[1]Supported in part by Grant MH 10400, National Institutes of Mental Health, U. S. Public Health Service.
[2]Now at the University of Maryland.

territory. We chose the latter and hence in the following account there are many lacunae of theoretical and empirical detail.

The experiments to be described were about the communication between a speaker and a listener and relied, for the most part, on spontaneous speech as inputs and outputs. We hypothesized that the speech signal often did not correspond well to what the speaker intended, but that this fact was allowed for in the way the listener perceptually processed the signal. Before describing the experiments, however, it is convenient to look at some examples of spontaneous speech generated by the subjects and to consider the problems these examples raise when contrasted with work on sentences, which are the usual type of materials employed in psycholinguistic experiments. The following are some spontaneous descriptions of Thematic Apperception Test (TAT) cards:

(1) *Oh this looks like out in the forest or woods or someplace an' there's it's either a fire or something like that explosion*

(2) *Somebody looks like a girl sitting down looks like she's crying or something somethin' happened sad*

These examples are far from atypical. While these utterances are easy enough to understand, it is difficult to analyze them grammatically, that is, to give them an exact surface structural description. This problem in itself seems to provide the challenge and justification for pursuing a communication model of spontaneous speech.

In order to talk about this work it is convenient to begin with the first experiment and a brief summary of its rationale (Martin, 1967). On the encoding side of the model, we thought that the speaker, as he intends a message, is provided immediately with the semantic and syntactic structure of his message, but not necessarily all of the words to appear in the message. Word selection was another process depending upon psychological factors such as vocabulary access. That is, the determination of a word and its acoustic realization were two different operations. As the speaker commenced, he often came to a place where a word hadn't been chosen, or he changed direction in midsentence, and, at these points, he introduced noise into the signal in the form of pauses and false starts.

The listener, given the speech with these distorting characteristics, had to recover from it the speaker's intention. As he detected message elements, the acoustic noise such as pauses in the signal was biased out, or at any rate failed to register. In short, speaker pauses and other distortions revealed psychological processes, but they gave false information about his message and were not registered.

The general experimental procedure we used involved speakers describing TAT cards in short utterances. Each speaker was paired with a listener who heard his speech, one utterance at a time, and attempted to reproduce it. The speakers were called encoders, the listeners, decoders.

A decoder's reproductions should reflect something of the way he perceptually organized what he had heard, causing hesitation phenomena to differ in encoder production and decoder reproduction. Many workers have reported that hesitation phenomena, usually pauses, tend to precede high-information words during productive speech, for example, oral examinations (Tannenbaum, *et al.*, 1965), cartoon interpretation (Goldman-Eisler, 1961a) or psycholinguistic conferences (Maclay & Osgood, 1959). These pauses mark momentary encoding uncertainty but convey little linguistic information. Since an efficient speech perception mechanism might be expected to filter out pauses in the course of detecting the grammatical structure underlying the message, these pauses would not appear in decoder reproductions. It is only a small step from that thought to the suggestion that encoder pauses mark both uncertainty and constituent boundaries, while decoder pauses mark only the constituent boundaries. This would show up in the data as a relatively lower proportion of pauses preceding high-information (i.e., content) words in the decoder compared with encoder protocols. By assuming that function words tend to initiate grammatical constituents, the result could be taken as indicating a displacement in the distribution of pauses from within to between grammatical constituents.

The following examples illustrate what might be expected by this theory. Slashes indicate pauses of some kind. One encoder said:

(3) *It looks like a girl who is / standing / at the top of a hill and just / trying to / maybe find herself*

The decoder reproduced it as:

(4) *It looks like a girl just standing at the top of the hill thinking / and trying to find herself*

Pauses usually preceded content words in the encoder's speech, but the decoder's pause was followed by a function word. Most of the encoder's pauses seemed to fall within phrases and could even be called ungrammatical pauses, whereas the decoder's pause fell at a phrase boundary. These examples illustrate rather clearly the relationship of pauses to boundaries, but consider the next:

(5)   *Somebody / looks like a girl / sitting down looks like / she's crying or something somethin' happened / sad*

The reader is invited to look at example 2 again, and note where he might have guessed boundary markers to be. Now, in example 5, with the pauses indicated, are the pauses within or between major grammatical constituents? (It is necessary to say major, since all words, being constituents in themselves, mark constituent boundaries in a trivial sense.) Of course, we cannot use the pauses to say where the boundaries are because that would be circular.

Given this speech, there were several possible solutions to the problem of assigning grammatical structure to it, at least in relation to the pauses. One was to locate a pause and then try to determine from context whether or not it was "grammatical." This seems to be the approach, for example, of two of the more recent Goldman-Eisler studies (Henderson, *et al.*, 1965; 1966). To classify gaps in speech (100 msec or more), these workers used six rules to identify those gaps which were located at "grammatical junctures." Four of the rules involved judgments that a "natural" punctuation point, indirect question, parenthetical reference or adverbial clause had been identified, two rules relied solely upon the presence of a single word from certain word classes, e.g., conjunctions, to establish a gap as grammatical. Gaps not meeting the six rule criteria, such as, presumably, all the pauses in example 5, would be counted as ungrammatical.

Another possible solution was to use only utterances, or portions of utterances, in which the grammatical structure was clear, and ignore the rest of the data. This was the approach taken by Maclay and Osgood (1959) in the section of their study concerned with between and within-constituent pauses. Using the well-known Fries (1952) scheme for classifying lexical and function words, Maclay and Osgood isolated all and only the two to four-word phrases in their protocols which were described by sixteen selected word frames, and then tallied the frequency of pauses around or within these phrases.

A third possible solution, which we adopted, was to postulate all function words as initiating constituents in a probabilistic sense and identify words in the function class by means of a list. Miller, Newman and Friedman's (1958) list of 363 function words served this purpose. Their list included all function words listed by Fries as well as other words added intuitively by them after an analysis of selected printed text in English. These function words were clearly low-information; they represented 6 percent types but 59 percent tokens in the printed text. However, this convenient list allowed an empirical test of the intuitively highly plausible assumption that function words initiate grammatical constituent boundaries, at least in formal printed text. Function words were counted at the beginning and end of sentences in Miller, Newman and Friedman's text (Martin & Strange, 1968a). The results were that 84 percent of the sentences began with one of the function words on the list but only 18 percent ended with one of these words.

Following word classification, the encoder and decoder protocols from the experiment were scored blind for hesitation phenomena. Maclay and Osgood's classification as Repeats, False Starts, Filled Pauses and Unfilled Pauses was used; for convenience, however, we will use pauses hereafter to refer to all four types except where indicated. The two scorers knew nothing of the content-function classification or the purpose of the experiment. Their independent counts were averaged.

The results, seen in Figure 1, indicated that encoders placed a higher percentage of pauses before content words than function words, while decoders placed a higher percentage of pauses before function words than content words. This relative displacement in the distribution of pauses within and between grammatical constituents, which was the dependent variable generally observed in our experiments, was called the *hesitation shift*.

These results were interpreted to mean that encoder pauses mark not only "junctures" but also momentary uncertainty within grammatical constituents, while decoder pauses usually mark only the "junctures." It was tempting to speculate that the hesitation shift indicated that decoders were ignoring the noninformative aspects of the speech signal, that they were not "hearing" the pauses in the encoder speech at all, but instead were organizing the message at some higher level.

The experiment provides the basis for organizing the remainder of the paper. In the next section experiments on speech perception question whether or not the listener can attend to acoustic elements while decoding speech. Then experiments turn to the speaker's task and to what the pausal phenomena will reveal about it.

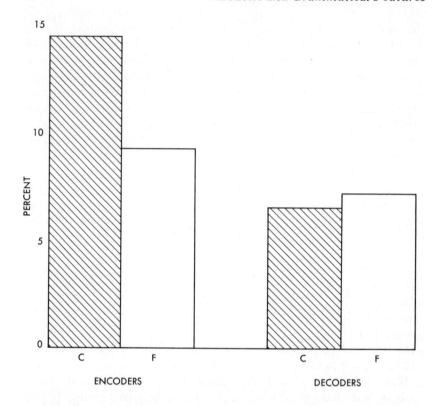

FIGURE 1. **Percentages of content (C) and function (F) words preceded by hesitations.**

Some characteristics of pause judgments are considered, particularly their reliability and the possible cues that might be in the acoustic signal. Finally, some data are presented to bear on the grammar of spontaneous speech and hypotheses about its underlying structure, the knowledge of which is shared (more or less) by the speaker and listener.

SPEECH PERCEPTION

Experiments in this section concern the perception of pauses during speech decoding (Martin & Strange, 1968b). In the case of speech perception, looking at pauses may be particularly valuable. Because pauses in speech are usually linguistically noninformative, the task of discriminating or detecting these acoustic effects should be separable from decoding or understanding the message in the sound signal. The separation, however, does not seem possible if listeners are asked to identify or detect, say, words, which are part of the message. Both of these kinds of tasks have been called perception, by Garner (1966), Gibson (1966), Lane (1965), Liberman (1957) and many others. One question underlying these experiments, then, was whether or not these two tasks refer to perceptual processes which, in the case of the perception of speech, are psychologically distinct.

The general approach was to ask subjects to listen to speech in one pass, attending to pauses and decoding the message at the same time. We expected the two tasks to be incompatible and consequently the listeners would either show disruptive performance on one of them or, if the alternative were available, avoid one altogether. This was the weaker of two hypotheses; in the stronger, one might say that pauses and perhaps other linguistically noninformative acoustic features cannot be "heard" at all during speech decoding. In short, listeners will resist attending to pauses if they are also required to decode the message. Asked to detect pauses but unable to do so without attending to the message as well, they will be unable to correctly place the pauses.

The experiment described earlier was consistent with these notions, but there were several alternative interpretations. It was possible that decoders heard pauses perfectly well but did not regard pause placement as a part of the task. Second, asked to place pauses it was possible that they still did not fully understand the task. Third, decoders might have heard pauses yet simply forgotten them by the time of reproduction. Fourth, while easy to hear, pauses might have been difficult to reproduce, that is, the hesitation shift between encoding and decoding might simply reflect the response characteristics of the decoder's task. Finally, decoders given the instruction to attend to pauses and words might have chosen words because they are easier, or, said another way, the hesitation shift might demonstrate nothing but the failure of instructions. All of these alternatives were considered in the following work.

The design and rationale of the first pause perception experiment (Martin & Strange, 1968b) was similar to the one discussed earlier. Decoders reproduced the encoder's speech. A second decoder did also, but under explicit instructions to include pauses and other irregularities, that is, to reproduce the utterances *exactly*. The three subjects then made a triple, including an encoder, an "ordinary" decoder and an "exact" decoder, in order to insure that exact decoders regarded pause placement as part of their task.

The results of this experiment indicated that both ordinary and exact decoders paused relatively more often at constituent boundaries, that is, prior to function words. Exact decoders paused more frequently overall, however, suggesting that the instructions to reproduce pauses exactly produced a motivational effect without any change in the hesitation shift.

Most hesitation phenomena in these experiments were Unfilled Pauses, but the remaining types were potentially of special interest. Repeats and Filled Pauses are obvious and should be easily heard in encoder speech when pauses are heard at all. To check this point, these two hesitation types were counted for overlap between encoder and decoder protocols. To provide the most liberal comparison, a pause was counted as a decoder imitation if either scorer heard the pause before the same word in the paired encoder and decoder protocols, but as a decoder production if both scorers marked it in the decoder transcript but neither in the encoder transcript.

One clear feature of the comparison was the small number of decoder pauses that could be called imitations. It is true that exact decoders did insignificantly better than ordinary decoders, but both groups imitated poorly (around 8 and 16 percent for ordinary and exact decoders, respectively; the remaining 92 and 84 percent were productions). Even so, imitative success is probably overestimated by the liberal scoring method.

It was possible, of course, that exact decoders were not responding consistently, if at all, to the instructions to imitate pauses. Perhaps they regarded pauses as secondary, or perhaps they did not fully understand what counted as a pause to be imitated. The next experiment introduced a practice session during which decoders demonstrated their grasp of the task by imitating pauses to a performance criterion, after which experimental utterances were presented as before. A single encoder was used in this experiment, one selected for a particularly high content-pause rate.

The results were rather similar to the previous experiment. Exact decoders again paused more frequently overall in their reproductions than ordinary decoders, but both groups paused relatively more frequently at constituent boundaries and to about the same degree. Practice in the pause reproduction task apparently did not improve performance. This conclusion was supported by a comparison of imitation rates for the infrequent but "obvious" Repeats and Filled Pauses. In this experiment, the exact decoders, though given practice in their task, were even less successful than the ordinary decoder group. It seems paradoxical that the practiced exact decoders imitated less well (relative to their comparison ordinary decoders) than the unpracticed exact decoders in the previous experiment; it is not, however, since the single encoder utterance used in the second experiment was longer than the average utterance in the first. Hence, it was more difficult to track, resulting in a higher exact decoder pause rate with a correspondingly lower imitation rate. In short, given brief utterances, a few pauses were easy to reproduce. Given longer utterances, attempting exact reproduction stimulated higher pause rates with the result that overlap with encoder pauses approached the rate to be expected by chance.

Continuing on the theory that attending to pauses and decoding messages were incompatible operations, another possibility was examined. Attending to pauses in speech should disrupt speech decoding. Rote reproduction of words heard is not a good measure of effectiveness of speech decoding and was not ordinarily used in these experiments. In the experiment just discussed, however, it was particularly convenient to count correct imitations of both words and pauses. The results of this comparison also supported the notion that the two processes were mutually interfering. Exact decoders produced more total words and total pauses, but, of these, a lower proportion were correct. Apparently the exact instructions stimulated a higher output rate without a corresponding increase in accuracy.

The next experiment considered the possibility that the hesitation shift was due to a memory factor. While there are problems with any theory of memory that proposes content pauses are forgotten more quickly than function pauses, a change in hesitation shift after a delay in reporting what was heard would be instructive. Decoders listened to a composite tape of 60 utterances selected from the protocols of various encoders in earlier experiments. The experimental variable was delay between listening and reproduction. The three intervals were zero, four and eight seconds. The result again was a substantial hesitation shift, but of about the same magnitude for all three groups. It seemed reasonable to conclude that if memory contributes to the shift it must be during the time of listening.

In the subsequent experiment the subjects were required to listen to speech and simply mark the pauses they heard in it on transcripts of the speech rather than repeating the speech so that pause distributions in their reproductions could be determined. The purpose was primarily to assess the difference between detecting pauses as a single task and detecting pauses and decoding messages as a double task. In addition, it seemed possible to consider hesitation shift without the potential complications of a normal speaking tendency toward between-constituent pausing. This tendency is not inconsiderable and could apply to the decoder's reproduction task.

The experimental variations were as follows. Four groups listened to the composite encoder tape and marked pauses on transcripts. One group listened to each utterance twice through headphones, marking it as they listened (the Mark-2 condition). A second group heard the recording once and simultaneously marked each utterance (Mark-1). Another group heard the utterance once, marked it simultaneously, and then wrote the utterance from memory (Mark-Write). The last group listened to the utterance without looking at the transcript; when the utterance had finished they marked the transcript from memory (Recall-Mark). These tasks seem to depart from the simple task of scoring pauses in order of decreasing similarity to the scoring task while simultaneously increasing order of difficulty. Mark-2 was similar to the research assistant's scoring task, Mark-1 less so. The Mark-Write subject, provided with a transcript while listening, nevertheless had to decode the speech if he were to write it later. Finally, the subject in the Recall-Mark group, with no transcript while listening, nevertheless had to remember at least part of the utterance to keep track of where the pauses were; that is, he presumably had to remember words even though his instructions asked only for pauses. In short, the first two groups needed only to detect pauses, the latter two were required to decode and store the words as well. If the tasks were successively dissimilar, the four groups should show a progressive shift away from the scorers' judgments.

To measure the hesitation shift in this experiment, the results were first considered in terms of the number of content-word pauses marked over the total pauses marked. This proportion yields a straight-forward measure of relative shift comparable to the measure used in earlier experiments (pauses divided by words where both are variables), despite the fact that words in this experiment were constant. Figure 2 shows the results. Included for comparison are data from the research assistants who scored the composite encoder tape and the decoders of the previous experiment who listened to it but whose task was reproduction.

The decreasing content-pause rate as one goes from left to right represents increasing hesitation shift. The results look like a task

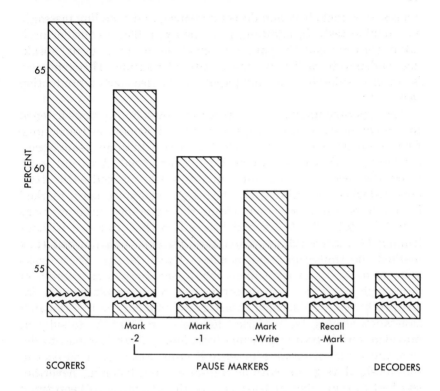

FIGURE 2. Percentages of words marked for pauses which were content words.

continuum representing relative ease and accuracy of pause detection, with practiced scorers at one end and decoders at the other.

These results were consistent with expectation, but the hesitation shift hypothesis implies more than this. It is possible that the decoder's task involves the imposition of new structure on the acoustic signal. The real meaning of hesitation shift then could be the decoding of grammatical segments (constituents) as "units" despite disunitizing elements (within-constituent pauses) in the acoustic signal. On this theory the shift results not only from forgotten content-word pauses but from the listener's contribution of function-word (constituent-boundary) pauses which were not "there" in the input signal, that is, incorrectly marked.

The marker data were scored as correct or incorrect, using pauses detected by the practiced scorers as criterion. The proportion, correct over correct plus incorrect, was used as the measure of accuracy. Again, according to the hypothesis of decreasing similarity to the scorer's task, the groups differed in appropriate order, with accuracy of marked function-word pauses decreasing most rapidly. This interaction was expected on the theory that the hesitation shift depends upon a disproportionate increase in function-word pauses supplied by the listener. The largest shift appeared in the Recall-Mark group, the group that used no transcript during marking and presumably could correctly place pauses only by remembering the words as well. For this group the hesitation shift probably should not be attributed to failure of instructions.

Summarizing these experiments, each required the subjects to attend simultaneously to pauses and messages in speech. Since speaking bias, memory and failure of instructions seemed to be largely ruled out, the hesitation shift suggested inattention to pauses during the linguistic organization of the input. Obviously subjects can judge pauses in a speech signal on the one hand, or remember its message on the other. The question perhaps is the way in which these two different mental operations are incompatible. It could be concluded that the subjects were alternating, however unevenly, between words and pauses as different segments of the signal. We preferred, however, the conclusion that the subjects were alternately attending to information at different levels, to information in the acoustic signal sometimes, but, mostly, to information at some higher level.

SPEECH PRODUCTION

This section turns to experiments primarily concerned with the encoder, again using pause distributions as the data of interest. Looking at the literature on the distribution of pauses in spontaneous speech (as opposed to speech reproduced, repeated, read aloud, etc.), it was difficult to find a consistent relation between pauses and grammatical structure, which is hardly surprising in view of the problems of grammatical analysis discussed earlier, and considering the variety of methods and analyses employed. For example, some of Goldman-Eisler's early studies (1958 a; b) were interpreted as showing that pauses tend to precede high-information (within-constituent) words. Boomer (1965) found a spike in hesitation-pause probability preceding the second (rather than the first) word in "phonemic clauses." This result was largely a consequence of the decision to regard pauses between clauses as junctures following the first clause rather than hesitation pauses preceding the second, unless a Filled Pause or word fragment intervened between the two clauses. If Boomer had added (a) pauses preceeding the first word, and (b) juncture pauses which were not included at all in the analysis because they contained no within-clause pauses, to the between-clause junctures, then the result might have shown a fairly close relation between pauses and constituent boundaries. Finally, as an indication of the difficulty in finding a clear relation between pauses and grammatical structure, Maclay and Osgood's (1959) work has been cited as evidence both for within- (Osgood, 1963) and between-constituent (Garrett and Fodor, 1968) pauses.

Going beyond the obvious point that pauses do occur at both places, it seemed to us that these studies were not inconsistent, because our experiments suggested that encoders yield disproportionate content-word pauses, that is, within-constituent pauses, only under certain conditions. Two of these conditions were that the speaker is motivated to choose informative words, but that the words he needs are not immediately accessible. These are far from unusual conditions, but they do seem to be required. As an illustration of this point, we did an exercise in which some encoders were asked to give one sentence only in their TAT-card descriptions while for others the one-sentence restriction was not mentioned (Martin, 1968). The results showed that "unrestricted" encoders gave almost double the number of words per card, but, in doing so, they paused predominantly between constituents. In other words, subjects who talk more, think less, at least about word choice, and therefore they tend to pause between rather than within constituents. These results also explain the seemingly inconsistent data mentioned above. As a later section will show, there is reason to believe that relaxed, conversational speech abounds in function words and between-constituent pauses. Boomer's speakers were interviewees engaged in conversation, and they paused often at phonemic clause boundaries. Goldman-Eisler's and Maclay and Osgood's speakers generally were engaged in more demanding tasks.

Turning now to some experiments in speech production, we assumed that selecting the syntactic-semantic structure of a sentence, and realizing the sentence acoustically, were really two different speaker processes, or at least two different levels. Since function words tend to initiate grammatical constituents it follows that at least some of the early words will be determined first, and hence the encoder can begin to speak immediately, pausing, however, as he reaches the slot containing an as yet incompletely selected word. This word will be most likely a content word, and even though it has been *selected* simultaneously with every other word in its structure, it draws a pause if it is not ready for articulation at the needed moment. The content word requiring a pause will usually be the first one in a constituent for the simple reason that each content word following it in the constituent has more time to become accessible.

This theory might be supported if it could be shown that encoders pause less before content words when these words are unusually accessible. One way to accomplish this was to provide the encoder with content words to use in describing TAT cards. In the first experiment, subjects were assigned into triples made of an (ordinary) encoder and decoder as usual, and a second "primed" encoder who, prior to describing a TAT card, was read a list of content words appropriate to it. The words were, in fact, those used earlier for that card by the ordinary encoder in his triple, in scrambled order. Thus two kinds of encoders could be compared, those with the benefit of priming words for their descriptions and those required to find their own. According to the hypothesis, the primed encoders should place pauses between grammatical constituents rather than within them. Decoders would provide a baseline.

The results were as expected. The ordinary encoders paused relatively more often within constituents but the primed encoders paused between them. In addition, they paused less prior to the primed content words they used than prior to the content words they had to select for themselves. It would seem that the primed encoders' decreasing content-word pause rate was specific to the primed words they used (Martin & Strange, 1968a).

This experiment was however subject to another interpretation. Perhaps the very fact of reading to an encoder a list of words led him to construct utterances before speaking, so that it was his interpretation of the task rather than word-search time that determined the distribution of pauses. This notion was tested by comparing encoders primed with content words against other encoders given function words, though with the latter necessarily arranged to provide some kind of sensible albeit "content-less" utterance frame. In the second experiment, one primed encoder in a triple was given the content words supplied by the ordinary encoder. Another was given the same encoder's complete utterance except that every content word was deleted and replaced by the word *blank*. Number and tense suffixes were retained. An example might proceed, *A blank of blank blanks blanking in a blank blank.* Thus, there were content-primed and function-primed encoders.

The results of this experiment were that content-primed encoders paused relatively more frequently prior to function words, i.e., between constituents, while function-primed encoders paused more frequently for content words, i.e., within constituents. This effect was marked when primed words only were scored. In other words, the pause distributions from function-primed encoders were a lot like those from ordinary encoders and suggested that the word-priming effect on pause distributions was specific to content words.

A reasonable interpretation of this experiment, and of two others similar to it, might be that by the time a content-primed encoder has arranged his primed content words into an utterance, the function words have fallen into place also, and hence his pauses will precede constituents. Given function words on the other hand, the choice of informative words remains.

The next experiment investigated a rather obvious variable on the theory that pauses indicate search time for words. Three ordinary encoder groups described TAT cards, but they were allowed to begin their descriptions only after a delay interval of zero, four or eight seconds. Thus they looked at each card, presumably constructing a description, but began talking only after signal from the experimenter. One might expect within-constituent pauses to diminish after the delay interval, but they did not. The experiment was similar to the previous ones in that the basic factor in within-constituent pause rates seemed to be whether or not content words were easily accessible during composition.

The results of all these experiments seemed to mean that a speaker who had the content words in a constituent to be uttered, had the function words also, but not necessarily vice versa. The result was consistent with the notion that speech production is neither wholly hierarchical nor wholly left-to-right, as well as with the idea of separate processes for deciding what to say and acoustically realizing the words to say it. Having the structure of what he will say, the talker has to speak in a left-to-right sequence, but the words he uses do not become accessible to him in a left-to-right order.

PAUSES

Most workers investigating hesitation phenomena have relied upon the physical measurement of silent intervals of some arbitrary length when they have considered Unfilled Pauses (Goldman-Eisler, 1958 a, b; Boomer, 1965; Levin, *et al.*, 1967). Our experiments, however, have used listener judgments to identify all types of hesitation phenomena. Since Unfilled Pauses are by far the most frequent, it is worth asking, first, how reliably listeners can identify them and, secondly, what cues in the signal are used.

In experimental effects, reliability is not an issue, since blind scorers consistently separated encoder and decoder protocols. Moreover, subjects asked to mark pauses on transcripts placed 88 percent of their pauses in agreement with the scorers, despite the fact that they were inexperienced in this task and probably varied greatly in motivation and other factors (Martin & Strange, 1968 b). There were, however, differences between scorers, and types of hesitation. Scorer agreement was usually highest for Repeats and Filled Pauses, with Unfilled Pauses next. False starts were lowest since grammatical judgment is required, but probably for another reason as well. Scorers have informally admitted that they "tune out" (ignore words) while listening for pauses, which is only to be expected by the theory motivating the experiments. Between pairs of scorers, agreement over all four types of hesitation combined ranged, in terms of percentage overlap, from in the 80's to the 90's. Informal observation suggests that ROC curves for pause judgments vary somewhat between and within scorers and are susceptible to personality and sociological factors as well (one scorer allowed she sometimes felt others were marking more hesitations than she), but since the same scorers were always used within experimental comparisons these facts present practical, not interpretational, problems.

The question of the acoustic correlates of, or cues for, pause judgments deserves some consideration. The physical records of the 60 utterances comprising the composite encoder tape (see above) were analyzed by a spectrograph, with separate frequency and amplitude displays on the same time line (Martin, in press). Silent intervals were taken to be identifiable stretches at background noise level on the amplitude record. Background noise was fairly constant but substantial and hence the length of "real" silent intervals by this measure is over-estimated. For this reason, silent intervals of less than 50 milliseconds were ignored, but with no effect on the tentative conclusions which follow.

Analysis showed there was little reason to separate content and function pauses, or judgments of one, as opposed to two, scorers; hence they were combined. There were 206 locations in the 60 utterances at which at least one scorer or the machine "heard" a "pause." Table 1 summarizes the results of spectrograph analysis. At least

TABLE I

MEDIAN PAUSE AND SYLLABLE LENGTHS.

(in msec)

	Scorer-Machine	Scorer Only	Machine Only
N	150	23	33
Pause	470	—	70
Syllable Preceding	290	320	130
Syllable Following	190	200	190

one scorer agreed with the machine in 150 cases, or 82 percent of the silent intervals, while hearing pauses at 23 nonsilent locations. The second line of Table 1 shows that the silent intervals judged to be pauses were larger than those for which no judgments were recorded. Pause judgments in the absence of silent intervals were, however, of greater interest. On listening to them one forms the impression that the speaker is changing pace, that his speaking rate slows briefly but then is followed by a "burst" of words. This impression was checked by measuring syllable length before and after each silent interval and syllable length prior and subsequent to the judged-pause location when there was no silent interval. A technician naive about the purpose of the research measured three syllables in each direction, but the results were clearest for the syllable immediately preceding and following a pause location. See Table 1. When scorers judged a pause where there was no measured silent interval, the last syllable of the word preceding the pause was longer than the first syllable of the following word in nearly every case. When there was a silent interval, there was usually an elongated syllable prior to the pause interval. When, however, the machine detected a silent interval but the scorers did not, the syllable following the interval was usually longer. It does appear that elongated syllables at the end of a word may serve as a cue for pause judgments. It also appears that the presence of a relatively longer syllable *following* a silent interval may cancel the effect of the interval as a cue for a pause judgment, if the interval is quite short. To conclude, momentary tempo changes in speaking, which apparently were frequently what the scorers were hearing, seem to be logically at least as close to psychological hesitation mechanisms as short silent intervals. This suggests that, except where one's theory requires an Unfilled Pause to be a silent interval of some minimal length, one may as well use scorer judgments as physical measures to locate them, particularly since all the other usual types of hesitation, Filled Pauses, Repeats and False Starts, must be identified by listener judgment.

WORDS

Our work with spontaneous speech has been primarily directed toward hesitation phenomena, but it was difficult to avoid speculating about what its grammatical structure might be. We first considered the ways it might be different from formal text. One may be that real speech deviates (when it does) toward a closer approximation to some kind of intermediate of deeper structure. Another is that real speech contains only the structure required by the speaker's circumstances. These and the following considerations suggested a hypothesis about the grammatical structure of spontaneous speech, more specifically, about the distribution of content and function words.

First, function words in a sentence would be thought of as representing features of underlying lexical units, that is, that they were surface realizations of certain deeper structure features. This notion of course has a formal counterpart in linguistic analysis (see, e.g., Postal, 1966). Perhaps function words, as surface (phonetic) realizations of relatively uninformative features of deeper units, tend to be omitted under certain conditions, such as when the encoder ordinarily has difficulty in expression, or when he wishes to communicate clearly what he means but does not feel compelled to encode everything in a formally correct fashion. In short, intermediate structures can be incompletely encoded, and, speaking very loosely, there may sometimes be a tradeoff between formal and communicative accuracy.

There was a variety of evidence and speculation consistent with all of this. Apparently, some aphasics delete function words (see, e.g., Fillenbaum, *et al.*, 1961; Luria, 1958). Children speak "telegraphese" (Brown & Bellugi, 1964), which amounts to omitting function words. Perhaps children "talk base strings directly" (McNeill, 1966), or perhaps they talk in topic-comment constructions, which are said to be more fundamental (and universal) than subject-predicate constructions (Gruber, 1967). These considerations, as well as the fact that some function-word classes, e.g., auxiliaries, appear to differ widely in their use and importance across languages, seem to support the notion of content-word utterances as "closer" to underlying structures.

Aphasics and children speak content-word language. Some of our data suggest that adult speakers do also, during points of difficult word search. It had been believed earlier (Martin, 1967; Martin and Strange, 1968a) that the distribution of content and function words was about the same for real speech as for written text. This was true for the typical encoding experiment, which, like Miller, Newman and Friedman's (1958) formal text, yielded about 41 to 42 percent content words on the average. But on the composite encoder tape, composed of utterances *selected* for high content *pause* rates, the *content* word rate was also higher, 45 percent. On the other hand, unrestricted TAT card descriptions (no one-sentence limit) yielded 39.9 percent content words, the only encoder group to fall below 40 percent. And further, our count of function words in ordinary interview conversation from Davis Howes' (1967) published word count of spoken English yielded around 37 percent content words (using the Miller *et al.* list as the basis for classifying words). If high rates of content pausing signal careful word search, and if the Howes interview minimized word search (subjects apparently were made comfortable and encouraged to talk about anything), then there may be a continuum of word-choice difficulty, with the ordinary encoders falling between the Howes interviewees and the composite encoders.

If the foregoing is correct then momentary differences in word-choice difficulty, correlated with differences in content-word rate, should also occur *within* encoders. This prediction was tested by matching every composite encoder utterance with another from the same encoder but selected for low content pause rate; the pairs were augmented with 58 others. As expected, the utterances selected for high content pause rate also had a higher content word rate. On the theory that function words were deleted during vigorous word search, the question next asked was which function words were "missing" in the content-pause speech.

It was first considered that function words appearing frequently in formal text but relatively less frequently in real speech might constitute words that have a higher syntactic than semantic "value" in correct English. As a start, the 50 function words with the greatest differences in relative frequency (percentage of total function words) between written and spoken count were determined. For example, the first word on this derived list was *the*; highest on both written (12 percent) and spoken (6 percent) counts, the difference was also the largest. The 50 words on this derived list as well as several articles were counted in the pairs of utterances selected for extremely high and extremely low content-pause rates. According to theory, articles should appear less frequently in hesitant speech (high content-pause rate), and perhaps auxiliaries and certain prepositions as well.

The findings which seemed to be most consistent and also to make the most sense were the following. Of the eight definite and indefinite articles, seven were relatively less frequent in hesitant speech (one difference was zero). In short, articles, which carry little information, drop out of hesitant speech. On the other hand all the conjunctions on the list appeared more frequently in hesitant speech. These words, *if*'s, *and*'s, *or*'s, *but*'s and *so*'s could be regarded as "hem-and-haw" words. The case for auxiliaries and prepositions was less clear, but for articles and conjunctions at least, hesitant speech seemed to be low in certain words which carry very little information, but high in words which can be used as "fillers."

These results suggest that the adult trying to say what he means shows certain similarities to the child in the same situation. The similarity is a coarse one, having to do with content and function words only, but it suggests, we believe, that the study of how people actually speak and listen may be as important for understanding the mature language user as for understanding the language learner; we need to look at the spontaneous speech of adults as well as children. Surely this will be true for an account of the mechanisms involved in the production of connected speech. In the case of speech perception, it just might be that what the spontaneous speaker omits or distorts without detriment to the listener's understanding will reveal something of what the necessary and sufficient conditions really are for communication to take place.

REFERENCES

Boomer, D. S. Hesitation and grammatical encoding. *Language and Speech*, 1965, 8, 148-58.

Brown, R., & Bellugi, Ursula. Three processes in the child's acquisition of syntax. In E. Lenneberg (ed.), *New directions in the study of language*. Cambridge: MIT Press, 1964.

Fillenbaum, S., Jones, L. V., & Wepman, J. M. Some linguistic features of speech from aphasic patients. *Language and Speech*, 1961, **4**, 91-108.

Fries, C. C. *The structure of English*. New York: Harcourt, Brace, 1952.

Garner, W. To perceive is to know. *American Psychologist*, 1966, **21**, 11-19.

Garrett, M., & Fodor, J. A. Psychological theories and linguistic constructs. In T. R. Dixon and D. L. Horton (eds.), *Verbal behavior and general behavior theory*. Englewood Cliffs: Prentice-Hall, 1968.

Gibson, J. J. *The senses considered as perceptual systems*. New York: Houghton-Mifflin, 1966.

Goldman-Eisler, Frieda. Speech production and the predictability of words in context. *Quarterly Journal of Experimental Psychology*, 1958, **10**, 96-106. (a)

Goldman-Eisler, Frieda. The predictability of words in context and the length of pauses in speech. *Language and Speech*, 1958, **1**, Part 3, 226-231. (b)

Goldman-Eisler, Frieda. Hesitation and information in speech. In C. Cherry (ed.), *Information theory*. London: Butterworths, 1961. (a)

Goldman-Eisler, Frieda. The significance of changes in the rate of articulation. *Language and Speech*, 1961, **4**, 171-74. (b)

Gruber, J. S. Topicalization in child language. *Foundations of Language*, 1967, **3**, 37-65.

Henderson, A., Goldman-Eisler, Frieda, & Skarbek, A. Temporal patterns of cognitive activity and breath control in speech. *Language and Speech*, 1965, **8**, 236-42.

Henderson, A., Goldman-Eisler, Frieda, & Skarbek, A. Sequential temporal patterns in spontaneous speech. *Language and Speech*, 1966, **9**, 207-16.

Howes, D. A word count of spoken English. *Journal of Verbal Learning and Verbal Behavior*, 1967, **5**, 572-604.

Lane, H. Motor theory of speech perception: A critical review. *Psychological Review*, 1965, **72**, 275-309.

Levin, H., Silverman, Irene, & Ford, B. Hesitations in children's speech during explanation and description. *Journal of Verbal Learning and Verbal Behavior*, 1967, **6**, 560-64.

Liberman, A. Some results of research on speech perception. *Journal of the Acoustical Society of America*, 1957, 117-23. Reprinted in S. Saporta (ed.), *Psycholinguistics: A book of readings*. New York: Holt, Rinehart & Winston, Inc., 1961.

Luria, A. R. Brain disorders and language analysis. *Language and Speech*, 1958, **1**, 14-34.

Maclay H., & Osgood, C. E. Hesitation phenomena in spontaneous English speech. *Word*, 1959, **1**, 19-44.

Martin, J. G. Hesitations in the speaker's production and listener's reproduction of utterances. *Journal of Verbal Learning and Verbal Behavior*, 1967, **6**, 903-09.

Martin, J. G. Two psychological mechanisms specified by hesitation in spontaneous speech. *Proceedings of the 76th Annual Convention of the American Psychological Association*, 1968.

Martin, J. G. On judging pauses in spontaneous speech. *Journal of Verbal Learning and Verbal Behavior*, in press.

Martin, J. G., & Strange, Winifred. Determinants of hesitations in spontaneous speech. *Journal of Experimental Psychology*, 1968, **76**, 474-79. (a)

Martin, J. G., & Strange, Winifred. The perception of hesitation in spontaneous speech. *Perception and Psychophysics*, 1968, **3**, 427-38 (b)

McNeill, D. Developmental psycholinguistics. In F. Smith and G. A. Miller (eds.), *The genesis of language*. Cambridge: MIT Press, 1966.

Miller, G. A., Newman, E. B., & Friedman, A. E. Length-frequency statistics for written English. *Information and Control*, 1958, **1**, 370-98.

Osgood, C. E. Psycholinguistics. In S. Koch (ed.), *Psychology: A study of a science*. Vol. 2. New York: McGraw-Hill, 1963, pp. 244-316.

Postal, P. M. On so-called 'pronouns' in English. *Monograph Series on Language and Linguistics*, 1966, **19**, 177-207.

Tannenbaum, P. H., Williams, F., & Hillier, Carolyn S. Word predictability in the environments of hesitations. *Journal of Verbal Learning and Verbal Behavior*, 1965, **4**, 134-40.

THE IMPORTANCE OF LINGUISTICS FOR THE STUDY OF SPEECH HESITATIONS

HERBERT H. CLARK[2]

Carnegie-Mellon University

Why should psychologists study speech hesitations? The answer, of course, is that hesitations are presumed to be psychological in origin. Martin, in his paper on speech hesitations, makes that assumption: hesitations indicate something about the process of encoding and decoding speech. He also assumes that these two processes should be described in terms of linguistic entities. These two assumptions are clearly appropriate for the psychologist studying hesitations. But, it is on Martin's models or theories that I would like to make some comments. Martin is working from a model or theory which is inadequate for his purpose. First, he is using too weak a linguistic theory. Second, because he has used such a weak linguistic theory, he draws weak and sometimes misleading conclusions about encoding and decoding. And third, Martin's study of decoding is confounded with his study of encoding. I will comment on these three points in turn and suggest what I think are some refinements for his model.

[1]This work was supported in part by Public Health Service research grant MH-07722.
[2]Now at Stanford University.

A general comment on much present day work in psycholinguistics is that it pays more attention to the *psycho-* than the *linguistics*. This criticism can also be made of Martin's paper. He has chosen for his linguistic theory one which makes only one distinction—that between content and function words. He has ignored sentences, phrases, embedding, subordinate clauses, and many other things previous psychologists—not to mention linguists—thought were important. The differences between content and function words certainly are important, but not in themselves. They are a product of a far more intricate linguistic theory and become important only in the context of this broader theory of language. It is the broader theory of language, of course, that should lie at the base of psychological theorizing. Previous investigators — such as Goldman-Eisler, Maclay and Osgood, and Boomer — have shown an increasing awareness of the need and importance of linguistic theories to the proper study of hesitations; they have gone far beyond content and function words.

Content and function words constitute a small subset of the theory of parts of speech. Where does this theory let the psycholinguist down? Martin infers an important result about constituents by way of content and function words. He reasons as follows: Most constituents begin with function words and end with content words, and encoder hesitations tend to occur more often before content words; therefore, encoder hesitations tend to occur more often within constituents. The logic is correct, but the conclusion is misleading. Taken at face value, the inference would say that the more deeply embedded the constituent, the more likely an encoder will pause within it. Some of Maclay and Osgood's data contradict this conclusion. In phrases of the type, *under the big houses*, the deepest constituent boundary is between *big* and *houses*, yet speakers hesitated more often between *the* and *big*. A constituent consisting of an adjective modifying a noun, of course, is just one of the exceptions to Martin's generalization about constituents: it begins and ends with content words. There are indeed large classes of exceptions: (1) verbs with particles, as in *look up the telephone number*; (2) nouns with any kind of prenominal modifiers, as in *telephone number*; (3) verbs or adjectives with preceding or following adverbs, as in *walked slowly, quickly ran*, or *exceedingly gallant*; and so on. Later, I will take up some reasons for the hesitations before the adjective instead of after, but for the moment, I want to emphasize that the within-constituent hypothesis clearly does not predict this fact and might not work for others of the exceptions.

To make hesitation phenomena much clearer, I want to bring out a fundamental distinction between two kinds of pauses — conventional and idiosyncratic pauses. Linguists have made this distinction for some time, identifying conventional pauses as part of their study of linguistic competence and idiosyncratic hesitations as part of speech performance. This is what Martin has been studying, but without saying so. The conventional-idiosyncratic distinction is a simple one. A speaker who knows what he is going to say uses conventional pauses only. He pauses at various places in speech because he has to breathe, but he will not breathe just anywhere. He will take the opportunity only at places where the syntax allows him to do so. These conventional pause points are the junctures linguists have studied as part of intonation patterns. The speaker may breathe or pause at junctures, but he is not forced to: junctures are points of *possible* pausing. On the other hand, a speaker who composes as he speaks shows other kinds of hesitations. He pauses where there are no junctures — at places where the idealized speaker who knows what he is going to say would never pause. These are idiosyncratic hesitations.

There is ample evidence for this differentiation in the pause literature. In Goldman-Eisler's laboratory, Henderson, Goldman-Eisler, and Skarbek (1965) studied people reading aloud and people speaking spontaneously. They showed that the readers paused very rarely except to breathe, and when they did breathe, they did so only at grammatical junctures. Their spontaneous speakers, however, breathed not only at junctures, but elsewhere, and they hesitated elsewhere. Martin's encoders and decoders appear to be comparable to the spontaneous speakers and readers, respectively, of Henderson *et al.* Martin has shown that someone who knows what he is going to say — he has just listened to another speaker — talks more like a reader than a spontaneous speaker. The decoder's speech has become more conventional, more fluent. Even the "primed encoder," the speaker who was given the content words of another person's description, sounds more like a reader — more conventional in his pauses — because he has some idea of what he will say. This part of Martin's work is a very nice replication of Goldman-Eisler's continuing research findings and similar results by Maclay and Osgood (1959).

The encoder-decoder "hesitation shift," as Martin calls it, does not seem to be a shift at all. Decoders merely eliminate the encoder's idiosyncratic pauses from their speech, since the decoders know what they are going to say. They eliminate very few of the encoder's conventional pauses, since they are an integral part of language.

It is the idiosyncratic pauses, then, that tell the psychologist something about the encoding process, a part of performance and not competence. The implication is that the spontaneous speaker — Martin's encoder — does not know exactly what he will say before he starts talking. Previous experiments have shown that an encoder's hesitations are related to various kinds of mental activity. First, there is the cognitive difficulty hypothesis. Goldman-Eisler (1961) has shown that when people give mere descriptions of cartoons they hesitate less than when they give explanations of why the cartoons are funny. Levin, Silverman, and Ford (1967) have shown a comparable result with children. Closely related to this hypothesis is the anxiety hypothesis. Mahl (1956) has shown that in psychiatric interviews patients hesitate more during periods of anxiety than during periods of calm. This might be the result of cognitive difficulty also: an anxious person has more difficulty expressing anxiety-laden non-verbal thoughts than other kinds of thoughts.

To understand encoding itself, we must understand the *kind* of encoding difficulty the spontaneous speaker faces. The results of Maclay and Osgood (1959), and Goldman-Eisler (1961) show that spontaneous speakers, put under cognitive strain, hesitate more before content words than before function words. Martin's results confirm this finding. From this, we can only conclude that speakers have trouble deciding on high information content words. Boomer (1965) has gone one step further. He first looked for the phonological junctures in spontaneous speech. These can be identified from the intonation pattern and are not dependent on the pauses in speech. Calling the stretches of speech between junctures "phonemic clauses," he found that hesitations tended to come early in the clauses, especially after the first word. The first word, of course, is most often a function word, so Boomer has no quarrel with the results of Maclay and Osgood, Goldman-Eisler, or Martin.

To explain the kind of difficulty an encoder encounters, Maclay and Osgood and Goldman-Eisler have proposed the following theory: A speaker has syntactic and semantic processes which go on in coordinated but separate fashions. The speaker knows, for example, that he will begin a sentence with a noun phrase, so he says *The*, but hesitates while deciding, in some implicit process, on the semantic content of the noun phrase he is going to use. After he has decided upon the first noun in the phrase, the following few related phrases are more or less constrained semantically and therefore are spoken more fluently, as Boomer found. With the arrival of the next "phonemic clause," the process starts all over again.

This description of the encoding process, however, has been almost devoid of linguistic theory. I would now like to suggest where modern linguistic theory can help. Again, consider a noun modified by an adjective, like *big houses*. Maclay and Osgood looked at such a constituent contained within larger constituents, such as *the big houses, into big houses*, and *under the big houses*. In each case, pauses were more likely to occur just before *big* than anywhere else within the constituents. Transformational generative theory about the derivation of the prenominal adjective in English syntax suggests a reason for this. Underlying the sentence *The big houses burned* are the two kernel strings (underlying) *The houses burned* and *The houses are big*. Embedding the latter into the former we get *The houses which are big burned*. And finally, there is a set of transformations which deletes the relative and preposes *big* in front of *houses*, making, *The big houses burned*. It is unlikely, of course, that speakers go through this exact process, even implicitly (see Fodor, this volume), but this linguistic analysis does suggest an interesting point. A speaker composing the sentence *The big houses burned* must decide on the noun *houses* before he can decide on the adjective *big* which modifies *houses*. In the typical pause before *big*, the speaker, in effect, is choosing the noun at the same time he is choosing the adjective, so he does not need to pause again before the noun. This explanation has the virtue of characterizing the vague notion of semantic constraint in a motivated way: *big* constrains *houses* severely, because in the underlying structure *houses* is chosen at the same time or before *big* (because *houses* and *big* come from the same kernel string). There are other constructions with properties similar to the prenominal adjective. One is the noun modifying a noun, as in *manor houses*. Maclay and Osgood also looked at this constituent contained within larger constituents, such as, *the manor houses, into manor houses*, and *under the manor houses*. Hesitations were more frequent before *manor* than before *houses*, again in keeping with the linguistic analysis.

This thinking has led me to two hypotheses about pauses in spontaneous speakers (as opposed to readers): first, conventional pauses will increase. Second, idiosyncratic hesitations will tend to occur just before the first lexical item in a surface structure constituent, all of which comes from one kernel string in deep structure. Idiosyncratic hesitations will occur just before the first lexical item in simple sentences, subordinate clauses, relative clauses, predicate complement constructions, and coordinated clauses. They will occur more often before prenominal nouns and adjectives than after, more often before preverbal and preadjectival adverbs than after, and so forth.

The new point of these hypotheses is that the kernel string is the principle unit of semantic encoding. When a speaker comes to utter a lexical item, he decides not only on that lexical item, but on the whole kernel string that it comes from, at the same time. This allows the rest of the lexical items in the same kernel string to be spoken more or less fluently, unless some other embedding intervenes and forces the speaker to change syntactic levels. The hesitation before the embedded sentence is clearly illustrated in the adjective-noun construction given above and fits Boomer's data nicely. This characterization is a natural way of bringing hierarchical processes into encoding. Each new embedding brings with it the tendency for hesitations to occur near the beginning of the embedded clause.

The two kinds of hesitations are now more closely implicated in the two separate encoding processes: (1) conventional pauses, which occur at breaks in the intonation pattern and between major sentence constituents, give the speaker time for syntactic planning — for deciding the syntactic form of the speech about to come. And (2) idiosyncratic hesitations which allow the speaker to decide on the semantic component once he has chosen the syntactic form of his message. This, of course, is only a rough division of labor between conventional and idiosyncratic pauses, for semantic planning undoubtedly also goes on during conventional pauses.

I will consider the process of decoding next. As I pointed out above, Martin found, generally, that listeners who tried to repeat what some other speaker had said, left out idiosyncratic pauses but left in conventional pauses. By definition, idiosyncratic pauses are of little value to the listener since they carry no semantic information. We would expect the listener to leave them out, just as he will not repeat the speaker's uninformative mistakes in grammar or phonology. To ask him to notice them puts added strain on his memory capacity, as Martin observed, so we should not expect him to transcribe hesitations optimally. What Martin does not emphasize, however, is that his decoders do leave in the conventional pauses. They do because they are dictated by the syntactic and thematic structure of the material. The conventional pauses *are* information-bearing elements of the sentences.

Some examples will clarify the importance of conventional pauses. There are two kinds of relative clauses in English, appositive and restrictive. Appositive clauses are set off by commas in writing and by comma intonation in speech, while restrictive clauses are not, (Smith, 1964). Compare the following two sentences (from Halliday, 1967):

> *My brother/the dentist/came home.*
> *My brother the dentist came home.*

Here the intonation pattern, and with it the possibilities of conventional pauses, differentiates the two sentences syntactically. Also consider the pauses in the following two sentences (Halliday, 1967):

> *I saw John/and Mary/too.*
> *I saw John and Mary/too.*

In both pairs of examples we would expect a listener to notice, remember, and frequently reproduce the pauses, because they are conventional and distinguishing.

The decoders in Martin's experiments were both decoders and encoders: they first listened to speech and then tried to repeat it. Martin measured the hesitations of the repeated speech. This confounding of the decoding task with its later encoding has some real drawbacks for one who wants to study only the decoder's task. Some of the problems are indicated in Martin's last experiment in which he compares a mechanical pause indicator and a human scorer. The human scorers agreed with the mechanical scorer only 72 percent of the time, whereas two human scorers agreed more frequently — between 80 and 90 percent of the time. Why should the agreement between human and mechanical scorers be as low as it is? One hypothesis is that human scorers consistently misperceive the pauses that are actually there. The pauses they score are based more on syntactic considerations than on the actual acoustic signal. The analogous phenomenon occurs when professional phoneticians score spoken English sentences for Trager and Smith's four degrees of stress. Lieberman (1965) has shown that they hear more degrees of stress than are actually there. This suggests, of course, that stress judgments, which are consistent across phoneticians, are based to some extent on syntactic information — knowledge of the rules of the language.

One suggestion, then, is that detecting pauses might pose perceptual problems for the listener. If so, it would affect even Martin's trained scorers. A slight pause within a constituent might be easily detected, although the same length pause at a natural syntactic boundary might be completely passed over. These two possible ways of perceiving pauses would depend only on the syntactic and thematic structure of a sentence. If true, this type of misperception would be very important for characterizing the properties of the decoding process.

A graduate student, George Madaras, and I have looked at this possibility of misperception in some pilot experiments. The results are still not well explained, but I can describe what happened. We were interested in whether a half-second break in a sentence would be perceived in the same way no matter where it occurred in the sentence. We chose many simple sentences of the form, *The boy caught the ball*, that is, a definite noun phrase, a transitive verb, and a definite noun phrase as object of the verb. After splicing a half-second's worth of blank tape into a tape of the normal reading of each sentence, we had listeners judge which of two pauses in two successive sentences seemed longer. The half-second pauses were placed in one of the four positions between words. We expected the judgments of relative length to follow the phrase structure of the sentence: a half-second pause would seem long at minor constituent boundaries and short at major ones.

The results did not come out as expected. The first of the four word breaks in the sentence (between *The* and *boy*) was perceived as shortest; the next word break (between *boy* and *caught*) appeared longer; finally, the last word break was perceived as longest. This pattern of pause perception does not coincide with phrase structure boundaries, no matter how conceived, for the longest and shortest perceived pauses occurred within the two simple noun phrases. The results look suspiciously like Boomer's analysis of hesitations with a slight twist. First, we assume that the listener judges the half-second pauses after the first *The* in the sentence, so he would judge the actual pause to be shorter than what he expected. Similarly, he would judge the other pauses as longer than expected. Whether this is the explanation or not will take further testing — we expect that shorter pauses might give the expected results. But, notice that the perceptual part of the decoding process can be tested more directly than Martin does in his experiments.

Just as idiosyncratic pauses could be misperceived, they could also affect the listener's understanding of the spoken sentence.

Presumably, a passage spoken with many interruptions would be more difficult to understand than the same passage read fluently. The question then becomes, what psychological processes are disrupted by hesitations? Here again, conventional and idiosyncratic hesitations seem to differ in function. The speech of thoughtful experienced speakers is marked by the careful placement of conventional pauses. This is apparently meant to allow the listener time to reconstruct and digest the meaning of just-finished phrases. Conventional pauses help understanding. But the speech of inexperienced speakers is marked by many idiosyncratic hesitations. They act to break up constituents and natural intonation patterns, making it more difficult for the listener to understand what is said. Breaking up constituents is already known to disrupt rapid reading (Graf & Torrey, 1966) and learning (Suci, 1967). Idiosyncratic hesitations hinder understanding. Here also there are direct tests of decoding done by the listener.

With these ideas in mind, a student, Mike Schulman, and I carried out a pilot study which demonstrates the effects of disruptions on understanding and memory. Relying on the Archimedes principle of immediate memory (Savin & Perchonock, 1965), we asked our subjects to recall sentences of the form, *The boy found the penny*, as well as eight following nouns. Difficulties in understanding the sentences will show up in how *few* of the following nouns they can recall. The sentences, however, were interrupted at one of their word boundaries by a one-and-a-half second pause or by a three-digit number which subjects were also required to recall after recalling the sentence. Where did the interruptions help, or hinder? With the unfilled interruptions, subjects were helped most when the pause came between the subject and verb, i.e., at the major constituent break in the sentence. With the digit-filled interruptions, it mattered very little where the interruption came. Apparently, an interruption is helpful to the listener only when it allows him time to digest a completed phrase. The experienced speaker's carefully placed conventional pauses serve the same purpose; only idiosyncratic hesitations should be very disruptive to understanding.

I have emphasized that hesitations in speech should be studied, not for themselves, but for what they tell the psychologist about the underlying cognitive processes. This, however, necessitates strong theories about those processes, theories based on as much knowledge of the language as we can muster. In this direction, I have pointed out the important distinction between conventional and idiosyncratic pauses and their relation to various underlying processes. The conventional pauses seem to have evolved in the language mainly for the benefit of the listener, whereas idiosyncratic hesitations are the product only of an overburdened speaker and give no help to the listener. It is important to show that the speaker and listener are different, but they do have one thing in common — the language. The psycholinguist should exploit this common knowledge of speaker and listener, if he is ever to describe their differences and understand what both of them are doing.

REFERENCES

Boomer, D. S. Hesitation and grammatical encoding. *Language and Speech*, 1965, **8**, 148-58.

Goldman-Eisler, Frieda. Hesitation and information in speech. In C. Cherry (ed.), *Information theory*. London: Butterworths, 1961.

Graf, R., & Torrey, Jane W. Perception of phrase structure in written language. *Proceedings of the 74th Annual Convention of the American Psychological Association*, 1966, 83-84.

Halliday, M. A. K. *Some aspects of the thematic organization of the English clause.* (Memorandum RM-5224-PR). Santa Monica: The RAND Corporation, 1967.

Henderson, A., Goldman-Eisler, Frieda, & Skarbek, A. Sequential temporal patterns in spontaneous speech. *Language and Speech*, 1966, **9**, 207-16.

Levin, H., Silverman, Irene, & Ford, B. Hesitation in children's speech during explanation and description. *Journal of Verbal Learning and Verbal Behavior*, 1967, **6**, 560-64.

Lieberman, P. On the acoustic basis of the perception of intonation by linguists. *Word*, 1965, **21**, 40-55.

Maclay, H., & Osgood, C. E. Hesitation phenomena in spontaneous English speech. *Word*, 1959, **1**, 19-44.

Mahl, G. F. Disturbances and silences in the patient's speech in psychotherapy. *Journal of Abnormal and Social Psychology*, 1956, **53**, 1-15.

Savin, H. B., & Perchonock, Ellen. Grammatical structure and the immediate recall of English sentences. *Journal of Verbal Learning and Verbal Behavior*, 1965, **4**, 348-53.

Smith, Carlotta S. Determiners and relative clauses in a generative grammar of English. *Language*, 1964, **40**, 37-52.

Suci, G. J. The validity of pause as an index of units in language. *Journal of Verbal Learning and Verbal Behavior*, 1967, **6**, 26-32.

4

THE PERCEPTION OF TIME COMPRESSED SPEECH[1]

EMERSON FOULKE

University of Louisville

Time compressed speech is speech that is reproduced in less time than was required for its original production. One effect of time compression is the acceleration of the rate of speech sounds. If speech, when accelerated, remains comprehensible, the savings in listening time should be an important consideration in situations in which extensive reliance is placed on aural communication. However, current data suggest that although individual words and short phrases may remain intelligible after considerable compression by the right method, when these words are combined to form meaningful sequences that exceed the immediate memory span for heard words, as in a listening selection, comprehension begins to deteriorate at a much lower compression. Compression may affect the intelligibility of single words and the comprehension of connected discourse differently because different cognitive processes underlie the behavior on which their measurement is based. In the

[1]The author's research, reviewed in this paper, was performed at the University of Louisville, with financial support from the Office of Education under projects 1005, 1370, and 2430.

pages that follow, several methods for the time compression of speech will be described, and compared with the way in which they influence the intelligibility of speech sounds and the comprehension of connected discourse. Following this, we will try to analyze the perceptual and cognitive problems confronting the listener of compressed speech.

ALTERNATIVE METHODS FOR THE TIME COMPRESSION OF SPEECH

The speed changing method

The word rate of recorded speech may be changed simply by reproducing it at a different tape or record speed than was used originally. If the playback speed is slower than the recording speed, the rate at which the speech sounds occur is reduced, and the speech is expanded in time. If the playback speed is increased, the rate at which speech sounds occur is increased, and speech is compressed in time. Changing speech rate in this manner is technically easy. However, the change in rate is accompanied by a shift in the component frequencies of the voice signal that is proportional to the change in tape or record speed. For instance, if the speed is doubled, the component frequencies of a voice signal will be doubled, and the overall vocal pitch will be raised one octave. This distortion in vocal pitch interferes with the intelligibility of time compressed spoken words.

Sampling methods

In 1950, Miller and Licklider demonstrated the signal redundancy in spoken words by deleting segments of the speech signal. This was accomplished by a switching arrangement that permitted a recorded speech signal to be turned off periodically during its reproduction. They found that as long as these interruptions occurred at a frequency of ten times per second or more, the interrupted speech was easily understood. The intelligibility of monosyllabic words did not drop below 90 percent, until 50 percent of the speech signal had been discarded. Thus, it appeared that a large portion of the speech signal could be discarded without a serious disruption of communication. Garvey (1953a), taking cognizance of these results, reasoned that if the samples of a speech signal remaining after periodic interruption could be abutted in time, the result should be compressed intelligible speech without distortion in vocal pitch. To test this notion, he prepared a tape of speech, by periodically cutting out short segments of tape, and splicing the free ends of the retained tape together again. Reproduction of this tape achieved the desired effect. Garvey's method was, of course, too cumbersome for anything but research purposes. However, having shown the success of the general approach, an efficient technique for accomplishing it quickly followed.

In 1954, Fairbanks, Everitt and Jaeger published a description of an electromechanical apparatus which makes possible the time compressed or expanded reproduction of tape recorded speech. In the Fairbanks apparatus, a continuous tape loop passes over a recording head used to place on the tape the signal to be compressed. Next, it passes over the device used to reproduce samples of this signal. Finally, it passes over an erase head which removes the signal from the tape loop so that the tape can be rerecorded. The sampling device is a cylinder with four playback heads embedded in it, equally spaced around its circumference. The tape, in passing over the curved surface of this cylinder, makes contact with approximately one quarter of its circumference. When the cylinder is stationary, and one of the playback heads is contacted by the moving tape, the signal on the tape is reproduced as recorded. However, when the apparatus is adjusted for some amount of compression, the cylinder bearing the four playback heads begins to rotate in the direction of tape motion. Under these conditions, each of the four heads makes and loses contact with the tape. Each head reproduces the material on the portion of the tape with which it made contact. When, as it rotates, the cylinder arrives at the position where one head is losing contact with the tape while the preceding head is making contact with the tape, the segment of tape wrapped around the cylinder between these two heads never makes contact with a reproducing head and is not reproduced. The segment of the tape that is eliminated from reproduction is always the same length, one quarter of the circumference of the cylinder. The amount of speech compression depends upon the frequency with which these tape segments are eliminated, and this frequency, in turn, depends upon the rotational speed of the cylinder. The temporal value of the segments not reproduced depends upon the speed of the tape loop, since this determines the amount of tape that will pass over the recording head during a given time interval. Since the cylinder rotates in the direction of the tape motion, the speed of the tape loop is reduced, and the retained samples scanned by the four playback heads are reproduced at a lower frequency. The output of the compressor is recorded on tape, and this tape is reproduced at a speed that is enough faster than the speed at which it was recorded to restore the frequencies represented in the original signal. The final product of this process is time compressed speech that is unaffected with respect to vocal pitch.

Mr. Anton Springer, relying upon the same basic principles, developed a simpler device.[2] In the Springer approach, the continuous tape loop, the record head and the erase head are eliminated. Previously recorded tape passes from a supply reel, over the surface of the cylinder bearing the four playback heads, and then to a takeup reel. The tape is sampled in the manner just described. However, as the cylinder rotates in the direction of tape motion, the speed of the tape is increased enough to hold tape speed constant. Thus, the output of the Springer device is already compressed and the vocal pitch is not distorted.

A computer may also be used to compress speech by the sampling method (Scott, 1965). In this approach, speech that has been transduced to electrical form (for example, the output of a microphone or tape reproducing head) is temporally segmented by an analog-to-digital converter, and these segments are stored in the computer. Then, the computer samples these segments according to a sampling rule for which it has been programmed (for example, discard every third segment). The duration of both retained and discarded segments can be varied. The retained samples are abutted in time and fed to the input of a digital-to-analog converter, and the signal at the output of this converter, compressed in time, is appropriate for transduction to acoustical form again.

Electromechanical compressors, of the Fairbanks or Springer type, are unselective about the parts of a message that are discarded. Portions are discarded on a periodic basis, and may be discarded anywhere within or between words. It is unlikely that a given message would be sampled in exactly the same way on consecutive passes through these devices. With the computer, it is feasible to employ a great variety of sampling rules. For instance,

---

[2]The current version of the Springer device, known as the Information Rate Changer, is distributed in this country by Gotham Audio Corporation, 2 West 46th Street, New York, New York 10036.

the computer might be programmed to dispose of empty time intervals between words, and to sample differently the time intervals occupied by words, discarding larger fractions of those speech sounds with higher signal redundancy.

It would appear that the computer, because of its flexibility, offers the most satisfactory method for the time compression of speech. At present, however, computer time is too expensive to justify its use for anything other than research.

The technique of speech synthesis suggests another possibility for the production of accelerated speech without distortion in vocal pitch (Campanella, 1967). The speech synthesizer generates electrical analogs of the acoustical materials needed for the construction of speech sounds. A program of rules is provided for generating these analogs for the proper durations, the proper intensities and in the proper conjunction or sequence. These rules may be varied to produce speech at any desired rate. Though this method has, as yet, received little development, it should share with the computer the ability to shorten speech sounds in accordance with their signal redundancy.

Another device for the time compression of speech, now under construction at the American Foundation for the Blind, is the harmonic compressor, an outgrowth of the research at Bell Laboratories. In this approach, a speech signal is passed through an elaborate filter network that divides the speech spectrum into a large number of narrow frequency bands. The portion of the signal appearing in each of these bands is reduced in frequency by one half, and these derived signals are combined to produce speech, the component frequencies of which have been halved. If a recording of this speech is reproduced at twice the recording speed, the result is speech that has been compressed to 50 percent of the original production time without distortion in vocal pitch. Since the prototype of the harmonic compressor is still under construction, there has, as yet, been no opportunity to evaluate its output. Unfortunately the harmonic compressor cannot be adjusted for any desired amount of compression. It can only shorten the time required for the reproduction of a message by one half.

To summarize, five methods for the acceleration of speech have been discussed. Three of these — the computer sampling method, the speech synthesis method, and the frequency dividing method employed by the harmonic compressor — have not yet been developed sufficiently to permit an adequate evaluation of their products. For the remaining two methods — the speed changing method and the electromechanical sampling method — the necessary apparatus is available and good. By now, a number of experiments evaluating the products of these methods, have been performed, and it is possible to draw some conclusions about their merits.

THE EVALUATION OF TIME COMPRESSED SPEECH

Two general approaches have been employed in the evaluation of time compressed speech — tests of the ability to repeat brief messages accurately, and tests of the comprehension of listening selections. Brief message reproduction is taken as an index of the intelligibility of time compressed speech. In the typical procedure, single words are compressed in time by some amount, and presented, one at a time, to a listener. The listener's task is to reproduce these words, orally or in writing, and his intelligibility score is the fraction, usually expressed as a percent, of correctly identified words. This procedure is sometimes referred to as an articulation test (Miller, 1954, p. 60).

Disjunctive RT (reaction time) may also be taken as an index of intelligibility (Foulke, 1969). The underlying rationale in this case is that, in the disjunctive RT experiment, reduced intelligibility means reduced discriminability. It has been shown that as stimuli are made less discriminable, choice RT is increased (Woodworth & Schlosberg, 1954, p. 33). The procedure, under this approach, is to acquaint the subject with a short list of words, for example three, and then present them to him one at a time in random order for identification. The subject indicates his choice with a discriminative response, for instance, pressing the appropriate response key. The subject can then be scored for RT and accuracy. The experiment is performed with words that have been compressed by several amounts, and changes in RT and/or accuracy are regarded as indicative of changes in intelligibility. The RT method may be more sensitive than other methods, since a change in the amount of compression may produce a change in RT to words that are discriminated without error.

Calearo and Lazzaroni (1957) report the use of a procedure familiar to those in clinical audiology for detecting the effect of compression. The minimum intensity required for words to be intelligible is determined at several levels of compression. Threshold intensity is defined as that intensity at which some percent of a list of words, for example 50 percent, is correctly identified. If a change in the compression of a list of words is accompanied by a change in threshold intensity for that list, it is concluded that time compression has altered intelligibility.

In the other common approach for evaluating the effects of the acceleration of speech the listener first hears a listening selection at some accelerated word rate, and then is tested for knowledge of the facts and implications of that selection. Any kind of test may be used, but researchers have, in general, preferred objective tests with specifiable reliability.

FACTORS AFFECTING THE INTELLIGIBILITY AND COMPREHENSION OF TIME COMPRESSED SPEECH

Factors that have been shown to have an effect upon the intelligibility and the comprehension of time compressed speech can be divided into two general classes. One class includes stimulus variables associated with the context in which the speech signal is presented and characteristics of the signal itself. The second class includes organismic variables, such as the listener's age, sex, education, intelligence, and prior relevant experience. No effort will be made here to present the results of studies of all of these factors. Instead, only the research which concerns factors believed to have an important bearing on the argument to be developed will be reviewed. Readers interested in a more complete review of research regarding these factors are referred to "A Review of Research on Time Compressed Speech" (Foulke & Sticht, 1969).

Intelligibility and the method of compression

The intelligibility of time compressed words depends upon the method used for compression. When the speed changing method is used, reproduction of words in two-thirds of the original production time results in a 40 percent or more loss in intelligibility (Fletcher, 1929; Garvey, 1953a; Klumpp & Webster, 1961). Garvey (1953a), using his manual sampling method, found only a 10 percent loss in the intelligibility of words that were reproduced in 40 percent of the original production time and a 50 percent loss in the intelligibility of words reproduced in 25 percent of the original production time. Kurtzrock (1957), using the electromechanical sampling method, obtained an intelligibility score of 50 percent for a list of words reproduced in only 15 percent of the original production time. Using a similar method and similar materials, Fairbanks and Kodman (1957) obtained an intelligibility score of 57 percent for words reproduced in 13 percent of the original production time.

The relationships displayed in Figure 1 (based on the figure in Garvey's 1953a article) are fairly typical. In this figure, the percent of the original production time required for the compressed reproduction of words is shown on the X-axis. Mean percent of words correctly identified is shown on the Y-axis. The dotted curve describes results obtained with the speed changing method, and the solid curve describes results obtained with the manual sampling method.

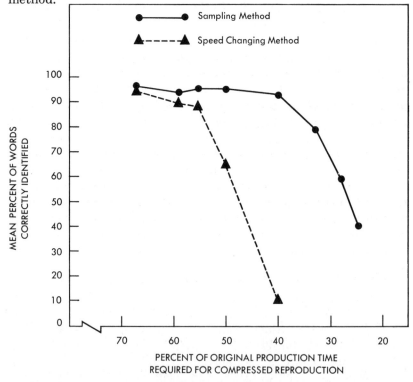

FIGURE 1. Word intelligibility as a function of method of compression (based on the figure in Garvey, 1953a).

Compression by either method increases the rate at which the discriminable elements of speech occur. However, while vocal pitch is unaffected by the sampling method, it is elevated by the speed changing method. The difference in the intelligibility of words compressed by the two methods, then, is probably due to the distortion in vocal pitch, since it is the factor that is not common to the two methods.

Intelligibility and the sampling rule

The message to be compressed may be conceived as consisting of a succession of temporal segments, called sampling periods. Compression is accomplished by discarding a fraction of each sampling period and by abutting the remainders of sampling periods. It is the retained fraction of the sampling period that determines the amount of compression. When the sampling method is used, the effect that a given amount of compression will have on the intelligibility of words depends upon the duration of the discarded portion of the sampling period, and hence upon the duration of the sampling period itself. The duration of the discarded portion must be shorter than the durations of the speech sounds to be sampled. If it is not, a speech sound may fall entirely within the discarded portion of a sampling period, in which case it would not be sampled at all.

With spondaic words, compressed to 50 percent of their original durations, Garvey (1953a), using discard intervals of 40, 60, 80, and 100 msec., found corresponding intelligibility scores of 95.33, 95.67, 95, and 85.67 percent. In a two factor experiment in which five discard intervals were employed for each of eight compressions, Fairbanks and Kodman (1957) found a substantial loss in intelligibility when the duration of the discard interval exceeded 80 msec.

The intelligibility of a word may be degraded if the word is sampled too frequently. Speech that is compressed by the sampling method has a succession of abutted samples of the original speech. If the transitions from sample to sample occur with sufficient frequency, the result is an audible tone with definite pitch. If the sampling rate is high enough, the pitch of this tone will intrude into the speech spectrum, and mask some speech frequencies. Fairbanks and Kodman (1957), using a discard interval of 10 msec., found 90 percent intelligibility for words compressed to 20 percent of their original duration. When this discard interval was changed to 40 msec., they found 94 percent intelligibility. When a 10 msec. discard interval is used to compress speech to 40 percent of its original time, the retained samples are 2.5 msec. in duration, and they occur at a rate of 400 per second. The 400 cycle tone corresponding to this rate is well within the speech spectrum and might be expected to interfere with intelligibility. If, however, a 40 msec. discard interval is used in compressing speech to 20 percent of its original duration, the retained samples are 10 msec. in length, and they occur at a rate of 100 per second. The audible tone of corresponding frequency is below the speech spectrum in this case, and there should be little interference.[3]

Intelligibility and the rate of occurrence of speech sounds

Garvey (1953a) compared the intelligibility of compressed time words by the sampling method with the intelligibility reported by Miller and Licklider (1950) for words that had been interrupted periodically. Garvey's words, and Miller and Licklider's words were treated alike since portions of sampling periods were discarded. However, the retained samples of Garvey's words were abutted to produce time compressed speech, while the retained samples of Miller and Licklider's words were not abutted and the resulting speech, though interrupted, was not compressed. There was no difference between the intelligibility of time compressed words and interrupted words when 50 percent of each word was discarded. However, when 62 percent of each word was discarded, interrupted words were 40 percent more intelligible than time compressed words. Since the two groups of words were alike in the amount of speech information that had been discarded, the poorer intelligibility of the time compressed words, when 62 percent of the speech information had been discarded, was probably due to the accelerated rate of occurrence of speech sounds.

Intelligibility and word structure

In a study in which the number of phonemes in a word was varied from three to nine, Henry (1966) found that increasing the num-

---

[3]The equipment used for the compressed reproduction of speech in the experiments reported hereafter samples with a discard interval of 40 msec.

ber of phonemes improved the intelligibility of words that had been compressed by the sampling method. In a similar vein, Klumpp and Webster (1961) found short phrases, compressed in time by the speed changing method, to be more intelligible than single words. The findings of Henry, and Klumpp and Webster are probably explained by the cues the subjects can derive from the context of multiphonemic words and short phrases.

Intelligibility and prior experience of the listener

Using the sampling method, Fairbanks and Kodman (1957) compressed words so that they were comparable to the interrupted words of Miller and Licklider in the amount of speech information discarded. They found the compressed words to be more intelligible than the interrupted words. However, the subjects of Fairbanks and Kodman had received extensive familiarization with the words, before the tests were made, whereas the subjects of Miller and Licklider were relatively naive. Miller and Licklider (1950), using interrupted words, and Garvey (1953b), using words compressed in time by the manual sampling method, found that repeated exposure to these words improved their intelligibility.

If a group of listeners agree that a particular speech sound in a word compressed by the sampling method is unrecognizable, it may be concluded fairly that the difficulty lies with the signal itself. However, Garvey (1953b) found that subjects disagreed about the speech sounds that were rendered unintelligible by compression of the words in which they occurred. Garvey explained this finding in terms of the differential experience of subjects with the words in question. In this connection, Henry (1966) found that words which occur with greater frequency in general language, as indicated by the Lorge-Thorndike count, are more intelligible when time compressed by the sampling method than less frequently occurring words.

Intelligibility and anatomical damage

The intelligibility of time compressed words is influenced by hearing capacity. In research reported by deQuiros (1964), subjects with normal hearing, subjects with hearing losses due to peripheral damage, and subjects with hearing losses due to central damage were given articulation tests with short sentences presented at 140, 250, and 350 wpm. For normal subjects, an increase in intensity of 10 db was required to reach threshhold intensity (50 percent of the words identified correctly) with each increase in word rate. For subjects with hearing losses due to peripheral damage, the intensity required increased as the word rate was increased in a similar manner, but each threshold intensity was somewhat higher than the corresponding intensity for subjects with normal hearing. For subjects with hearing losses due to central damage, the increase in intensity required for threshold as the word rate was increased, was relatively large and positively accelerated.

Comprehension and word rate

There are several studies in which comprehension has been measured as a function of word rate. Within the range extending from 126 to 172 wpm, Diehl, White, and Burk (1959) found listening comprehension to be unaffected by changes in word rate. In the range extending from 125 to 225 wpm, Nelson (1948), and Harwood (1955) found a slight but insignificant loss in comprehension. Fairbanks, Guttman, and Miron (1957) found little difference in the comprehension of listening selections presented at 141, 201, and 282 wpm. Thereafter, comprehension, as indicated by percent of test questions correctly answered, declined from 58 percent correct at 282 wpm to 26 percent correct at 470 wpm. Foulke, Amster, Nolan, and Bixler (1962), using both technical and literary listening selections, found comprehension to be only slightly affected by increasing the word rate up to 275 wpm. However, in the range extending from 275 to 375 wpm, they found an accelerated decrease in comprehension as word rate was increased. The two studies last cited agree in the finding that comprehension declined only slightly until a word rate in the neighborhood of 275 wpm was reached, but much more rapidly thereafter.

In each of the studies just mentioned, the word rate was varied through a limited range. It is possible, by combining their results, to gain an impression of the relationship between word rate and listening comprehension over a wide range of word rate values. However, because these studies were conducted at different places and times, and with different subjects, listening selections and measuring instruments, the picture that emerges may not be completely dependable. For this reason, an experiment was performed

(Foulke, 1969) in which twelve groups of subjects, drawn at random from the same population, were tested for listening comprehension at twelve word rates, starting at 125 wpm and progressing in steps of 25 wpm through 400 wpm. After listening, each subject completed a multiple choice test, covering the facts and implications of the listening selection.

A test score, corrected for guessing, was determined for each subject, and these corrected scores were averaged for each experimental group to produce the means used in plotting Figure 2. In this figure, the X-axis is scaled in terms of word rate, and the Y-axis is scaled in terms of mean percent of corrected comprehension scores. Although the curve shows some fluctuation, the relationship it suggests is one in which listening comprehension is little affected by increasing the word rate in the range bounded by 125 and 250 wpm. Beyond this point, however, comprehension begins to decline at an accelerated rate. The significance of this relationship was

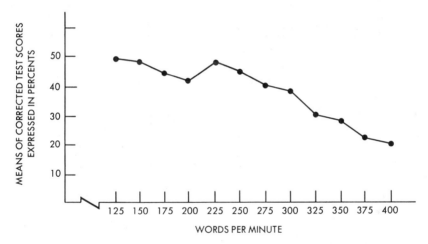

FIGURE 2. Listening comprehension as a function of word rate.

revealed by an analysis of variance. The significance of the differences among means was examined by the Newman-Keuls Test for Ordered Pairs of Means (Winer, 1962, p. 80). The results of this analysis are shown in Table 1. This table is cast in matrix form with the word rates at which tests were conducted arranged down the left hand margin and across the top of the matrix, in order of increasing magnitude. Entered in each row, under the appropriate column heading, are the word rates for which comprehension scores were not significantly different from the comprehension score associated with the word rate in the left hand margin that identifies that row. The results presented in Table 1 reinforce the impression suggested by Figure 1. The pattern formed by the entries in this table clearly depicts the nature of the relationship between word rate and listening comprehension. Listening comprehension does not vary significantly as the word rate is increased in the range extending from 125 to 250 wpm. However, further increases in word rate result in losses in comprehension that are too large to be accounted for by chance fluctuation of test scores.

TABLE 1

NEUMAN-KEULS ANALYSIS OF THE SIGNIFICANCE OF
DIFFERENCES AMONG GROUP MEANS.

WPM	125	150	175	200	225	250	275	300	325	350	375	400
125	125	150	175	200	225	250		300				
150	125	150	175	200	225	250	275	300				
175	125	150	175	200	225	250	275	300				
200	125	150	175	200	225	250	275	300				
225	125	150	175	200	225	250	275	300				
250	125	150	175	200	225	250	275	300				
275		150	175	200	225	250	275	300	325	350		
300	125	150	175	200	225	250	275	300	325	350		
325							275	300	325	350		
350							275	300	325	350	375	
375									325	350	375	400
400											375	400

Comprehension and the method of compression

McLain (1962) and Foulke (1962), using subjects who were naive about compressed speech, and unaccustomed to reading by listening, compared the comprehension of speech compressed by the sampling method with the comprehension of speech compressed by the speed changing method. In both instances, a slight but statistically significant difference was found in favor of the sampling method. However, in a similar experiment in which blind school children, who were accustomed to reading by listening, served as subjects, Foulke (1966) found no statistically significant difference favoring either method.

The relationship between word rate and listening comprehension for speech compressed by the speed changing method, and by the sampling method, is shown in Figure 3. In this figure, word rate, on the X-axis, is plotted against comprehension, on the Y-axis. The dotted curve describes results obtained with the speed changing method, and the solid curve describes results obtained with the electromechanical sampling method. The figure suggests that compression has approximately the same effect on comprehension in both methods.

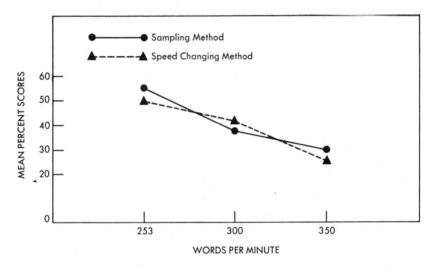

FIGURE 3. Listening comprehension as a function of method of compression.

The conclusion suggested by the results of the experiments just cited is that the superiority of the sampling method is slight, and that it may be erased by experience in reading by listening. It should be pointed out that this conclusion is only tentative. In these studies, all the subjects were naive about speech compressed in time by the sampling method. The blind subjects probably had varying amounts of experience in listening to speech compressed in time by the speed changing method, since many blind people listen to Talking Book Records at a faster speed than the one used during recording. Furthermore, the tests were made in a limited range of word rates.

THE DIFFERENTIAL EFFECTS OF COMPRESSION ON WORD INTELLIGIBILITY AND LISTENING COMPREHENSION

Experiments such as those reported by Garvey (1953a) Kurtzrock (1957), and Fairbanks and Kodman (1957), are in close agreement about the effect of comprehension by the sampling method on word intelligibility. When half or more of a word has been discarded, intelligibility is only moderately affected, and intelligibility is not completely lost when only 15 percent of a word remains. Experiments such as those reported by Fairbanks, Guttman, and Miron (1957a), Foulke, et al. (1962), and Foulke (1969), generally agree in suggesting that comprehension begins to decline when only 45 percent of each of the words comprising a listening selection has been discarded. Taking these results together, it seems clear that listening comprehension is affected differently than word intelligibility with the time compression of speech by the sampling method. However, this conclusion is weakened somewhat by its dependence upon experiments that differed in stimulus materials, subject populations, experimental plans, and techniques of measurement. A more satisfactory approach would be to demonstrate this differential effect in a single experiment. Consequently, an experiment was performed (Foulke & Sticht, 1967) in which listening material (PB words and a listening selection), compressed by 5 different amounts, was used in testing 5 experimental groups. Each subject received an intelligibility score (the percent of correctly identified PB words) and a comprehension score (the percent of correctly answered multiple choice items in a test of listening comprehension). Mean intelligibility scores and mean comprehension scores for the five experimental groups were used in plotting the curves in Figure 4. In this figure, the five time compressions are displayed along the X-axis. The entry below each compression value refers to the word rate that would result if connected discourse at a normal word rate of 175 wpm (Johnson, Darley, and Spriestersbach, 1963, pp. 202-03) were compressed by that amount. Percent correct for the two dependent variables is scaled on the Y-axis. As the amount of compression was increased, both intelligibility and comprehension decreased. However, comparison of the two curves reveals that by increasing the amount of compression intelligibility was always superior to comprehension. The impression conveyed by Figure 4 was confirmed by an analysis of variance of intelligibility and comprehension test scores. Both variables, and their interaction, were significant beyond the .001 level.

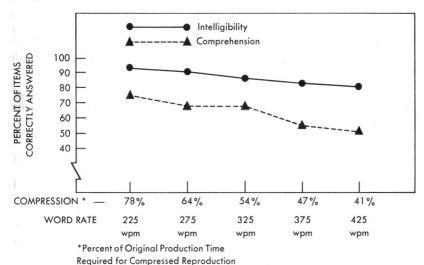

FIGURE 4. **Word intelligibility and listening comprehension as a function of percent of compression.**

It was, of course, expected that comprehension scores would be lower than intelligibility scores. The demonstration of comprehension imposes a much more complex task on the listener than the demonstration of intelligibility. It is the finding that the difference between intelligibility and comprehension scores increases as the amount of compression is increased that requires additional explanation.

One possibility is that the progressively larger loss in comprehension is a consequence of the cumulative effects of the relatively smaller losses in intelligibility. The data of the experiment were examined for this possibility in the following manner. All of the subjects tested at a given compression were separated into high and low scoring groups, on the basis of their comprehension test scores. The difference between the means of the intelligibility scores of the two groups, was tested for significance. In all but one case, (the 59 percent compression group) the difference between means did not reach significance at the 5 percent level. This finding suggests that poor comprehension cannot be satisfactorily explained by low intelligibility for individual words. In any case, it is well known that it is not necessary for all of the units of a message to be intelligible in order for the message to be received accurately (Miller & Selfridge, 1950; Attneave, 1954). Because of prior learning, the listener is able to reconstruct the message using reduced cues. He makes use of the sequential dependencies in grammatical speech and the meaningfulness of the message in supplying missed words.

The results of Garvey (1953b), Klumpp and Webster (1961), and Henry (1966), reviewed earlier in this paper (see pp. 88-89), are pertinent in this regard. They found that increasing the number of phonemes in a word, or the number of words in a phrase, while holding constant the amount of compression, improved intelligibility. Increasing the number of phonemes in a brief message should permit the listener to take advantage of his estimates of sequential dependency and reduce his uncertainty regarding elements of the message.

The net effect of the listener's ability to utilize cues should be to free him from strict dependence upon the intelligibility of single words in comprehending messages composed of sequences of words.

It has already been shown that listening selections composed of words differing in intelligibility are approximately equal in comprehensibility (see Figure 3). Of course, if words are completely unintelligible, messages formed from them will be incomprehensible. However, one is tempted to draw the conclusion that once words have reached a certain level of intelligibility, further improvements in intelligibility will contribute little to the comprehensibility of messages formed from these words.

It is possible, by combining the speed changing method and the sampling method, to hold constant the rate at which speech sounds occur while varying the amount of distortion in vocal pitch. That is, if for each of several versions of a listening selection, the two methods for speech compression are combined in different proportions to produce the same final accelerated word rate, then the resulting versions of the listening selections will vary in the amount of distortion in vocal pitch. Since there is a strong relationship between distortion in vocal pitch and word intelligibility, this scheme provides a way of varying word intelligibility system-atically. Of course, the versions resulting from this treatment will also vary in the amount of speech information that has been dis-carded. But, as already shown, the sampling method has a rela-tively small influence on word intelligibility.

Taking advantage of this possibility, an experiment was per-formed (Foulke, 1969) in which the intelligibility of words in a listening selection was varied while the word rate was held con-stant. Five groups of subjects listened to five different versions of a selection, presented at a rate of 325 wpm. Proceeding from version 1 to version 5, there was a progressive elevation in vocal pitch. Following this listening experience, subjects completed a multiple choice test of the facts and implications of the selection.

Each subject's score was the number of test items correctly answered. The mean of these test scores, for the five experimental groups, are shown in Figure 5. The vocal pitches employed in the experiment, arranged in order of increasing pitch, are shown on the X-axis. The Y-axis is scaled in terms of test scores, expressed as percents. It is clear from this figure that differences in vocal pitch, and therefore presumably in word intelligibility, had prac-tically no effect on listening comprehension. An analysis of variance of test scores indicated no significant difference in listening com-prehension that could be associated with the experimental treat-ments. Therefore, it seems reasonable to conclude that within the

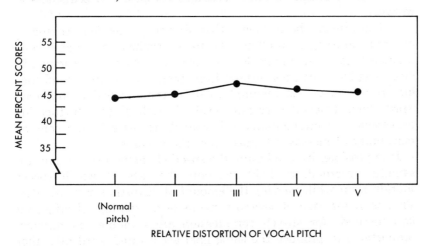

FIGURE 5. Listening comprehension as a function of word intel-ligibility.

range in which intelligibility was varied, it had no influence on listening comprehension.

Evidence of another sort for the hypothesis that, within limits, variation in the intelligibility of single words has little effect on the comprehension of meaningful discourse composed of these words was provided by the results of another experiment (Foulke, 1969). A professional oral reader produced three renditions of a listening selection: one at 149 wpm, one at 164.6 wpm, and one at 195.7 wpm. These renditions were then compressed, by the sampling method, to the same final word rate of 275 wpm. In order to achieve the same final word rate, it was necessary to compress the three selections to 71, 60, and 50 percent respectively of their original durations. It seems reasonable to assume that, in most cases, the durations of individual words were compressed by the same fraction as the durations of the renditions in which they occurred.

Three groups of subjects heard and were tested for comprehension of the three compressed renditions of the listening selection. Mean test scores for the three groups were practically the same, and an analysis of variance of test scores revealed no differences among means that could be associated with the experimental treatments provided.

Since the three renditions differed considerably in their discarded fractions of words, there should be a systematic change in word intelligibility from rendition to rendition. This change would not be large since the compressions used in the experiment were not large enough to have a profound effect upon intelligibility. Nevertheless, the differences among the three renditions in their word intelligibility should have been at least measurable. To the extent that word intelligibility did vary from rendition to rendition, it is clear that it had no effect on listening comprehension.

Within the range in which intelligibility was varied in the two experiments just cited, it exerted no influence on the comprehension of connected speech. If intelligibility had been degraded sufficiently, there no doubt would have been a loss in comprehension. Nevertheless, within limits, comprehension does not appear to depend heavily upon the intelligibility of single words. There is apparently enough redundancy in spoken language that many words can be transmitted imperfectly or not at all without interfering seriously with listening comprehension. As a listener acquires experience with his language — its grammar and conventional forms — he acquires information about the probabilities associated with the occurrence of particular words, given the occurrence of particular preceding words. Similarly, the context of meanings, aroused by a listening selection, reduces the listener's uncertainty, at any given instant, about the words and phrases that are to follow. The listener is able to use his information about the occurrence of words, phrases, and sentences in reconstructing imperfectly transmitted speech.

COMPREHENSION AND THE RATE OF OCCURRENCE OF THE DISCRIMINABLE ELEMENTS OF SPEECH

When the results of these experiments are considered collectively, a pattern of relationships begins to emerge. Word intelligibility, defined by the measuring operations employed in its assessment, is seriously degraded when words are compressed by the speed changing method. When the sampling method is used, a substantial compression is required before word intelligibility is seriously degraded (see Figure 1). Listening comprehension, defined by the measuring operations employed in its assessment, is only moderately affected by compression until a compression sufficient to produce word rates in the neighborhood of 275 wpm is surpassed (a compression of this magnitude would have little effect upon word intelligibility) but seriously affected thereafter (see Figure 2). Thus, over a wide range, the relationship between compression and listening comprehension is not the same as the relationship between compression and word intelligibility (see Figure 4).

The demonstration of comprehension imposes a much more complex task on the listener than the demonstration of intelligibility. The behavior upon which the measurement of intelligibility depends implies registration of the stimulus word, some kind of short term memory storage, and the transduction of the stored item to an overt response. On the other hand, the behavior on which the measurement of comprehension is based implies continuous registration and short term storage of stimulus material, as well as the continuous encoding, or simplification by reorganization, and selective discarding of stimulus material so that it can be transferred to long term memory storage, and a final decoding step for the transduction of material in long term storage to overt behavior.

The model implied by these operations resembles the models proposed by Sperling (1963), or Broadbent (1957). It seems reasonable to suppose that these processing operations would require time. With the additional assumption that the stored traces of stimulus events decay, so that after a short period of time they are no longer available for processing, it is possible to offer a tentative explanation of the differential effects of compression on word intelligibility and listening comprehension. In the situation in which the listener is tested for the intelligibility of words or short phrases or sentences, he receives stimulus input at a relatively slow rate. There is ample time to perform the processing operations required to transduce the stored effects of stimulation to an overt response. And, even though the memorial representation of the stimulus begins to decay immediately, it can be processed soon enough after registration that its availability is not impaired. When the listener must perform those processing operations needed to prepare a stimulus input, consisting of a meaningful sequence of spoken words, for the subsequent demonstration of comprehension, he must continuously process a store to which new additions, in the form of the memorial representations of stimulus events, are being made. If items are added to short term storage at a faster rate than the rate at which they can be processed, they will begin to accumulate. This accumulation will be limited by the decay of items in store. When, because of a fast word rate, processing lags behind the addition of items to storage, some selection must be made among the accumulated items for processing. This selection may be made in terms of the relative availability of items. Those memorial representations of stimulus events that have been added recently to storage will have had less time to decay, and will therefore be more available for processing. Consequently, when word rate does not exceed the processing rate, words will be processed in the order of their arrival. However, when word rate exceeds the processing rate, there will be a confusion of the order in which they are processed.

Many experiments in the general area of verbal learning and cognitive processing have produced results consistent with the point of view presented here. It has been shown repeatedly, in studies of verbal learning, (Miller, 1951, p. 212; Osgood, 1953, p. 505) that the difficulty of a learning task is increased by increasing the number of items in the list to be learned, and by decreasing the interstimulus interval. Of course, when continuous speech is compressed, the number of words per unit time is increased, and the intervals between words are decreased. On the other hand, compression cannot have this effect when the intelligibility of a single word is determined.

An experiment has been reported by Aaronson (1967), in which the subjects were required to repeat sequences of heard digits. The acoustical durations of digits were adjusted by means of time compression so that the reproduction of each digit required 150 msec. Three different interstimulus intervals were represented in the experiment. In repeating sequences of heard digits, the number of errors, both omission and order, made by the subjects increased with decreasing duration of the interstimulus interval. Since the stimulus "on" time was the same for all spoken digits in the experiment, this change in performance must have been the direct result of reducing the duration of the interstimulus interval, and hence the time available for perceptual processing. Insufficient processing time should, according to the model suggested here, result in errors of both omission and order.

Another variable in Aaronson's experiment has at least parenthetical relevance for the present discussion. It seems reasonable that stimuli which are, to some degree, unclear or unintelligible should require more time for registration than clear stimuli. To test this hypothesis, stimuli were presented at three different signal to noise ratios. As expected, more errors were made in repeating sequences composed of stimuli presented with a poorer signal to noise ratio. Using the speech compression devices presently available, there is some deterioration of signal quality when speech is compressed by the sampling method, and this deterioration increases slightly as the amount of compression is increased. This deterioration may be regarded as a degradation of the signal to noise ratio and hence, in addition to processing problems, there may be registration problems that interfere with the perception of highly compressed speech.

In an experiment now in progress at the University of Louisville, subjects are required to repeat as many words as they can from sentences that are presented at an approximate rate of 500 wpm. When sentences are long, many words are missed, and the remaining words are often not repeated in the order in which they were presented. Again, as in the case of Aaronson's study, these are the kinds of errors that one would expect when the memorial representations of stimulus events accumulate at a faster rate than the rate at which they can be processed.

The two experiments just reported constitute examples in which discrete sequences of items have been used to demonstrate the functioning of the model. In describing the manner in which continuous speech is processed, it may be useful to introduce the concept of channel capacity (Miller, 1953; 1956). According to this concept, a communication channel, in this case the listener, has a finite capacity for handling information. (This capacity would be defined by the rate at which the memorial representations of stimulus events could be processed for long term storage.) As the amount of information applied to the input of the channel is increased, there is a corresponding increase in the amount of information transmitted by the channel, until channel capacity is reached. At this point, the input rate would match the processing rate. Further increases in the input rate cannot be handled by the channel, with the result that some information is lost. Assuming normal speech to occur at a rate that is well below channel capacity, increasing the word rate should have little effect on listening comprehension until channel capacity is reached. Beyond this point, further increases in the word rate should result in progressively larger losses in listening comprehension. This is the situation that is described by the curve in Figure 2 and, in general, by the results of other studies of the effect of word rate on listening comprehension.

The facts regarding silent visual reading rates may seem to constitute an obvious objection to the kind of explanation attempted here. Silent visual reading rates considerably in excess of 275 wpm, the word rate at which listening comprehension begins to deteriorate, are commonplace. However, because of the spatial display of information on the printed page, the reader is able to perform the perceptual operation referred to by Miller (1956) as "chunking." In order to keep the input rate below his channel capacity, the visual reader reduces the number of elements with which he must contend by this "chunking" operation. With experience in reading, he learns to perceive not single words, but entire phrases or sentences. However, when language is displayed orally, it is displayed sequentially in a temporal dimension, and the listener cannot perform the "chunking" operation.

Though detailed neurological support for the point of view presented here is not possible, it is always tempting to suggest a neurological basis for a psychological model. The evidence presented by deQuiros, and reviewed earlier in this paper (see p. 89), is interesting to consider. It will be recalled that when articulation testing was conducted with accelerated speech for subjects with hearing losses due to peripheral damage, an increase in word rate had approximately the same effect on the increase in intensity required for threshold intelligibility as for normal subjects. But at each word rate at which tests were conducted, threshold intensity for subjects with peripheral damage was somewhat higher than threshold intensity for normal subjects. The primary effect of peripheral damage should be a loss in the sensitivity of the hearing organs, and the results reported by deQuiros should be a reasonable consequence of the damage. The positively accelerated increase in the intensity required for threshold with increasing word rate, obtained from subjects with central damage, suggests that the increased rate at which words were presented constituted a more serious problem for these subjects than for subjects with normal hearing. Damage to the central nervous system might be expected to interfere with perceptual or cognitive operations. It may be, therefore, that subjects in this category found the reproduction of sentences presented at accelerated word rates an especially difficult task because of a decreased ability to perform the processing operations required for the perception of those sentences.

In summary, an effort has been made to account for the observed differences in the effect on word intelligibility and listening comprehension of increasing word rate, by appealing to a model for short term memory that bears a general resemblance to the models suggested by Sperling (1963). It is recognized that the proposed model, in its ability to account for the perception of time compressed speech, is only rudimentary in conception. Its parameters would have to be more carefully quantified before the predictions needed to test its adequacy could be made, and this quantification would require a great deal of research that has not yet been performed. Nevertheless, at its present stage of development, the model does seem to render a plausible account of the results of many of the experiments that have been reported.

CONCLUSION

In this chapter's introductory statement, it was claimed that time compressed speech is interesting for both practical and theoretical reasons. In closing, it seems appropriate to draw some general conclusions regarding the extent to which this claim has been supported by the research literature that has been surveyed.

Although the results of experiments on the comprehension of time compressed speech have been disappointing to those who hoped to demonstrate the feasibility of reading by listening at very fast word rates, it may be fairly concluded that one can read, with good comprehension, by listening to undistorted recorded speech, the rate of which has been accelerated enough to produce a significant savings in reading time.

In the experiments reviewed here, messages have been compressed unselectively, and only the gross effects of unselective acceleration have been determined. Nevertheless, it has been possible to reveal the limitation on comprehension imposed by the listener's need for time in which to process the elements of continuous speech. The finding that word intelligibility and listening comprehension are affected differently by compression suggests that an effort to bring about a further increase in the aural reading rate will have to consider the listener's need for processing time. There is a need for experiments in which listeners are tested for the comprehension of selections in which words, phrases, sentences, or other syntactical units have been highly compressed, while the intervals between these units have been left intact in order to make processing time available.

In addition to the practical value of this research, the ability to control the time required for spoken words in isolation, or in sequence, that is possible by the sampling method, permits an exploration of the extent to which the cognition of spoken language is influenced by its temporal organization. An interesting hypothesis to be examined by subsequent research is that, at normal word rates, the temporal organization of spoken language is relatively unimportant, but that as the word rate is increased, temporal organization becomes more critical to comprehension. If this is the case, experiments in which the temporal organization of accelerated messages is varied may reveal the organization that is most efficient for comprehension. From a knowledge of what constitutes efficient temporal organization, it may be possible to make useful inferences regarding some of the cognitive operations performed by a listener who comprehends spoken language. A related group of research questions have to do with the way in which the word rate and temporal organization of spoken language interact with variables such as grammatical structure and redundancy in determining listening comprehension.

Man's ability to produce and understand spoken language stands as one of his most impressive cognitive accomplishments. The possibility of varying speech rate, while holding constant other characteristics of speech, such as vocal pitch and timbre, suggests a

new and useful method for inquiring into the processes that underlie this ability.

REFERENCES

Aaronson, D. Temporal course of perception in an immediate recall task. *Journal of Experimental Psychology*, 1968, **76**, 129-40.

Attneave, F. Some informational aspects of visual form perception. *Psychological Review*, 1954, **61**, 183-93.

Broadbent, D. W. A mechanical model for human attention and immediate memory. *Psychological Review*, 1957, **64**, 205-15.

Calearo, C., & Lazzaroni, A. Speech intelligibility in relation to the speed of the message. *Laryngoscope*, 1957, **67**, 410-19.

Campanella, S. J. Signal Analysis of Speech Time-Compression Techniques. *Proceedings of the Louisville conference on time compressed speech*. Louisville: University of Louisville, 1967.

deQuiros, J. B. Accelerated speech audiometry, an examination of test results. *Translations of the Beltone Institute for Hearing Research*, #17, 1964.

Diehl, C. F., White, R. C., & Burk, K. Rate and communication. *Speech Monographs*, 1959, **26**, 229-32.

Fairbanks, G., Everitte, W. L., & Jaeger, R. P. Method for time or frequency compression-expansion of speech. *Transactions of the Institute of Radio Engineers Professional Group on Audio*, AU2, 1954, 7-12.

Fairbanks, G., Guttman, N., & Miron, M. S. Effects of time compression upon the comprehension of connected speech. *Journal of Speech & Hearing Disorders*, 1957, **22**, 10-19.

Fairbanks, G., & Kodman, F., Jr. Word intelligibility as a function of time compression. *Journal of the Acoustical Society of America*, 1957, **29**, 636-41.

Fletcher, H. *Speech and Hearing*. New York: D. VanNostrand, 1929, 293-94.

Foulke, E. A comparison of two methods of compressing speech. Symposium Paper, Southeastern Psychological Association, Louisville, March, 1962.

Foulke E. Comparison of comprehension of two forms of compressed speech. *Exceptional Children*, 1966, **33**, 169-73.

Foulke, E. The comprehension of rapid speech by the blind—Part III. Final Progress Report, Cooperative Research Project #2430, Office of Education. Washington, D.C.: U.S. Department of Health, Education, and Welfare, 1969.

Foulke, E., Amster, C. H., Nolan, C. Y., & Bixler, R. H. The comprehension of rapid speech by the blind. *Exceptional Children*, 1962, **29**, 134-41.

Foulke, E., & Sticht, T. G. A review of research on time compressed speech. *Psychological Bulletin*, 1969, **72**, 50-62.

Foulke, E., & Sticht, T. G. The intelligibility and comprehension of accelerated speech. *Proceedings of the Louisville conference on time compressed speech*. Louisville: University of Louisville, 1967, 21-28.

Garvey, W. D. The intelligibility of speeded speech. *Journal of Exceptional Psychology*, 1953, **45**, 102-08. (a)

Garvey, W. D. The intelligibility of abbreviated speech patterns. *Quarterly Journal of Speech*, 1953, **39**, 296-306. (b)

Harwood, K. A. Listenability and rate of presentation. *Speech Monographs*, 1955, **22**, 57-59.

Henry, W. G., Jr. Recognition of time compressed speech as a function of word length and frequency of usage. Unpublished doctoral dissertation, Indiana University, 1966.

Johnson, W., Darley, F., & Spriestersbach, D. C. *Diagnostic methods in speech pathology*. New York: Harper & Row, 1963. Pp. 202-03.

Klumpp, R. G., & Webster, J. C. Intelligibility of time-compressed speech. *Journal of the Acoustical Society of America*, 1961, **31**, 265-67.

Kurtzrock, G. H. The effects of time and frequency distortion upon word intelligibility. *Speech Monographs*, 1957, **24**, 94.

McLain, J. A comparison of two methods of producing rapid speech. *International Journal for the Education of the Blind*, 1962, **12**, 40-43.

Miller, E. C. Effects on learning of variations in oral presentation. Unpublished doctoral dissertation, University of Denver, 1954.

Miller, G. A. *Language and communication*. New York: McGraw-Hill, 1951.

Miller, G. A. What is information measurement? *American Psychologist*, 1953, **8**, 3-11.

Miller, G. A. The magical number seven, plus or minus two: some limits on our capacity for processing information. *Psychological Review*, 1956, **63**, 81-97.

Miller, G. A., & Licklider, J. C. R. The intelligibility of interrupted speech. *Journal of the Acoustical Society of America*, 1950, **22**, 167-73.

Miller, G. A., & Selfridge, J. A. Verbal context and the recall of meaningful material. *American Journal of Psychology*, 1950, **63**, 176-85.

Nelson, H. E. The effect of variations of rates on the recall by radio listeners of straight newscasts. *Speech Monographs*, 1948, **15**, 173-80.

Osgood, C. E. *Method and theory in experimental psychology.* New York: Oxford University Press, 1953.

Scott, R. J. Temporal effects in speech analysis and synthesis. Unpublished doctoral dissertation, University of Michigan, 1965.

Sperling, G. A model for visual memory tasks. *Human Factors*, 1963, (Feb.), 19-31.

Winer, B. J. *Statistical principles in experimental design.* New York: McGraw-Hill, 1962.

Woodworth, R. S., & Schlosberg, H. *Experimental Psychology,* New York: Henry Holt & Co., 1954.

A PERSPECTIVE ON THE PERCEPTION OF TIME COMPRESSED SPEECH

DAVID B. ORR

Software Systems, Incorporated

In discussing Prof. Foulke's paper I shall adhere fairly closely to the organization of his presentation. Little attempt will be made to extend the discussion beyond the scope of his presentation or to emphasize and describe the wide applications of time compressed speech which are now under study or in progress. Whatever the theoretical characteristics of the perception of time compressed speech are, from a practical standpoint, a good case can be made for the judicious use of the technique in a number of applied situations.

ALTERNATIVE METHODS FOR THE TIME COMPRESSION OF SPEECH

Foulke's paper presents an overview of five possible methods for the compression of speech. One or two additional comments might be made about each of these methods, from the standpoint of their imminent practicability.

Speed changing

While this method, as stated, is technically easy in the laboratory, it is not easily accomplished on standard home playback instruments. To be sure, tape recordings can be played at twice their recorded speeds, e.g., 3¾ i.p.s. at 7½ i.p.s. However, since standard playback machines are arranged so that the only alternative is to double the speed which produces a full octave shift upward, it is unlikely that this procedure can be used much by the average person who wishes compression but can tolerate only a modest pitch shift. The situation is better in playing a 33⅓ rpm recording at 45 rpm, a standard phonograph option, in which only a 35 percent compression is obtained. As the reader may demonstrate for himself, intelligibility and comprehensibility remain good at this level. However, the use of this method will probably await the widespread availability of devices which permit a continuously variable change in the playback speed of recorded material, so that individual differences in ability to handle compression and pitch changes can be met. These devices are now becoming available, so that this method of compression will soon be practical for modest degrees of compression (probably no higher than 50 percent).

Electromechanical sampling

As Foulke points out, these devices have a serious limitation as the portions of the tape record to be discarded are removed on a strict periodic basis with *no* regard for the message contained on the tape record. Furthermore, the Fairbanks device is difficult or impossible to use in real time (the compressed material must be stored and replayed to restore the frequencies to normal pitch); but, most importantly, at this writing, it is a one-of-a-kind, laboratory device, not available on the commercial market.[1]

On the other hand, the Springer device is distributed in this country and can be used in real time (although limited to a single, fixed discard interval of about 35-40 msec.). It is, however, expensive (about $4,000 as well as playback equipment), and limited by its design characteristics to a maximum compression of approximately 50 percent. Nevertheless, if one were to compress material tomorrow (e.g., for educational presentations), the Springer device would probably be the most logical choice of the methods. (Furthermore, the distributor has recently indicated that significant modifi-

---

[1]As this paper is going to press, a very limited number of these devices, modified, are becoming available.

cations planned for the next model may eliminate some of its limitations.) All of the research on compressed speech carried out by this writer and his colleagues at the American Institutes for Research in the past five years has employed this device.

Speech synthesis method

Although, as Foulke points out, this method has great potential flexibility for compressing speech in accordance with specific, selected speech sound redundancies, its present key limitation has been the inability of its acoustical generators to reproduce adequately the complete formant structure of human speech sounds. This deficiency results in a loss of voice identification and in the metallic quality we typically associate with artificial speech. No doubt, these technical problems will be solved, but these devices are likely to be expensive and less satisfactory than the electro-mechanical method in the immediate future.

Harmonic compressors

As Foulke has indicated, these devices depend on the division of the speech spectrum into narrow frequency bands and the application of frequency halving and doubling circuits. In addition to the limitations imposed by the lack of flexibility in producing a variety of speeds, a technical breakthrough is required in the development of low cost, precision filters. Because of the frequency halving and doubling, it is critical that the filter bands be clearly separated; otherwise, the band overlap interaction with the harmonics of the speech spectrum produces intolerable distortions.

Computer sampling

The present writer would agree with Foulke that perhaps the most promising future approach to speech compression lies in the further development of computer techniques. Present explorations of this area have required a somewhat unusual computer configuration (a general-purpose digital computer as well as analog/digital — digital/analog capabilities), and have proved expensive. However, the rapid rate of technical developments in the field of

computers suggests that these limitations may become less con-
strictive in the near future.

It is in its flexibility that the computer approach seems most
promising. In addition to offering the option of setting up the discard rule in a wide variety of forms, periodic or message-linked,
other novel approaches have become possible. For instance, R. J.
Scott (1967) has explored the production of stereo-compressed
(dichotic) speech. In this variation of the computer method, the
sampled material is routed to one of the listener's ears through
Channel A of a stereo system; some or all of what would otherwise
be discarded is simultaneously routed to the other ear via Channel
B of the system. Surprisingly, this procedure appears to improve
intelligibility and comprehensibility, particularly of speech compressed to less than 50 percent of the original recording time. Scott
reported that 11 of his 14 subjects expressed a preference for this
form of compressed speech over the Fairbanks/Springer method.

A further elaboration has been suggested by H. L. Cramer
(private communication) who calls it *braided* speech. In this procedure the computer is instructed to divide the speech into segments as close to pitch periods as possible and overlap segments
by sequentially displacing some of them temporally. The signal
may also be treated dichotically, depending on the degree of compression desired. The exact mechanics of this procedure are too
involved to discuss here, but the concept emphasizes the great
flexibility provided by the computer approach to compression.

THE EVALUATION OF TIME
COMPRESSED SPEECH

As Foulke points out, the evaluation of time compressed speech
is a complex question depending on the evaluation of the actions
and interactions of a number of classes of factors including the
mechanics of compression, the characteristics of the stimulus
material, situational variables, and the organismic characteristics
of the listeners. In addition, however, the researcher must opera-
tionally define his terminal behaviors in terms of measurements.
It is here that questions of intelligibility and comprehensibility become entwined. Clearly, a message is not comprehensible unless
it is intelligible; but, of course, the converse does not hold true.

Beyond the difficulty inherent in deciding at what point (and how much) declining intelligibility has degraded comprehensibility, the problem of measuring comprehensibility is crucial to the evaluation of time compressed speech. The common approach has been to develop a test, usually objective, based on a listening selection. Most of the research to date, including our own, has employed this measure of comprehension. Nevertheless, serious difficulties in this measurement approach have impaired our ability to draw dependable conclusions about the factors associated with time compressed speech. This is not the place to indulge a treatise on measurement, but the issue is sufficiently important to warrant some discussion.

The major concern is the extent to which performance on the test actually represents accurately the acquisition of the information in the listening selection. Two conditions must be true to support the assumption that it does: first, the test questions must cover and represent the material contained in the selection (which is extremely difficult to demonstrate); second, the differential prior knowledge and experiences of the various listeners must be entirely uncorrelated with test performance (a condition which is virtually impossible to accept). Thus, we are led to the conclusion that, for almost any practical listening selection and its related test, the measurement of comprehension derived from this method is invalid to an unknown degree.

A second concern deals with the problem of measuring change and/or improvement over a period of time in the comprehension of time compressed speech. Either tests must be repeated, raising questions of partial memory, multiple exposure to the stimulus, and statistical problems in treating gains scores; or equated tests must be used at the different points in time. In this case, not only must the tests be equivalent, but the listening selections themselves must be comparable. Otherwise, the measurements will reflect the differences in instrumentation to an unknown degree as well as actual listener changes.

While these criticisms apply to the measurement of comprehension in general, and are certainly not novel, they do emphasize the wisdom of marshalling a variety of measures of comprehension, particularly in the study of new fields, such as time compressed speech. One possibility might involve the presentation of a variety of oral directions pertaining to a relatively simple response device. In this situation, comprehension would be defined as the number of correct responses, indicating the number of situations in which the listener was able to understand the directions well enough to select the correct response. In any case, further work on the measurement of comprehension is crucial to the evaluation of time compressed speech.

INTELLIGIBILITY AND THE SAMPLING RULE

Foulke also indicates that the intelligibility of speech compressed by the sampling method depends, to some extent, on the size and frequency of the discard interval, citing the work of Garvey (1953a; b), and Fairbanks and Kodman (1957). Certainly, a discard interval that permits the loss of entire speech units will degrade intelligibility; and, it is likely that an interruption frequency in the audible range of speech will produce interference. It must be emphasized, however, that both the experimentation carried out by Foulke himself and by the writer and his colleagues has employed the Springer device which features a fixed discard interval of about 40 msec. This value represents a compromise which virtually eliminates the loss of entire speech units and does not produce an objectionable interference tone. It does introduce another problem.

With a fixed discard interval, the retained sampling interval must of necessity vary with variations in compression, specifically growing smaller as compression increases. For example, it seems clear that as compression increases the discard interval is removed more frequently, so that the sampling intervals must become progressively smaller as compared to the discard interval. The situation for a message of 320 msec. is illustrated in Figure 1 for 50 percent and 37½ percent compression. The hatches in Figure 1 indicate the discard segments.

Foulke reports several studies which suggest that as compression increases beyond the 50 percent point, both intelligibility and comprehension begin to decline. Our own results also show little degradation until about the 50 percent point. Is it significant that at this point, the fixed discard begins to exceed the sampling interval in length? Certainly, smaller and smaller bits, originally separated by segments larger than themselves, are being abutted to form the output as compression increases. Theoretically, this would make for disjunctive transitions from segment to segment that might distort the overall sound pattern.

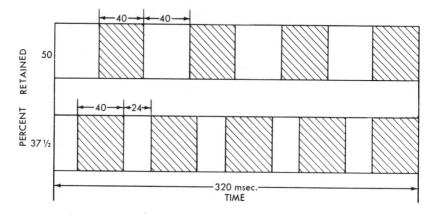

FIGURE 1. Sampling and discard segments for different degrees of compression.

Cramer (1967), however, has reported on intelligibility studies conducted at degrees of compression much higher than those employed in the studies reported by Foulke. Cramer reasoned that intelligibility should be studied in terms of what remained (sampling intervals rather than discard intervals), and presented extensive evidence to show that the optimal intelligibility for his material occurred at sampling intervals of 10-15 msec., *regardless* of degree of compression. (Compressions to 43½ percent of original time were used.) Cramer computed the fundamental frequency of his speaker's voice and concluded that a sampling interval of 15 msec. was just the value necessary to ensure that, on the average, there was at least one pitch period of the voice in each sample of speech. Cramer's conclusion emphasized that the sampling interval for compression should be selected in keeping with the characteristics of the speaker's voice.

It is also interesting to note that Cramer's data show that the Springer device is far from the optimum sampling interval at all degrees of compression within its design range (and even as modified by both Foulke and the present writer to extend its range). While the findings reported may not (and probably do not) invalidate the research carried out with this device to date, they certainly suggest that great caution is necessary in building a theoretical structure about compressed speech which is based only on the Springer compressor.

COMPREHENSION AND WORD RATE

It is difficult to argue with the data presented by Foulke in summarizing the relationship of comprehension test performance and degree of compression (pp. 92-93), particularly since these results are similar to those obtained by the writer (Orr, Friedman, and Williams, 1965). However, it must be brought out clearly that Foulke's results (Figure 2) pertain to a single exposure to (presumably) naive subjects. It would help to know how Foulke computed his "mean percent of corrected comprehension scores" in Figure 2, but the shape of the curve appears to be correct. However, Foulke's Table 1 indicates clearly that comprehension scores hold up through 300 wpm rather than 250 wpm as Foulke states on page 90. The 300 wpm figure is also in better agreement with our work (Orr, et al., 1965; 1967).

THE DIFFERENTIAL EFFECTS OF COMPRESSION ON WORD INTELLIGIBILITY AND LISTENING COMPREHENSION

In this section of his paper Foulke offers the hypothesis that, within limits, variation in the intelligibility of single words has little effect on the comprehension of a meaningful discourse composed of these words. He cites a variety of experimental evidence to support this contention. However, in the experiment (pp. 94-99) in which five groups received both PB materials as a test of intelligibility, and then a test on a listening selection as a measure of comprehension at five different compression rates, the measure of intelligibility is *not* a specific measure of the intelligibility of the listening selection itself. Therefore, the lack of difference in intelligibility means for high and low comprehension groups does not seem to justify the conclusion that poor comprehension cannot be explained by low single word intelligibility. Such a conclusion demands a measure of the individual word intelligibility *of the listening selection*, not just the PB materials. Furthermore, Foulke tends to de-emphasize the significant difference in his intelligibility means at the highest speed (if indeed this is what he means by "59 percent compression;" note that Figure 4 does not show this value, but rather 41 percent compression) and the fact that the data presented in his Figure 4 look just like one would expect if the progressively larger loss in comprehension were indeed attributable to the cumulative effects of relatively smaller losses in intelligibility.

In further support of his hypothesis Foulke reports an experiment (Figure 5, for which the X-axis is less than fully meaningful) in which "Springer" (sampling) compression was apparently mixed in varying degrees with the speed change method, presumably producing an output at a constant 325 wpm, but with varying degrees of distorted intelligibility via pitch shift. However, one might ask whether or not the 325 wpm speed used in this experiment was high enough to be in the range where speed change produces measurable distortion of intelligibility. Reference to the data in Foulke's Figure 1 does not provide a complete answer, but, certainly, 325 wpm was not in the range of great or perhaps even measurable loss of intelligibility as a function of speeding. A similar criticism can be made of the unpublished experiment reported on pages 88-89. Clearly, it is difficult to come to a solid conclusion in favor of his hypothesis.

It might be logically argued that as the organism approaches the limits of its information processing capability, any factors which induce additional processing load (such as distortions of intelligibility) should result in loss of comprehension. Furthermore, as Foulke points out, some intelligibility is a necessary condition for comprehension. If Foulke's hypothesis holds, it appears that the limits within which it can be expected to hold may be narrow, and this reviewer considers it improbable, particularly for higher degrees of compression, that further improvements in intelligibility at almost any level will not affect comprehension. Of course, context and redundancy are employed by the listener to help reconstruct imperfectly transmitted messages. Nevertheless, this does not negate the importance of continued efforts to improve the intelligibility of compressed speech, if it is to be used in any practical ways.

COMPREHENSION AND THE RATE OF OCCURRENCE OF THE DISCRIMINABLE ELEMENTS OF SPEECH

While the nature of the relationship between word intelligibility and comprehension discussed in Foulke's paper may be in doubt, the fact that comprehension falls off more rapidly with increasing compression than intelligibility cannot be disputed. Cramer (1967) found comparatively high intelligibility for short sentences at word rates above those used by Foulke and certainly above the rates at which both Foulke and the present writer have found serious losses in comprehension. Even if some loss of comprehension can be attributed to the cumulative effects of imperfect intelligibility, both logic and experimental results to date tend to support the arguments presented in favor of a breakdown in cognitive processing as the information flow increases to high rates. There is even considerable support for the theoretical process proposed by Foulke. However, perhaps the more interesting question is whether or not the loss of comprehension experienced at some level (whether it is 275 wpm or higher) can be offset by some training or practice procedures. In other words, is the "channel capacity" referred to by Foulke amenable to enlargement? The work of this writer and his colleagues suggests that it is.

Foulke argues essentially that the "capacity" of the visual channel cannot be taken as an index of the potential capacity of the auditory channel, because the visual process of reading is a "chunking" or quantum process, whereas the auditory process is serial and "cannot be chunked." There are several problems with this argument. First, it is conceivable that the auditory input can be stored in short term memory and processed from there in sequential chunks similar to those acquired during the fixations in reading. Available evidence does not support or refute this possibility, but parsimony certainly suggests that the central information handling process might be similar for both auditory and visual channels. Second, while many persons read more rapidly than 275 wpm, little is known about the ability of fast readers to listen to rapid material; and, it may be argued that the imperfect intelligibility of present compression devices makes it difficult to obtain the required comparisons. In fact, the present writer and his colleagues have noted some tendency (not yet formally tested) for the comprehension of compressed material to drop off at or near the listener's reading rate. More experimentation on this point is needed. However, in spite of these facts, *considerable evidence exists* to suggest that good comprehension may be possible at higher rates than 275 wpm.

A major portion of our research over the past five years has been devoted to the proposition that comprehension of compressed speech can be improved (Orr, Friedman, and Williams, 1965; Orr and Friedman, 1968; Friedman and Orr, 1967). Results of this research have shown conclusively that variations of simple practice routines can improve comprehension of literary/historical passages presented at speeds up to 475 wpm to a highly significant degree.

For example, the combined mean scores for four different experimental groups reached 66 percent of their normal speed comprehension scores at 425 wpm after only 12-15 hours of practice listening, compared with initial scores of about 40 percent. In another series of experiments, mean comprehension scores of over 90 percent of normal speed comprehension were reached at 375 wpm. (Orr and Friedman, 1967).

It is, of course, not clear from these data what the mechanism of improvement is, but, certainly, the suggestion exists that information processing in the auditory dimension can be improved. An interesting possibility worthy of study is that the average person processes a flow of language at a rate no faster than his usual reading rate (which is in itself limited by a variety of physiological and experimental factors). This condition could be expected to lead to an *habituated rate* of information processing. Perhaps compressed speech research provides a unique opportunity to probe the characteristics and limitations of human information processing in general.

In an effort to shed further light on the nature of the comprehension of time compressed speech, research is continuing to try to determine the factors associated with individual differences in comprehending compressed speech. Preliminary data has already suggested that speech fluency, spelling skill, and general language ability are among the factors most relevant to listening comprehension performance, while specific memory skills have shown a tendency to be *inversely* related to listening scores, particularly at the early stages of high speed listening. This finding suggests that excessive attention to detail may be antithetical to good listening (perhaps overloading the processing capability with excessive encoding). Certainly, much remains to be done in this area of research, but these beginnings seem to hold promise for an improved understanding of the factors associated with comprehending time compressed speech.

CONCLUSION

Foulke's paper represents an important effort to summarize and integrate some of the research in the area of time compressed speech. It clearly makes the point that intelligibility and comprehension are different though related phenomena, and presents a rudimentary and tentative model or view of the process of comprehending aural input as its specificity increases. The discussion presented above has emphasized the importance of improved measures of comprehension and attempted to draw attention to several related problems about which further research is needed.

No attempt has been made to assess the implications of time compressed speech for practical applications, such as the improvement of educational efficiency, reading improvement, and language learning, (though research is proceeding on these and other topics). However, the point has been well made that time compressed speech may prove to be a most useful tool, the ingenious use of which may lead to a greatly improved understanding of language perception and human information processing in general.

REFERENCES

Cramer, H. L. The intelligibility of time-compressed speech. In E. Foulke (ed.), *Proceedings of the Louisville conference on time compressed speech*. Louisville: University of Louisville, 1967. Pp. 3-20.

Fairbanks, G., & Kodman, F., Jr. Word intelligibility as a function of time compression. *Journal of the Acoustical Society of America*, 1957, **29**, 636-41.

Friedman, H. L., & Orr, D. B. Recent research in the training of compressed speech comprehension. In E. Foulke (ed.), *Proceedings of the Louisville conference on time compressed speech*. Louisville: University of Louisville, 1967.

Garvey, W. D. The intelligibility of speeded speech. *Journal of Exceptional Psychology*, 1953, **45**, 102-08. (a)

Garvey, W. D. The intelligibility of abbreviated speech patterns. *Quarterly Journal of Speech*, 1953, **39**, 296-306. (b)

Orr, D. B., & Friedman, H. L. The effect of listening aids on the comprehension of time compressed speech. *Journal of Communication*, 1967, **27**, 223-27.

Orr, D. B., & Friedman, H. L. Effect of massed practice on the comprehension of time-compressed speech. *Journal of Educational Psychology*, 1968, **59**, 6-11.

Orr, D. B., Friedman, H. L. & Williams, J. Trainability of listening comprehension of speeded discourse. *Journal of Educational Psychology*, 1965, **56**, 148-56.

Scott, R. J., Computers for speech time compression. In E. Foulke (ed.), *Proceedings of the Louisville conference on time compressed speech*. Louisville: University of Louisville, 1967. Pp. 29-35.

5

CURRENT APPROACHES TO SYNTAX RECOGNITION[1]

JERRY A. FODOR

Massachusetts Institute of Technology

An important theme in recent psycholinguistic discussions has stressed the 'psychological reality' of the generative syntactic models proposed by transformational linguists. This is hardly surprising. The work of contemporary grammarians has provided numerous insights into a wide range of structural phenomena in language. Nor does it seem reasonable to suppose that the linguists' successes have been merely fortuitous. Rather, linguistically sophisticated psychologists have assumed that the achievements of modern grammars can be accounted for by hypothesizing some intimate relationship between the mechanisms postulated by grammars and those that actually mediate the verbal behavior of the speaker/hearer. To hypothesize the psychological reality of a linguistic theory which succeeeds in explaining a variety of data about the linguistic capacities of speakers is, of course, entirely sensible;

[1]The ideas presented in this paper were, in large part, worked out in collaboration with Profs. Merrill F. Garrett and Thomas G. Bever. For whatever errors or unclarities the paper may contain I am, however, entirely responsible.

theories which explain the data have *ipso facto* some claim to be considered true.

But while accepting *some* version of the hypothesis that grammars are psychologically real would appear to be highly rational, it is unclear precisely *which* version of this hypothesis the grammarians' explanatory successes best support. This unclarity is not a mere matter of terminology: what is at issue is the problem of characterizing the relationship between the 'performance' devices psychologists investigate and the 'competence models' that grammarians study. In particular, at present there exists no satisfactory account of the relationship between a grammar capable of recursively enumerating the sentences and their structural descriptions, and a device (a performance model) capable of simulating the speaker/hearer by recognizing and integrating utterances of sentences. To study the relation between these devices is to study the sense in which grammars are psychologically real, and some of the more profound problems in current psycholinguistics are found in this area of investigation.

It is possible to find at least two ways of construing the hypothesis that grammars are psychologically real. What might be called the 'strong psychological reality' position holds that not only the structural description enumerated by grammars, but also the grammars themselves and the operations they employ in the specification of structural descriptions, are directly realized in an adequate performance model. In this view, a grammar is presumed to be a component of a performance model, and the operations involved in the grammatical derivation of a sentence are presumed to be a subset of the operations involved in its perceptual analysis or its motor integration.

The 'weak psychological reality' position claims that, insofar as the grammar assigns the correct structural descriptions to sentences, it specifies the structures that the performance model must recognize and integrate. But, according to this position, the grammar is neutral concerning the character of the psychological operations involved in sentence processing. In effect, the weak view claims that psychological reality exists for the structural descriptions enumerated by a grammar but for nothing else.

Experimenters who have directed their attention to the psychological reality of grammars have not always made it explicit whether it is the strong or the weak version of the doctrine with which they were concerned. Nevertheless, it is possible, at least in retrospect, to distinguish between the investigations which demonstrated that their subjects responded to the parameters of sentences marked by syntactic structural descriptions, and the investigations which examined the psychological reality of grammatical rules and operations. Among the first group of studies are the experimental investigations conducted by Miller and his colleagues on the 'coding hypothesis' (i.e., on the view that the syntactic deep structure of a sentence is the form in which the sentence is stored for long-term recall. See, for example, Miller, 1962 and Mehler and Savin, in press). Also pertinent to the psychological reality of structural descriptions (and hence to the weak version of the psychological reality claim) are a variety of studies on the interaction of surface structure variables with the perception of pausation, stress, stimuli interfering with speech, etc. (cf., for example, Martin, 1967; Johnson, 1968). Experimental investigations which bear directly on the psychological reality of grammatical operations (and hence on the strong version of the psychological reality claim) have been concerned with the examination of sentential complexity.

Sentential complexity is particularly pertinent to the assessment of the strong version of the psychological reality claim for one important reason. If one assumes that, in producing or understanding a sentence, the speaker/hearer literally runs through the set of operations a grammar employs in generating that sentence, then one must predict that the length of the derivational history of a sentence ought to be a very good index of the difficulty the speaker/hearer will have in processing that sentence. Any experimental indices of complexity (including, of course, ontogenetic indices) ought, therefore, to be affected by the length of the derivational history of a sentence, if the strong version of the psychological reality claim is true.

A number of psycholinguistic studies in generative grammar appear to have been motivated by the hypothesis that the relative difficulty a subject has in dealing with a sentence in any number of experimental procedures is predicted by the number of grammatical operations employed in the transformational derivation of that sentence. We shall refer to this hypothesis as the derivational theory of complexity (DTC).

DTC can be made explicit in the following way. Consider a generative grammar G of the language L and a sentence S in the range of G. It is possible, in principle, to define a metric which for every pair (G_i, S_i) specifies the number N of rules (or elementary operations or whatever) that G_i requires to generate S_i. DTC in its

strongest form is the claim that the size of N is an index
relative complexity of S_i. In particular, all other things equ
sentences assigned the same number are predicted to be equally
complex and, of two sentences assigned different numbers, the
larger number is assigned to the more complex sentence.

Much of the published experimental literature on DTC has been
reviewed elsewhere (Fodor and Garrett, 1966) and will not be
recapitulated here. Studies in which the results are compatible
with DTC are often equivocal as they are also, by and large, compatible with a quite different account of the contribution of syntactic variables to determining sentential complexity.

The difficulty arises in the following way. DTC has usually been
tested by comparing the complexity of sentences which have relatively few grammatical transformations in their derivational histories with the complexity of sentences that have a relatively large
number of grammatical transformations in their derivational histories. The experimental prediction is characteristically that sentences with a large number of grammatical transformations will
prove relatively difficult in experimental tasks. Unfortunately,
however, the effect of the application of a transformation in the
grammatical derivation of a sentence is normally to deform the
grammatical structures to which the transformation applies. The
typical effect of transformation is to destroy structure. It is precisely the deep syntactic structure upon which the semantic interpretation of a sentence is usually presumed to depend. As we
increase the transformational distance between the base and surface structure of a sentence, we normally *decrease* the extent to
which its surface structure exhibits the grammatical relations
among the parts of the sentence in the appropriate form for
semantic interpretation. If, for example, we turn a sentence into
the passive voice, we add a grammatical operation to its derivational history, but we also produce a linguistic object which
departs from the 'canonical' (base structure) English sentence
order, in which the first noun phrase is the subject noun phrase
and the second noun phrase is the object noun phrase. The
problem with many of the experimental results that demonstrate
the increased complexity of passive sentences as opposed to active
sentences is that the experimenters fail to tell us whether the
increase in complexity is due to the addition of a transformation
to the derivational history or to the fact that the surface structure
of the passive sentence is not in the canonical form for semantic
interpretation. In short: does the hearer find passives relatively

difficult because the grammatical operations are psychologically real and the derivational history of the passive contains one more grammatical operation than the derivational history of the active? Or, does he find them relatively difficult because his heuristics for the decoding of English sentences treat the cases in which the first noun phrase of a sentence is the subject noun phrase as the canonical case? (For example, the heuristics assume that the surface order of phrases in a sentence corresponds to their deep order unless the sentence is explicitly marked in a way that precludes this analysis. The presence of a by-phrase might supply this marking in the case of passive sentences.) Questions analogous to this one arise for most of the comparisons between type of sentences that have been made in the experimental investigation of the derivational theory of complexity. The successes that theory has had, in general, have failed to supply univocal support for the strong version of the psychological reality view.

There are, in fact, a number of considerations which suggest that the cases in which experimental predictions based on DTC have proved true ought to be explained by reference to the organization of the speaker/hearer's sentence processing heuristics rather than the psychological reality of grammatical operations. To name just three: 1) There appears to be a number of counter examples to the claim that *all* transformational operations effect the performance of the speaker/hearer. There is, for example, a well-motivated English translation which takes "John phones the girl up" from "John phones up the girl." It is hard to believe that the second of these sentences is simpler than the first in anything like the way that actives are simpler than passives; nor has informal experimentation thus far succeeded in measuring a complexity difference between sentences with and without displaced particles. Analogous remarks can be made in the case of sentences with full and reduced comparatives like "John swims better than Bill does" and "John swims better than Bill." Fodor and Garrett (1968) have shown that adjectivization does not measurably increase the complexity of self-embedded sentences on any of a number of experimental tasks. If adjective insertion is a transformational operation, currently a moot point, then these findings would appear to militate against the derivational theory of complexity.

2) There are a variety of findings which suggest that Aux-expansion does not significantly affect sentential complexity. Aux-expansion is probably not a transformational operation, but it is certainly a grammatical operation. Must we therefore say that the

operations specified by some types of grammatical rules are psychologically real while those specified by other types are not? A more plausible hypothesis might be that Aux-expansion does not affect grammatical complexity, precisely because expanding the Aux does not affect the more efficient surface structure clues to deep structure relations. In particular, Aux-expansion preserves canonical constituent order, while transformational operations often do not. Again, the suggestion appears to be that increasing the length of the derivational history of a sentence increases its complexity only in those cases where the added syntactic operations complicate the way in which the grammatical relations in a sentence are exhibited in its surface structure.

3) Slobin (1966) found no significant difference between actives and passives when the latter were 'irreversible', for example: "The car was driven by the boy." It seems clear that the difficulty with passives derives not primarily from the fact they contain, in their derivational histories, one more operation than actives; but only that the use of the passive voice, by destroying canonical phrase order, slightly obstructs the functioning of a decoding device which prefers to assume that the first noun phrase is a subject noun phrase.

Finally, it is worth remarking upon the *a priori* implausibility of the view that the kinds of experimental procedures psychologists have used to investigate the derivational theory of complexity are sufficiently sensitive to capture performance differences of the minute magnitudes that DTC would predict. If the computational operations involved in the perceptual analysis of a sentence are identified with the grammatical operations involved in its generation, then there must be hundreds, perhaps thousands, of these operations involved in analyzing any moderately complicated sentence, (it should be remembered that these operations include not only the ones involved in the syntax, but also those postulated by the semantic and phonological components of the grammar). To suppose that psychological tests like listening to sentences under noise, or memorizing them in rote recall tasks, or reconstructing them from anagrams, are sufficiently sensitive to register differences in the order of one or two parts in a thousand is excessively optimistic. It seems that whatever is causing the differences we measure must account for a fairly substantial part of the total computational difficulty of a sentence. But there would appear to be no way of reconciling that hypothesis with DTC.

These sorts of considerations, together with a variety of others, point to a model of sentence recognition, and hence of the relation between the 'performance device' and the grammar, different from the one which appears to motivate DTC. Instead of thinking of the grammar as a component of the performance device, and hence of grammatical operations as a subset of the psychological operations involved in the recognition of the structural descriptions, one might think of the grammar as simply a representation of the structural relations characteristic of the sentences of a language. The psychological counterpart of the grammar is some set of heuristics for inducing the deep structure representations of sentences from possibly fragmentary representations of their surface structure and for integrating well-formed surface structures which express whatever message a speaker wishes to communicate. The grammar, to repeat, is construed as 'psychologically real' only in that it provides a representation of the linguistic structures that these heuristics compute.

It is obvious that before we can test this hypothesis about the relation between grammars and performance devices against the hypothesis that underlies DTC, we shall have to know something about what kinds of heuristics can be postulated as functioning in integrating and recognizing sentences. Fodor and Garrett (1968) and Fodor, Garrett, and Bever (1968) have suggested that these heuristics might be organized in something similar to the following way. The program subjects use to recover the grammatical structure of sentences is hypothesized to have two primary components: first, a *lexicon* which classifies the lexical items in the language according to the deep structure configurations that they are able to enter. The lexicon may be thought of as effecting these classifications by the assignment of syntactic features to each

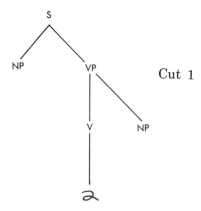

lexical item, and each feature, in turn, is thought of as designating a partially specified deep structure tree. Verbs might receive features like: *plus transitive, plus that-complement, plus infinitival complement*, etc. To say that a given verb has such a feature is to say that certain types of deep structure trees are well formed when they appear with that verb as their main verb. Thus, for example, to say of the verb ə that it is plus transitive is to say that trees like the one in Cut 1 are well formed. To say that a verb is plus that-complement is to say that trees like the tree in Cut 2 are well formed.

The claim that lexical items are cross-classified for the sort of base structures in which they appear has considerable empirical import. We could, for example, imagine that the system worked the other way around: that is, speakers cross-classify types of clauses by the lexical items which can select them. Examples like the following strongly suggest that this is not the case. Subjects find considerable difficulty in completing left deleted sentences like: "_____ the man come running through the trees." (Completion here means supplying any phrase in the blank which renders the whole a grammatical sentence.) On the other hand, the completion of the following left deleted sentence is relatively easy: "_____ saw the man come running through the trees," as is the completion of the right deleted sentence: "John saw _____."

It appears that certain verbs (in particular perceptual verbs) govern subordinated sentences in which tense is neutralized. In principle, this is a fact which the speaker/hearer might represent in either of two ways: either as a constraint upon the class of verb which can be chosen, given that one has chosen a subordinate

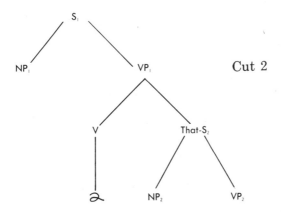

Cut 2

clause with neutralized tense, or as a constraint on the class of subordinated clauses that can be chosen, given that one has chosen a perceptual verb. In fact, the performance asymmetry just cited strongly suggests that the technique of representation actually employed is the latter one. That is, given only a subordinated structure with a neutralized tense, subjects find it difficult to select a verb compatible with that structure. However, given the dominating verb, subjects find relatively little difficulty in supplying subordinated phrasal material which satisfies the selection restrictions associated with the verb. It appears that subjects cross-classify lexical items by the material they dominate and not vice versa.[2]

For these and related reasons, we assume that the lexical items of a language are associated, in the speaker/hearer's lexicon, with sets of constraints on the deep structures in which these items can appear. If this is correct, then a plausible assumption is that the hearer employs the lexicon in sentence recognition by postulating for a given sentence just those types of deep structure compatible with the lexical items that the sentence contains. Since, moreover, it appears to be the verb of a sentence which dictates the more general features of the geometry of the deep structure of the sentence, we may assume, as a first approximation, that an early step in sentence recognition involves postulating any deep structure compatible with the lexical analysis of its main verb.

Even considered as a first approximation, however, this clearly cannot be the whole story. A given lexical item may, if we consider its entire distribution across the language, be compatible with a variety of types of deep structure trees. Barring cases of ambiguity, only one deep structure tree will represent the appropriate analysis of any given sentence in which the item occurs. Thus, granted that the hearer appeals to a lexicon to assign putative deep structure analyses to a sentence, and given that the putative analyses he assigns must be compatible with, and are determined by, the lexical entries for the words in the sentence, it remains an open question how the hearer decides between putative deep structure analyses when the lexical item is compatible with more than one analysis. The current suggestion is that the surface structure of a sentence must contain enough material to permit

---

[2]The example is owing to Forster, 1966 and 1967, as are a number of other interesting results on the completion of sentence fragments. I do not know whether he would accept the explanation of his findings that I have suggested here.

such decisions and that the speaker/hearer must be in possession of computational procedures adequate for the exploitation of the material.

Thus, for example, in analyzing a sentence like "John expected Mary to leave" we assume that the subject must ask which of the deep structure configurations possible for 'expect' the sentence exemplifies. In particular, we assume that the subject knows that 'expect' can take infinitival or *that*-complementation, or a direct object. Since he is capable of determining which of these patterns is exemplified by any given sentence containing 'expect', we must assume that the subject has and applies tests for each of the various base structure configurations that the verb may enter. It is at this stage that the appeal to surface structure features presumably plays its role. Thus, it is self-evident that the analysis of "John expected Mary to leave" as an example of infinitival complementation must be facilitated by the presence of 'to' in the surface structure of that sentence. Similarly, the *pos-ing* interpretation of "John expected Mary's leaving" must be facilitated by recognition of the surface 's,' 'ing'. In these cases, we might say that the surface material is a 'spelling' of certain deep structure configurations much as $/z/$, $/iz/$ and $/s/$ are possible spellings of the English plural morpheme. On this analogy, the heuristics available to the hearer must specify *which* surface configurations spell which deep configurations in the language he speaks.

The action of surface structure markers in facilitating the recognition of deep structure features like complement type can sometimes be dramatic. For example, *that*-complements are the only ones in English which simultaneously satisfy the two following conditions. First, they govern subordinated clauses which contain tense ("He thinks that John will be late" but not "He hopes for John to will be late") and second, they contain deletable complementizers ("He thinks that John is an idiot" vs. "He thinks John is an idiot.") In particular, complements like *whether*, which also govern subordinated sentences containing tense, are *not* deletable. Thus, we have "I wonder whether John will come" but not "I wonder John will come."

Since *that* is the only deletable complementizer which can govern subordinated structures containing tense, it is plausible to hypothesize that the presence of marked tense in a subordinated structure is an extremely efficient clue to *that*-complementation in reduced sentences. This is correct. Notice that "He felt the child trembled" is heard as a reduced form of "He felt that the child trembled" and as unrelated to the (tenseless) "He felt the child tremble." Correspondingly, "He felt the children tremble" is ambiguous between the two types of complement, depending on whether 'tremble' is heard as tensed. In these cases, it seems perfectly evident that an effective clue to the analysis of the complement is supplied by the presence or absence of tense in the surface structure of the subordinated clause. In fact, since "He felt the child trembled" and "He felt the child tremble" form, in the relevant respect, a minimal pair, it seems evident that *only* the presence of marked tense in the subordinated clause can be relevant to the operation of whatever perceptual heuristics are involved in distinguishing between them. (Theorists who are inclined to attribute precedence to the functioning of *semantic* cues in *syntactic* analysis ought to be embarrassed by this sort of case; we are clearly dealing with semantically distinct senses of 'feel' in these sentences, since in the one case 'felt' can be paraphrased as 'thought,' and in the other, it cannot. But, equally clearly, the relevant clue to disambiguation is a purely syntactic feature of the verbs — their behavior *vis à vis* the tense of the subordinated clauses they dominate.)

These examples point to an interesting relation between the heuristics employed by the sentence recognition device and the grammar proper. We have seen that, in determining the appropriate base structure for a sentence like "John felt the child trembled" the subject apparently uses information about the kinds of derivations that are possible in English. In particular, the information that a derivation in which the reduction of a complement follows the use of a complement in a sentence with marked tense in its subordinated clause is possible only when the complementizer is *that*. That is, the subject is using information that might be appropriately represented as a metatheorem about the possible derivations in a correct grammar of English. It is precisely this metatheoretic character of the subject's information that is interesting. There is no single grammatical rule which corresponds directly to the heuristic that the subject appears to be employing. Rather, the heuristic is viable because of certain features of the way that several grammatical rules interact in the course of permissible derivations. The grammar, in short, does not appear in the recognition procedure, though the recognition procedure works only because certain facts are true about the derivations permitted by the grammar.

These suggestions about the possible organization of a recognition procedure for syntax would appear to have two obvious

implications for experimental testing. There ought to be two theoretically interesting ways of increasing the complexity of a sentence on performance tasks. The first is by introducing into the
sentence lexical items compatible with a relatively wide variety of
deep structure types. The more types of deep structure a lexical
item in a sentence is compatible with in principle, the more alternative hypotheses the speaker must entertain about the deep
structure of the sentence. The second procedure suggested by this
proposal is the eliminating, or confounding, of surface structure
features which can serve to spell the deep structure underlying the
sentence. This should lead to increasing the performance complexity of sentences. A body of experimental and anecdotal literature
is rapidly developing on each of these points. We shall consider
only a few examples here.

Let us begin with the second prediction—namely, that the complexity of a sentence increases with decrease in the explicitness
with which its surface structure configurations represent its underlying deep structure. We remarked above that in a sentence like
"John felt the girl tremble" or "John felt the girl trembled" the
recovery of the underlying form of complementation depends upon
recognizing the tensed or tenseless character of the subordinated
verb. In these sentences, this would appear to be the only clue
subjects have to the relevant deep structure, and it is interesting
that subjects often find these sentences difficult to understand. In
particular, many subjects have difficulty in 'hearing' the *that*-
complement version correctly. It is equally interesting that this
difficulty can be remedied simply by increasing the redundancy
with which deep structure information is specified in the surface
structure. The most obvious way of doing this is by restoring the
lost 'that' to the reduced sentence, but there are less obvious,
though equally efficient, means of attaining the same end.

Notice that "John felt the girl tremble" comes from a reduced
infinitival — i.e., it is a reduced version of "John felt the girl to
tremble." We can see this from the fact that the reduced 'to' is
restored in the passive: "The girl was felt to tremble by John."
Infinitival complements differ from *that*-complements in an interesting way. "John felt the girl tremble" comes from an underlying
structure "John felt NP # the girl to tremble" by way of a transformation that replaces the NP in the matrix sentence with the
subject noun phrase of the constituent sentence, thereby producing an intermediate form in which 'the girl' is the direct object of
the verb 'feel.' Alternatively, "John felt the girl trembled" comes
from a deep structure of the form "John felt that S # the girl

trembled" by way of a transformation that replaces the 'S' in the matrix sentence with the entire constituent sentence.

This difference in the derivation of the two sentences has two interesting consequences; the first is the semantic fact that sentences of the form *NP₁ verb NP₂ infinitive verb* characteristically entail sentences of the form "NP₁ verb NP₂"; e.g., "John felt the girl tremble" entails "John felt the girl" though "John felt the girl" is *not* entailed by sentences like "John felt that the girl trembled." The second point is purely syntactic. Since 'the girl' appears as the direct object of the main verb in "John felt the girl tremble," pronominalization of that sentence yields a sentence with the pronoun in the accusative case; hence: "John felt *her* tremble." On the other hand, since 'the girl' in "John felt the girl trembled" is the *subject* of the embedded verb (rather than object of the main verb), pronominalization in that sentence produces a form with the pronoun in the nominative case; hence: "John felt *she* trembled." *That*-complements characteristically differ from infinitival complements in this way. Notice the difference between the (unreduced) forms "John hoped that *she* left" and "John asked *her* to leave."

In short, the difference in pronominal case between sentences like "John felt she trembled" and "John felt her tremble" can be construed as a spelling of the deep structure differences between the sentences. It is therefore interesting to notice the striking intuitive difference in complexity between "John felt the girl tremble" and "John felt the girl trembled," on one hand, and "John felt her tremble" and "John felt she trembled," on the other. It seems obvious that by increasing the richness with which deep structure relations are marked in surface structure, we get a corresponding decrease in complexity.

A variety of recent experimental results point to the same conclusion. Fodor and Garrett (1968) have shown that the elimination of relative pronouns in center embedded sentences (e.g., differences like the one between "The man that the girl knew got sick" and "The man the girl knew got sick") appears to lead to an increase in the difficulty subjects have in dealing with these sentences. Fodor and Garrett hypothesized that this is because subjects recognize the surface configuration # NP₁ relative pronoun NP₂ # as a 'spelling' of a deep structure pattern in which NP₁ appears as the object of a verb of which NP₂ appears as the subject. (Though Garrett has recently suggested, correctly I think, that the facilitation ought to be attributed to the fact that the relative pronoun marks the deep structure as one in which relativization has applied, thus permitting the subject to 'call' the appropriate recognition routines earlier in the case of the unreduced sentences than in the reduced ones.) Support for the facilitation effects of the relative pronoun also comes from a recent thesis by Henry Olds (1968). Olds, working with children, discovered that response latency (though not response accuracy) was facilitated in the non-deleted as opposed to the deleted relative pronoun condition.

An extremely interesting line of research, in which the manipulated variable is the relative explicitness with which surface structure expressed the deep structure, has been carried out by Carol Chomsky in her Ph.D. thesis (1968). In this study, two kinds of comparisons are made. The first is between deleted and non-deleted shared pronouns (e.g., pairs such as "Ask her what you should do" and "Ask her what to do"). The second comparison is between deleted and undeleted *wh* elements (e.g., pairs of sentences such as "Ask her the color of the ball" and "Ask her what the color of the ball is"). In both cases examined, the results appear to bear out the view that the sentence in which surface structure is most explicit about deep structure is the one with which the subjects (children between 5 and 10) find it easiest to cope. These results hold despite the fact that the explicitly marked sentences are also superficially more complicated in terms of indices such as length, frequency of grammatical words, and so on.

Although the results just discussed are fragmentary, they would appear to be encouraging. It seems possible to make some sort of case, both on experimental and on intuitive grounds, for the role of reduction (i.e., deletion or other kinds of distortion of the surface structure representation of base structure configurations) in increasing the difficulty that subjects have with sentences.

Analogous results have been forthcoming for the prediction that increasing the lexical complexity of the items occurring in a sentence ought to increase the difficulty subjects have with the sentence. The initial results, while by no means conclusive, are tantalizing. Fodor, Garrett, and Bever (1968), for example, have shown that it is possible to increase the complexity of a sentence simply by substituting for a verb that accepts a relatively small number of types of complement a verb that accepts a relatively large number. Using center embedded sentences in short-term memory paradigms and a variety of types of sentences in anagram paradigms, they showed that substituting a verb like 'believe' (which takes direct objects and a variety of types of complement) for a verb like 'hit' (which takes only direct objects) increases the difficulty of the experimental tasks.

It seems fair to argue that the initial experimental results support a view of sentence processing and syntax recognition in particular, which holds that the recovery of base structure involves direct inductions from lexical and arrangement features of the surface structure. The grammar appears to be related to heuristics which accomplish this induction in an indirect and curious fashion. By enumerating the structures characteristic of the sentences in a language, it specifies the objects that the recognition procedure must recover. However, by characterizing the deep structure configurations into which lexical items can enter, and the types of correspondences between deep and surface structures permitted in the language, the grammar does, in a certain sense, express the information upon which the recognition heuristics capitalize. It appears that the grammar fails to characterize this information *in the form required for sentence recognition.* Sentence recognition heuristics seem to be founded upon facts about the language that hold by virtue of the way grammatical rules interact in permissible derivations of sentences. It also seems probable that the grammatical rules are not themselves part of the recognition procedure and that the computational processes involved in generating a sentence in the grammar are distinct from the computational processes which underlie the actual performance of the speaker/hearer.

I should like to conclude with a few general (and extremely speculative) remarks on the conceptual situation *vis à vis* the psychological reality of grammars as it appears in light of these considerations.

I have argued that grammars are not psychologically real in the following important sense: the mental operations which underlie the behavior of the speaker/hearer are not identical to, and probably do not include, the grammatical operations involved in generating sentences. If these arguments are correct, then they immediately raise the question "Why suppose that grammars (as distinct from the structural descriptions that grammars enumerate) are psychologically real at all?" I think that this is a question which, in the present state of the art, deserves to be taken seriously.

If grammatical operations are not psychologically real, then it is possible to conceptualize linguistic models of competence in a way that differs radically from what has been characteristic of the literature of generative grammar. In particular, generative grammarians have assumed usually that a grammar is psychologically real in the sense that 1) a grammar is what the normal child learns when exposed to a corpus of 'primary linguistic data,' and 2) it is precisely by virtue of his having learned the grammar that the adult is enabled to perform adequately as a speaker/hearer of his native language.

If, however, a model of the speaker/hearer is as loosely related to a grammar as we have been supposing, it is possible that this position requires revision. Why suppose that what a child learns when he learns his language is a grammar if, as we have seen, the grammar does not provide a model of what the child becomes when he becomes a speaker/hearer? Is it not, rather, plausible to assume that the child, upon exposure to his language, develops *not* a grammar, but a sentence producer/recognizer; that is, a device related to a grammar only in that it manipulates the structural descriptions that grammars enumerate?

This is an issue on which it seems important not to dogmatize. I suspect that the suggestion, though it raises difficult and important questions, is probably in the long run misconceived. Even though it appears that grammatical operations are not literally involved in the perception/production of sentences, the following consideration appears to militate in favor of the view that the child's linguistic apprenticeship does eventuate in the internalization of a grammar of the traditional generative type.

Grammatical universals can be divided into two kinds. There are, in the first place, universals which constrain the structural descriptions sentences in natural languages can have; for example: that all sentences have at least one NP in their deep structure, that deep structure sub-trees dominated by S may be embedded into one another only in certain fixed ways, that the constituents of a sentence must be drawn from among a certain fixed set of constituent types. Since all universal linguistic principles of this kind have in common the determination of the properties of possible sentence descriptions, it is possible to think of them as, in the first instance, constraints upon the outputs of grammars. That is, for these kinds of cases, one might say (as generative linguists traditionally have said) that the claim that L is a linguistic universal should be interpreted as: nothing shall count as a correct grammar of a natural language which enumerates structural descriptions incompatible with L. In short, whenever we have a universal constraint upon structural descriptions, we can treat it as a universal constraint upon grammatical rules.

These cases are, however, equivocal; for when they *can* be treated as implicitly 'about' the character of grammatical rule, they need not be so treated. While we can interpret a universal constraint upon structural descriptions as being 'really' a universal constraint upon grammars, we can equally well interpret it as a universal constraint upon the input/output characteristics of sentence producer/recognizers. In short, we know that there are certain universal properties of structural descriptions. But from this it does *not* follow that grammars must be psychologically real, since it is possible that the explanation of the fact that these universals hold is the fixed character of the sentence producer/recognizer.

There is, however, another kind of grammatical universal; namely, one which directly states that some property is true not of the structural descriptions output by a grammar but of the rules of grammars themselves. Among such universals are: that all grammars contain some transformational rules; that the transformational rules in all grammars are ordered; that not all the rules in any grammar are of transformational power; etc. Unlike universals of the first kind, these generalizations cannot be interpreted as constraints upon the input/output characteristics of the sentence producer/recognizer. For, these principles are not about *structural descriptions*, but about the *grammatical rules* which generate structural descriptions. Strictly speaking, universals of the first kind 'quantify over' structural descriptions and may or may not be interpreted as constraints upon grammatical rules, but universals of the second kind explicitly quantify over grammatical rules. Hence, the existence of the second kind of universal presupposes the existence of grammars. But what could it conceivably mean to say that a grammar exists except that it is part of a true psychological theory of the speaker/hearer?

It seems, in short, that we must either admit the psychological reality of grammars or abandon the linguistic universals, the discovery of which make up the primary contribution of generative grammar to linguistic theory: linguistic universals which constrain the form of grammatical rules. This does not mean that it is impossible simultaneously to do justice to the linguistic and the psychological facts. It *does* appear to mean that our account of the relation between linguistic and psychological models will have to allow for the possibility of an abstract mapping of the grammar onto any model of the speaker/hearer. One way of doing this, which seems to me not entirely implausible, is to assume that the child's innate linguistic endowment is even richer than most transformational grammarians have supposed. In particular, that the child must be construed as having not merely an innate ability to select a correct grammar of a given natural language on the basis of exposure to a sufficiently rich corpus of primary linguistic data drawn from that language, but also that he must have available procedures for constructing a recognizer/producer for sentences in a language given an appropriate grammar of the language. That is, his innate information must somehow permit him to distinguish between the relatively small set of metatheoretic properties of grammars which are relevant to the construction of sentence producer/recognizers and the infinite set of metatheoretic properties which are not. The form of this information would, by hypothesis, be an algorithm for constructing a sentence recognizer/producer from a grammar in normal transformational form.

While these remarks amount, of course, to no more than a speculation, it is a kind of speculation that is capable of empirical examination in a variety of ways. It implies not only a claim about the character of the innate endowment of the normal human child, but also a claim about the kinds of formal relations that ought to obtain between well-confirmed models of the sentence recognizer/ producer for a given language and independently well-confirmed models of the grammar for that language. In particular, this view requires that the formal relations between the two theories be such that, given the grammar, it should be possible to construct the sentence producer/recognizer by the application of a universal algorithm (i.e., an algorithm which will construct the appropriate sentence recognizer/producer for *any* natural language given a correct grammar of that language.) If we assume the view of sentence recognition discussed throughout this paper, then one might imagine that such an algorithm would construct, first, a classification of the formatives in the language by reference to their base structure properties and, second, an analysis of the ways in which specified surface structure features in the language represent deformations of the base structure trees characteristic of the language. Very roughly, one might expect that the first part of this construction should exploit information provided by the lexicon of a generative grammar and that the second part should exploit information provided by the transformational component of a generative grammar. It is the lexicon of a grammar which characterizes the selectional restrictions characteristic of formatives, and it is the transformational component which expresses the types of correspondence between base and surface structure that are characteristic of the language. On this view, perhaps the fundamental theoretical problem now facing psycholinguistics is to characterize the algorithm that performs this construction.

REFERENCES

Chomsky, C. The acquisition of syntax in children from 5 to 10. Unpublished Doctoral dissertation. Harvard University, 1968.

Fodor, J., & Garrett, M. Some reflections on competence and performance. In J. Lyons and R. Wales (eds.), *Psycholinguistic papers.* Edinburgh: Edinburgh University Press, 1966.

Fodor, J., & Garrett, M. Some syntactic determinants of sentential complexity. *Perception & Psychophysics*, 1967, **2**, 289-96.

Fodor, J. Garrett, M., & Bever, T. Some syntactic determinants of sentential complexity, II: Verb structure. *Perception & Psychophysics*, 1968, **3**, 453-61.

Forster, K. Left-to-right processes in the construction of sentences. *Journal of Verbal Learning and Verbal Behavior*, 1966, **5**, 285-91.

Forster, K. Sentence completion latencies as a function of constituent structure. *Journal of Verbal Learning and Verbal Behavior*, 1967, **6**, 878-83.

Garrett, M., & Fodor, J. Psychological theories and linguistic constructs. In T. Dixon and D. Horton (eds.), *Verbal behavior and general behavior theory.* Englewood Cliffs, N.J.: Prentice-Hall, 1968.

Johnson, N. Sequential verbal behavior. In T. Dixon and D. Horton (eds.), *Verbal behavior and general behavior theory.* Englewood Cliffs, N.J.: Prentice-Hall, 1968.

Martin, J. Hesitations in the speaker's production and listener's reproduction of utterances. *Journal of Verbal Learning and Verbal Behavior*, 1967, **6**, 903-10.

Mehler, J., & Savin, H. Memory process in the language user. In T. Bever and W. Weksel (eds.), *The structure and psychology of language.* New York: Holt, Rinehart and Winston (in press).

Miller, G. Some psychological studies of grammar. *American Psychologist*, 1962, **17**, 748-62.

Olds, H. An experimental study of syntactical factors influencing children's comprehension of certain complex relationships. Doctoral dissertation. Harvard University, 1968.

Slobin, D. Grammatical transformations and sentence comprehension in childhood and adulthood. *Journal of Verbal Learning and Verbal Behavior*, 1966, 5, 219-27.

WHAT GRAMMAR IS IN THE BRAIN?[1]

JOHN B. CARROLL
Educational Testing Service

I have some difficulty in commenting on Fodor's paper because his orientation seems rather different from mine. Perhaps it would be well to start by sketching what I understand to be his orientation, and how my own differs from it.

It is hard for me to tell exactly how far Fodor accepts what might be called the "standard" view in contemporary grammatical theory of the transformational variety. According to this standard view, the grammar has been described, loosely, as "what the speaker must know" in order to be able to "understand" (assign structural descriptions to) any well-formed sentence he may hear in the language, or to produce a well-formed sentence that will communicate whatever message he intends. Linguists, using their intuitions about what sentences are well formed, attempt to write an account of this "grammar." Chomsky (1965, p. 25) has acknowledged the ambiguity of the term *grammar*, as referring either to "the native speaker's internally represented 'theory of his language'" or to the linguist's account of this. The account is *descriptively adequate* to the extent that it correctly describes the intrinsic competence of the idealized native speaker" (p. 24); it has explanatory adequacy if it "succeeds in selecting a descriptively

---

[1] I am grateful to my colleagues Roy Freedle and Terrence Keeney for critiquing an early draft of this paper. For the views expressed here, I am of course solely responsible.

adequate grammar on the basis of primary linguistic data" (p. 25)
—observation of linguistic performance, including both well-formed
and not-well-formed sentences. At many points in his discussion,
Fodor uses the term *grammar*, following Chomsky, with a "systematic ambiguity" — i.e., the term is to be understood as referring
both to a (written, codifiable) theory and to the internalized
knowledge that the theory is supposed to describe. The real problem he confronts, however, is the kind of relationship that can exist
between a written grammar (theory) and the internalized competence of the speaker/hearer, and, indeed, the nature of that
internalized competence.

According to the generative grammatical theory to which Fodor
presumably subscribes at least in part, the grammar contains certain "deep" structures, and rules by which entities in the deep
structure may generate "surface" structures, actual well-formed
sentences in the language. Generative grammarians have been
reluctant to state exactly how competence can reside in the
speaker/hearer, or how one could detect the structural description
assignments made by him. These issues are laid aside, it would
seem, in favor of holding that a grammar is a rationalistic theory
in which the rules postulated may be highly abstract. Sentence
generation is a formal process that in the hands of the linguist becomes analogous to mathematical derivation and proof and is not
held to have any necessary relation to processes occurring in sentence production/understanding in speakers/hearers. Apparently
this is what Fodor means in speaking of a grammar as "a device
capable of recursively enumerating the sentences [of a language]
together with their structural descriptions." If a grammar is merely
a "device," it is no wonder that Fodor and his colleagues can be
concerned about its "psychological reality." Seen in this light a
grammar occupies some indeterminate position between internalized linguistic knowledge and a written account of that knowledge.
Raising a question about the psychological reality of such a device
seems tantamount to raising a question about the possibility of its
ever having descriptive adequacy, let alone explanatory adequacy.

Fodor appears to accept that part of contemporary linguistic
theory that envisages a "performance" model that would be a
theory of the process (psychological and otherwise) occurring in
sentence production and understanding. (It would also include a
model for language acquisition.) Like the competence model, the
performance model is viewed as a "device," in this case, a device
"capable of simulating the speaker/hearer by recognizing and inte-

grating utterances of sentences." The performance model is neither the actual structure of relationships within the individual nor an account of that structure; it is essentially a theory. Nevertheless, within this theory, Fodor recognizes the problem of stating the part played by the "grammar" (device) of the competence model in the actual production of sentences.

My own basic orientation has been to attempt to fit all the facts about language and language behavior into one unified model. It is useful to make the distinction that psychologists have long made between "what is learned" and "what the individual does" or how he performs. This distinction corresponds roughly to that between *langue* and *parole* made by De Saussure. Linguistics is the study of a certain set of learnings that we call the language system. But the learnings are always intrinsic to behavior; in this sense they are *ipso facto* psychologically real.

There is, of course, a problem about deciding exactly which learnings are part of the "linguistic system" and which are not. The "competence model" advanced by transformational grammarians has been oriented around those learnings that have to do with "grammaticality" — i.e., construction and recognition of "well-formed sentences"; however, the "competence-performance" distinction could be applied to other aspects of language behavior, e.g., memorized speeches vs. performance in delivering them. I believe there is general agreement about what types of learnings linguistics ought to address itself to (see Bever, 1968, on this point).

I also feel that it is necessary to make a clear distinction between a "grammar" as a set of internalized learnings and a "grammar" as an account or analysis of those learnings. In fact, it is somewhat surprising to me that Chomsky allows ambiguity in the term, because he is concerned precisely with the degree to which a particular (written) grammar does in fact describe the internalized learnings that underlie "competence" (cf. his notion of "descriptive adequacy"). A truly *psychologically adequate grammar* would describe the internalized learnings and nothing else. However, a grammar stated in the form of a "device" that is capable of recursively enumerating the sentences of a language, may or may not be psychologically adequate; it may contain much more analysis than description. Some statements in a grammar may be "meta-statements." Clearly, a counting of the number of elements of a certain type would be a meta-statement, e.g., the statement that there are four tones in Mandarin Chinese. A speaker of Mandarin Chinese has to be able to discriminate the four tones, but he would not necessarily know that there are four. I wonder whether many of the statements in transformational grammar are not of this type, i.e., meta-statements. For example, a statement of the way in which a negative yes-no question can be formed from a base structure may be a meta-statement; speakers of the language must be able to discriminate negative yes-no questions from the corresponding positive affirmative surface structure, and form negative yes-no questions when they want to, but they would not be expected to be able to state the transformational rules, or to follow them literally in sentence production/recognition. They may be following different "rules" in so doing. If transformational rules are meta-statements, they have "psychological reality" only for the linguists who propose them. It seems to me that a (written) grammar should make a clear distinction between those statements that refer to demonstrable learnings of the language speaker/hearer and those that are meta-statements.

In describing "internalized learnings," a psychologically adequate grammar would of necessity describe the stimulus and response conditions surrounding these learnings. One difficulty I find in formal grammar as it has developed in the hands of the transformationalists is that it attempts to describe syntactic relations with minimal reference to the semantic or pragmatic component—at any rate to the external conditions that give rise to particular structures or define them in terms of behavioral discriminations. To return again to our negative yes-no questions, I would hope that a psychologically adequate grammar would state the cognitive and social conditions which motivate the utterance of these questions or that are referred to when they are recognized. Some years ago here in Pittsburgh, I reported on experiments that sought to explore some of these conditions (Carroll, 1958), including also the conditions for the emission of active and passive forms of sentences.

For me, the (written) grammar of a language is a subset of the total theory or account of language behavior; other parts of the theory deal with the circumstances under which people speak, with how language is learned, and with deviant language behavior. The fact that different speech communities use different languages is an historical accident that necessitates writing somewhat different grammars for different speech communities. The various grammars will be found to have certain features in common; these features are what may be called "linguistic universals," and may well correspond to universal psychological processes.

The grammar of a language does not necessarily include all the learnings relevant to sentence understanding and production. It should be possible to differentiate those learnings that relate to the structure of "well-formed" sentences from those learnings that have to do with their recognition or production. In fact, the processes involved in the recognition of sentences may overlap only partially with processes involved in sentence production. Both these processes would have connections with the "grammar" but would not be identical with it.

Fodor opens his discussion by attempting to distinguish between what he calls "strong" and "weak" positions on the psychological reality of grammar. In the "strong" position, the grammar is regarded as literally a component of a performance model, and "the operations involved in the grammatical derivation of a sentence are to be a subset of the operations involved in its perceptual analysis or its motor integration." In the "weak" position, however, the grammar merely "specifies the structure that the performance model must recognize and integrate," and "is neutral with regard to the character of the psychological operations involved in sentence processing." Notice that the meaning of the term "grammar" changes radically from the first position to the second. In the "strong" position, the grammar (as a component of a performance model) is something internalized in the speaker/hearer; in the "weak" position, it is merely an account or a "device" for specifying structural descriptions, which are claimed to have "psychological reality" (and which, presumably, have internal representation).

There is one surprising feature in the "strong" position. If in the "strong" position the grammar is regarded as a component of a performance model, the necessity of assuming any competence model at all is brought into question. The "device" described by transformational grammarians would be regarded as built into, or (to use Fodor's term) "realized" in the performance model. To the extent that a grammar is in some way built into a performance model, the "strong" position has some similarity to my own position, as briefly sketched above. The question would really become, then, how much of the (written) grammar corresponds to what is built into the performance model. But Fodor further characterizes the "strong" position by asserting that it would require "operations involved in the grammatical derivation of a sentence" to be "a *sub-*

set of the operations involved in its perceptual analysis or its motor integration" (author's italics). Why this is necessary is not clear to me. Operations involved in the grammatical derivation of a sentence could conceivably be, in an adequate performance model, logically separate from, but called upon by, operations involved in sentence recognition or production. The analogy would be a series of rules stored in one part of a computer memory and an algorithm for calling upon those rules in another part of the memory. Both the rules (the grammar) and the algorithm (heuristic principles for sentence recognition, say) could have "psychological reality."

In the "weak" position, I am not sure whether a "structural description" could exist independently of a grammar that provides its key. I would have thought that in a transformational grammar, a "phrase marker" becomes practically unintelligible or meaningless without some underlying theory. This may be also with a "structural description" somehow resident in cognition: it could not exist without the support of a network of interrelated learnings that would sum to a "grammar." Fodor describes the "weak" position as claiming "psychological reality for the structural descriptions enumerated by a grammar but for nothing else" — I assume he means "nothing else given by a grammar." But what else is given by the grammar, and where is it?

Thus, the "strong" and "weak" positions outlined by Fodor contain certain contradictions and vaguenesses. The main characteristic that distinguishes them, however, is whether the subject follows the grammar ("device") rule for rule in recognizing/producing sentences, as the strong position seems to claim, or simply utilizes "structural descriptions," whatever they are, as the weak position claims.

There are many complex theoretical issues involved here. One issue has to do with what might be expressed as "how much grammar is in the brain?" That is, does the brain somehow *include* the rules and transformational derivations specified by the grammar device? If so, in what form are they represented? If not, what is the status of this apparatus? If we assume that the brain *does* somehow include everything given by the grammar device (except for sheer meta-statements that arise only in the minds of linguists), there is another issue: in what way are transformational rules and derivations used in behavior? The "strong" position would claim that they play some part in behavior, i.e., sentence production and recognition, while the "weak" position would assert that while such an apparatus is somehow represented in the brain, it is not actually used in sentence production/recognition.

My own position seems to be somewhere between Fodor's "strong" and "weak" positions. I would claim that *all* grammar is represented in cognitive processes, but I would restrict my definition of "grammar" to exclude meta-statements; I suspect that some of the transformational grammar possesses a meta-statement character. Like Fodor, however, I would feel that there are additional processes ("heuristics") that are involved in sentence recognition and production.

Fodor dislikes the "strong" position because, in the form in which he states it, it is assumed by a "derivational theory of complexity" (DTC), a theory which he questions. According to the DTC, sentence recognition/production is accomplished by the individual literally running through "the set of operations a grammar employs" in generating a sentence, and the more operations, the more difficult the processing. Fodor claims that the evidence for this theory is equivocal, and I can agree. But, because of the confusion of his formulation of the "weak" position, I don't know where to go with the basic issue. Even if the subject does *not* literally run through grammatical operations in recognizing/ producing sentences, it does not preclude the possibility that these grammatical operations have some psychological reality or status.

There are further difficulties. Suppose, for example, that the empirical work that has sought to confirm the DTC is based upon an invalid grammatical theory? Fodor has already admitted that it is a "moot point" whether adjective insertion is a transformational operation; he cites evidence that adjective insertion does not in itself produce changes in subjects' ability to handle sentence recognition. As grammatical theory changes, it may be necessary to reconsider the validity of the DTC. Another possibility, suggested by my colleague Roy Freedle, is that the various rules and derivations of grammatical theory vary in difficulty. Fodor states the DTC in a form that assumes that every transformational rule is equally difficult — i.e., that there is a perfectly linear relation between sentence complexity and the number of rules involved. This might not be true; perhaps adjective insertion is an "easy" transformation while others, like the use of the passive voice, are more difficult. The results in DTC experiments might be re-examined to see whether they would fit a model refined along these lines.

I am not disposed to believe that transformational derivations will be found to have much to do with sentence handling, partly because I feel that these derivations are actually metatheoretic and not normally represented in behavior. I find the section which deals with postulated heuristics in sentence recognition the most interesting and acceptable part of Fodor's paper. He starts this section of his discussion by saying that "the program subjects use to recover the grammatical structure of sentences is hypothesized to have two primary components: in the first place it contains a lexicon which classifies the lexical items in the language according to the deep structure configurations that they are able to enter." I might remark, incidentally, that this is precisely where many mechanical recognition ("parsing") routines start. The second component of Fodor's "program" is presumably what he is referring to when he states "the hearer must be in possession of computational procedures for exploiting" the information provided by the lexical assignment component, based on knowledge of the kinds of sentence structures and derivations that are permissible in his language. Thus, in assigning a structural description to *John felt the girl trembled*, the subject, after responding to the *-ed* morpheme, exploits his lexical knowledge that the verb *feel* can take a *that*-complement. Similarly, in giving alternative readings of grammatically ambiguous sentences like *Flying planes can be dangerous*, the subject exploits his knowledge of the possible grammatical relations in which the lexical components can participate. What could be simpler? I am not even sure that it is necessary to appeal to the notion of "deep structure" to explain subjects' understanding; one is dealing merely with alternative "labelings" or "parsings" of surface structures that the subject can represent to himself.

I have been sufficiently persuaded that grammatical interpretation of sentences is controlled, in large part, by grammatical knowledge about lexical components to undertake a research project in which I hope to trace children's development of the ability to understand sentences containing words with multiple grammatical functions. In the course of this project I hope to accumulate data, not previously available, on the habitual and less habitual grammatical assignments of these words made by subjects of different ages. All of this would be in line with the suggestion of Fodor, Garrett and Bever (1968) that difficulty in understanding sentences depends upon the diversity of grammatical functions possible for the lexical items in the sentence, particularly the verbs. At the same time I would suggest that the effect may also depend upon the relative strengths of the habits associated with the grammatical assignments of lexical items. For example, many people would have difficulty understanding the sentence *He gave an earnest of his intentions* because they have high strength for the assignment of *earnest* as an adjective and low, or zero strength for its assignment as a noun. I am sure, in any case, that studies of the ways in which lexical assignments of words influence sentence recognition will yield much information, and I applaud Fodor's suggestions along these lines.

In the last part of his paper, Fodor indulges in a curious kind of brinkmanship. He comes almost to the point of saying that a grammar is not psychologically real at all, because it "does not provide a model of what the child becomes when he becomes a speaker/hearer." He raises the possibility that the child develops not a grammar but a sentence producer/recognizer, that is, "a device related to a grammar only in that it manipulates the structural descriptions that grammars enumerate." This proposal is strange to hear from Fodor, because it is almost what a behaviorally-oriented psychologist like myself might also propose. Fodor, however, quickly retreats from this position, arguing that since there are linguistic universals relating specifically to grammatical rules, these universals must presuppose the existence and psychological reality of grammars. This somewhat debatable argument leads him to the suggestion, which he considers "not entirely implausible," that the innate endowment of the child includes "available procedures for constructing a recognizer/producer for sentences in a language given an appropriate grammar of the language." He ends by commenting that "perhaps the fundamental theoretical problem now facing psycholinguistics is to characterize the algorithm that performs this construction" — an algorithm that would be valid for any particular language. Fine! that is precisely one of the tasks of psycholinguistics. But to allege that this specific algorithm would necessarily be a part of the *innate* endowment of the child is possibly unparsimonious. As I have suggested in a review of Lenneberg's *Biological Foundations of Language* (Carroll, 1968), the phenomenon of language acquisition (as with many other behavioral phenomena), even though it undoubtedly has a biological substrate, may not be innate; it may occur simply by virtue of the general learning capabilities of the organism, and the way those capabilities interact with what has to be learned and the conditions under which it is learned. At any rate, such an assumption would, in my opinion, be a more powerful guide to research strategies than the assumption of innateness.

REFERENCES

Bever, T. G. A survey of some recent work in psycholinguistics. In W. J. Plath (ed.), *Specification and utilization of a transformational grammar.* Report No. 3, Contract AF 19(628)-5127, International Business Machines Corporation, Thomas J. Watson Research Center, Yorktown Heights, N. Y., July 1968. [Document AD 679633, Federal Clearinghouse for Scientific Information.]

Carroll, J. B. Process and content in psycholinguistics. In R. A. Patton, (ed.), *Current trends in the description and analysis of behavior.* Pittsburgh: University of Pittsburgh Press, 1958. Pp. 175-200.

Carroll, J. B. Man is born to speak: Review of Eric H. Lenneberg's *Biological Foundations of Language* (New York: Wiley, 1967). *Contemporary Psychology,* 1968, **13,** 117-19.

Chomsky, N. *Aspects of the theory of syntax.* Cambridge, Mass.: M.I.T. Press, 1965.

Fodor, J., Garrett, M., and Bever, T. Some syntactic determinants of sentential complexity, II.: Verb structure. *Perception and Psychophysics,* 1968, **3,** 454-61.

6

SPEECH AND BODY MOTION SYNCHRONY OF THE SPEAKER-HEARER [1,2]

W. S. CONDON and W. D. OGSTON

Western Psychiatric Institute and Clinic,
School of Medicine, University of Pittsburgh

The use of sound films and slow motion projection techniques provides a method for the storage and examination of a variety of subject matters. They can be used to provide a visual and auditory microscope of the study of behavioral processes. Certain aspects of human, interactional behavior have been examined by the present investigators at 24, 48, 64, and, presently, at 96 frames per second. This paper will indicate some of the technical, methodological and conceptual difficulties, the attempt at their resolution, and some of the findings, particularly in speech and body motion parallelism.

---

[1]The following work is dependent upon the approach in the forthcoming book *The Natural History of an Interview,* authored by Bateson, G., Birdwhistell, R., Brosin, H., Hockett, C. and McQuown, N. (eds.). We are also deeply indebted to the work of Albert E. Scheflen among many others.
[2]This work is also indebted to an N.I.M.H. special fellowship grant which permitted one of the authors to obtain linguistic training.

Prior to the actual attempt at analyzing sound film of human interaction, there was no anticipation that it might present unsuspected problems. One would simply observe the film carefully, pick out the units of behavior and then determine how they were put together. We live contentedly with a view of the world composed of familiar discrete things which surround and support our lives. We are usually clear about what another person has said and meant. These sayings are composed, it seems, of words put together in serial strings accompanied by subtle pitch and stress variations. The recognizable and familiar universe before us is conveyed and shared by this means. What, then, is the nature and order of this conveying, that it is, when received, found redolent of meaning?

Confrontation with a sound film of human behavior overwhelms the observers with a rapidly flowing and shifting scene of sound and motion. There seem to be no clear boundary points dividing the flow of events into discrete segments. An understanding of what is said provides a segmentation of the sound stream into words, phrases, and utterances. But where is the location of the segmentation? Is it now clear where a word begins and ends, or is where a word begins and ends as sound not the same as where an understanding of the word begins and ends? The perspectives and instrumentation the investigator brings to the analysis of his subject matter are related to the ways in which it will be divided and the findings that will ensue from that division. Our instruments and perspectives are part of the universe they aid us in understanding and are not exempt from the laws of the universe. How beginnings and endings are determined, and in relation to what, are not separate from a "something" which begins and ends. We are seeking to convey some sense of the perplexity that results when we are suddenly bereft of productive, segmental perspectives when confronted by the flow of behavior. The work of Tinbergen (1942, 1960) and Lorenz (1952, 1966) suggests that what constitutes a stimulus may not be what you begin with, but on the contrary, only the result of long inquiry. What does a lowering of the voice, "while" the eyes lower, "while" the face flushes, "while" the head turns aside, "while" a leg and foot shift, have to do with what is said? How is this modified by or the result of the equally complex configurations which immediately, and not so immediately, precede it. How do they anticipate those changes which follow? And how are all of the above changes, in turn, related to the equally complex behaviors of the other person or persons in the interaction? It makes a difference if the behavior is that of a man and a maid or of a father reprimanding an errant son. Not only does "the how" of the saying modify "the what" that is said, but also where and to whom and for what covert or overt reasons. All seem part of the process of something said.

Natural events and experimentally controlled events are equally determined. It was, however, not clear how a rigorous experimental approach might be applied, since the controlling would itself constitute part of the surrounding. What would provide a control for the control? One cannot control the variables when the problem itself involves the discovery of those "somethings" which would constitute the variables. At this juncture it was assumed, for purposes of analysis, that human interaction constituted an unknown yet seemingly ordered process and that inquiry would not begin with units but, on the contrary, the classification of what constituted a unit would be the central problem of the inquiry.

The initial problem then became one of determining what, in the material, would provide a descriptive basis for the detection of possible units. A small, five-second segment of sound film involving a mother, father, and their four year old son at dinner was examined intensively for many months. The segment contained two, full utterances by the mother. In time, some sense of an order in their behavior, suggestive of units, began to emerge. This procedure involved a saturation in the material and, in essence, comprised the primary research methodology. While one could not predict when a re-seeing would lead to a recognition of regularities, after a time one became assured that this would occur. A pragmatic trust in the method developed and this saturation viewing was subsequently used in the examination of other dimensions in the filmed materials. The principles of linguistic analysis were also used as far as possible, becoming more relevant as knowledge about the structure of the behavior increased. An attempt was made to permit the system under investigation to reveal its regularities rather than impose them extraneously.

PRELIMINARY SEGMENTATIONS

The basic equipment used to study body motion was a *16 mm, Bell & Howell, Time Motion Analyzer*. This projector permits variable, manual scanning of film one frame at a time or across many frames. It gives the investigator an ability to contrast a selected series of frames with a selected preceeding or following series, including the ability to vary the lengths of the series so contrasted. Equipment was also constructed which permitted the segmentation of speech down to one frame at a commensurate level with body motion. It was now possible to obtain a micro-analysis of both speech and body motion and compare the change in their relationship to each other.

Intensive viewing suggested that changes of direction and velocity of the body parts might provide a basis for transcribing the behavioral process. This permitted a flow description of the body's complex changes through time. All detectable changes of all body parts, from head to toe, were recorded at every frame or 1/24 of a second for all the interactants. The form of change of the body as it was observed in actual movement provided the basis for description. The body joints with their characteristic modes of extension — flexion, pronation — supination, adduction — abduction, etc., constituted a major, descriptive focus. Movements of the head, eyes, brows, and mouth were described with as much accuracy as possible. Gross descriptions were replaced as increasing ability to detect change forced finer-grained discriminations. The upper eyelid, for example, was differentiated into two aspects in terms of the way it changed during actual behavior. There are also subtle changes within an eye blink that are not detectable at standard projection speeds. These body motion descriptions are not, as such, the units of behavior. The verbal material was similarly transcribed frame by frame. Little by little, the way in which the changes of the body parts changed in relation to each other and to speech were seen to be forming an ordered pattern.

Self-Synchrony

As a normal person speaks, his body "dances" in precise and ordered cadence with the speech as it is articulated. The body moves in patterns of change which are directly proportional to the articulated pattern of the speech stream. And as the speech stream is composed of multiple, wider aspects in its emergence so also, and again proportional, are the accompanying body motion emergents. There are no sharp boundary points but on-going, ordered variations of change in the body which are isomorphic with the ordered variations of speech. This has been called self-synchrony. It has been dealt with elsewhere (Condon and Ogston, 1966, 1967) and is included to provide background information for the later examination of the eye blink in relation to speech.

The predication of a precise isomorphism between speech and body motion implies that there are discernible boundary-forms such that those of speech and body motion can be said to occur together. (Simultaneity in the domain of filmed material is relative to the speed of occurrence of a frame, i.e., whether the film was taken at 24, 48, 64, etc., frames per second.) Figure 1 illustrates self-synchrony and serves to clarify the nature of a unit of behavior. (The descriptive notation was developed over time and an explanation of the symbolism would require considerable space. The points of the arrows indicate change of direction while the shaft indicates sustaining of direction.)

The sound film from which the data for Figure 1 was extracted was taken at 48 frames per second (fps), twice the speed of standard filming, to permit a more precise detection of body motion. The present flow transcription was done to the degree of accuracy obtainable with present equipment. A single system filming procedure was used to insure that sound would be synchronized precisely with the body motion at this speed.[3] The subjects in the film, two male psychiatrists, were sitting beside each other in separate straight-backed chairs. They were aware that they were being filmed. Subject B, who was born and raised in Scotland, says to Subject A, "I was gonna ask you *why do* you um . . . have difficulty keeping your legs uncrossed?" The entire statement was transcribed in micro, although only the two words "why do" (which take slightly longer than ⅓ of a second) were selected for illustration. Spatial limitations and the fact that Subject B blinks during these words were the factors leading to their selection. Since eye blink occurrence in relation to speech will be treated below, it was felt useful to include an example from slow motion film.

Behavior seems to occur in configurations of "whiles." In Figure 1 "while" Subject B emits the "w" of "why" / ŭ ŭ / his head moves right, forward and down slightly, "while" his eyes begin to close for an eye blink, "while" his brows move up slightly, "while" his mouth opens, "while" his trunk moves forward and right, "while" his right shoulder is locked (no detectable movement), "while" his elbow, right wrist and fingers also move in given, sus-

---

[3]The following equipment was used: Camera: Eastman Kodak Reflex 16 mm with wild motor and sound-recording head in camera; Lens: 1″ standard 35 mm normal; Film: +X reversal magnetic striped.

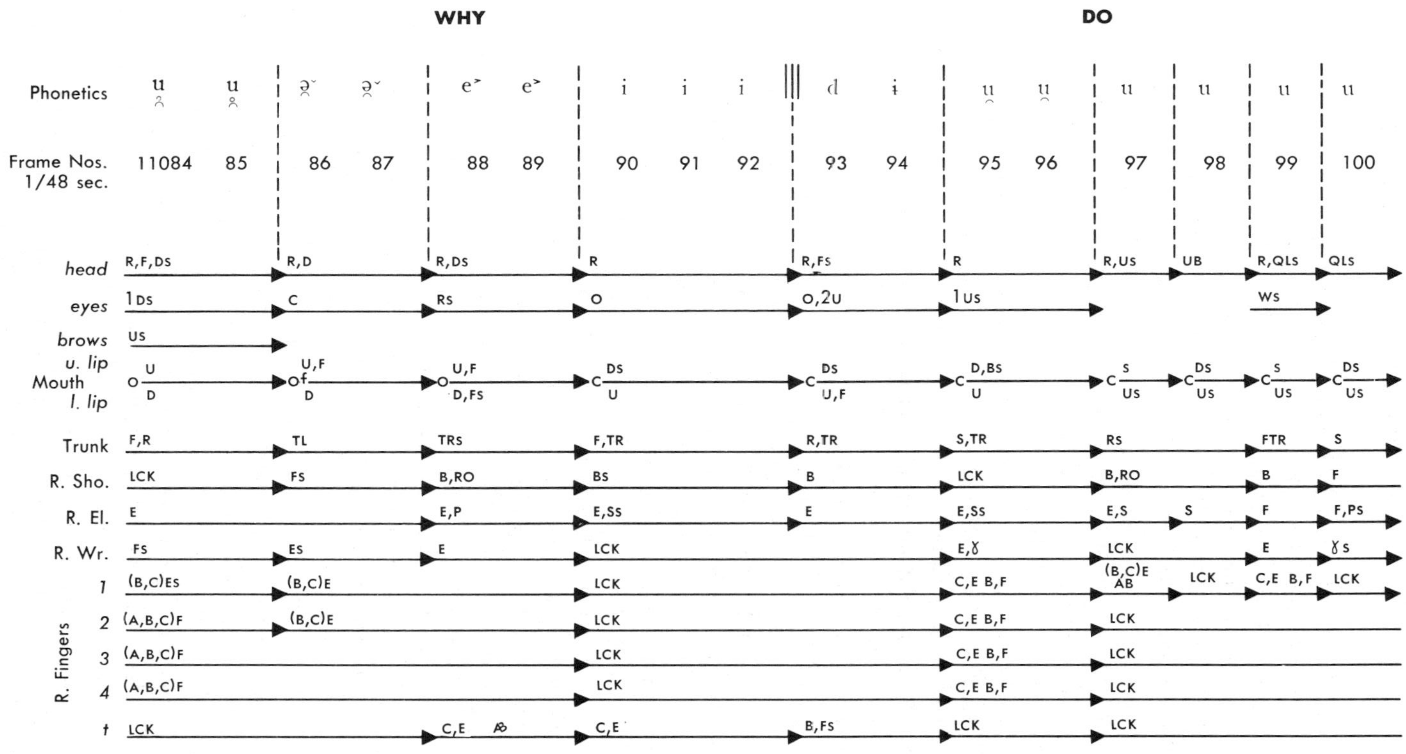

FIGURE 1. Self-synchrony in Subject B.

tained directions. Almost all these directions of movement are sustained precisely across the "w." (Some movements are sustained for a slightly longer interval, but when they do change it is in concert with the other changes then occurring.) The next segment to be passed through, as the tongue sweeps forward and up in the articulation of "why," is the mid central vocoid /ə̌ ə̌/. The body parts change direction in various ways at the end of / ṷ ṷ / and at the onset of /ə̌ ə̌ / and these new directions are sustained across this new segment until another new configuration of change begins at the onset of / ɚɚ/. This same pattern of sustaining and change occurs across / i i i /, / d i / and / ṷ ṷ /. It occurs in this same fashion throughout the total utterance and has been found to occur with similar consistency in all films of normal behavior thus far examined (over fifty films analyzed frame by frame). Unit boundary formation occurs through the massing or clustering together of directional change points. The redundancy at these change points, as seen in almost all body parts moving, aids in the boundary decision. These micro, configurational synchronies have tentatively been labelled "process units" to emphasize their on-going nature and to avoid the connotation of discrete entities, in the sense of a recurring identity which is the same at each occurrence.

The word "why" is formed by four articulatory pulses which coincide with four body motion clusters. The more major pulse which occurs across the word can also be divided into two aspects, (a) /ṷṷəəee/ and (b) /iii/. The mouth opens across the first aspect and closes across the second. Fingers three and four flex across the first aspect and remain still across the second. An eye blink begins exactly as the word begins, closing across the first aspect and opening across the second. Thus, there is a further massing of change, at a wider interval and using other contrastive criteria, that segments the word into two aspects, which are also harmonious with the four more micro aspects. The body also moves in a sustained pattern parallel with the emission of "why" as a total lexical event. The head moves primarily right and down across the word "why" and changes to largely right and forward across "do." This seems to be belied by the notation in Figure 1, but the micro changes smooth out when the wider aspects are contrasted. Head movement across "why," as a unit, contrasts with the head movement across "do," as a unit.

These three "levels" are thus represented in the organized unity of the emerging process and are not put together as discrete particles. The word "why" is not composed of three levels, but is formed in a way that allows three distinctions to be made, but the contrastive foci that permit each of these distinctions differ. The contrast between the body motion accompanying /ᵘ ᵘ/ and that accompanying /ɔ̆ ɔ̆/ reveals a difference that is not the same as the difference revealed by the contrast between /ᵘᵘɔ̆ɔ̆ee/ and /iii/. The former is not determined to be a unit in the same way since the latter, as a unit, could contain it. That which is intended to be said controls, to some extent, the saying of it. It is not composed of parts put together, but of a cumulative progression toward being said: such that the familiar, wider element, the word, is in the process of becoming what it is as its sub-orders are organized toward its expression. The total organism seems to participate in this, for body motion changes emerge synchronously with the physical articulatory changes of speech and at a variety of dimensions.

To summarize, a unit of behavior is an organized configuration which does not remain the same from moment to moment: what remains constant is the ordered form of the change. The body parts change direction of movement and sustain direction of movement, and the boundaries formed by the clusterings of such changing-and-sustaining-together, are isomorphic with the articulatory (as against abstracted segments) transformations of speech. Behavioral continuity (in the absence of speech as well) is formed through the constant but varying, on-going recurrence of these configurational clusterings, each one succeeding the other. A unit of behavior is defined by this recurrent order in the change. There are no points of non-organization. An arm may be moving at one moment and at rest during several succeeding moments. Thus the body parts, as isolates, do not provide a sustained descriptive continuity which devolves upon a unit. The body parts as organized participants in the on-going flow of behavior, however, display an order of change which does seem to fulfill the continuity requirement of primary unit status.

The abstracted, linguistic "classes" of sounds also do not form the actual basis of speech in the strictest sense. In overt speech the sounds seem to be "sounds-in-transition:" one sound follows from another, anticipating the next ensuing sound. It must be stressed that the relationship between speech and body motion is related to the sounds as they are actually said at a given moment. Changes in articulation, at the micro level, often occur within phone types, where the transition from a preceeding phone to the position of a following phone transforms, in turn, to the next phone. The sounds are not statically localized, but emerge as "being-passed-through" on the way toward.

The isomorphic relationship of speech and body motion occurs from the most micro level up through statement length utterances (and possibly at still wider levels). There are forms of body motion accompanying speech across sub-phone, phone, syllable, word, phrase, and statement length utterances. There is a relatively total bodily involvement in the accompaniment up to and including word length segments, with the "syllabic" change seeming to be a major cadence point in human behavior. A semi-individuation of body usage occurs across phrasal and wider elements. An arm may begin a sweep precisely at the beginning of a phrase and change direction precisely at the end of the phrase. Or, the feet may stop moving just as a long utterance begins, remain at rest throughout the utterance, then shift exactly as the utterance ends. There is also some indication that the "expression of emotion" does not violate the integrated patterns of behavior. A frown may begin to form, for example, exactly at the beginning of a small phrase, will sustain its expressive configuration across the phrase, then cease at the termination of the phrase. This does not necessarily mean that the frown is related to what is being said at that moment, only that its physical occurrence seems to be harmonious with the rest of behavior.

Interactional Synchrony

Further intensive film analysis led to the following observation. A hearer's body was found to "dance" in precise harmony with the speaker. When the units of change in their behavior are segmented and displayed consecutively, the speaker and hearer look like puppets moved by the same set of strings. In using a manually operated time-motion projector to show this phenomenon, a partial artifact arises. The subjects obviously begin to move together as the film begins and stop when the film stops. The important point, however, is that they sustain and change direction of body parts together. Thus the subject speaking may move his head down for three frames and then move it right for two frames. The listener may move his head left during those same first three frames and then up for the succeeding two frames. The starting and stopping of the projector has nothing to do with the changes of direction of movement of the interactants.

Two filmed experiments were conducted to rule out this artifact. In the first experiment two subjects were pulled out of their inter-action to interact with two separate subjects off camera. If inter-actional synchrony were an artifact of the projector, it should occur no matter with whom the subjects were interacting. In the above situation no interactional synchrony could be elicited.

In the second filmed experiment, the listener wore earphones which delayed the input of the speakers voice by ⅙ of a second. There was a marked dyssynchrony between the two that was in sharp contrast to the synchrony of normal interaction. The body of a hearer moves in synchrony with the speaker like a parallel system — as the pattern of the one varies so also does the other. The interactants also speed up and slow down together, and this appears to be related to stress and pitch variations.

The hearer's behavior is also organized self-synchronously, following the same principle as that of the speaker. There is a similar "sustaining-and-changing-together" of the body parts in an emergent flow. The units of the hearer's behavior are usually formed by different body parts moving or the same body parts moving in directions different than those of a speaker, but they sustain direction of movement as the speaker's sustain direction of movement and change when the speaker's change. Interactional synchrony is defined by this isomorphism of pattern of change between the speaker-hearer. This isomorphism is difficult to detect at the normal speed of body motion.

Figure 2 presents a flow transcription of interactional synchrony which can be seen in the vertical alignment of the arrow points. This figure is comprised of the material of Figure 1 as well as the further addition of the micro-analysis of the body motion of Subject A who is listening to Subject B as the two words "why do" are emitted. Interactional-synchrony, like self-synchrony, seems to occur constantly during normal interaction.[4] It has been observed in group behavior; in a group of eight persons listening to a ninth talking and in a group of four persons.

In the lower section of Figure 2, dealing with the body motion change patterns of Subject A, the similar principle of formation of units is evidenced — the body parts change and sustain together, giving rise to boundary clustering. The units formed by these clusterings are isomorphic with those of Subject B. Subject A sustains directions of movement while Subject B sustains directions of movement, then both change directions of movement at the same 1/48 of a second to again sustain directions of movement until the next change point. Subject A, when listening, appears to participate

---

[4]Fifteen films of various pathological disorders (including aphasia, petit mal, autism, retardation, schizophrenia, and Huntington's Chorea), analyzed frame by frame, revealed some form of dyssynchrony which has not, thus far, been observed in normal behavior.

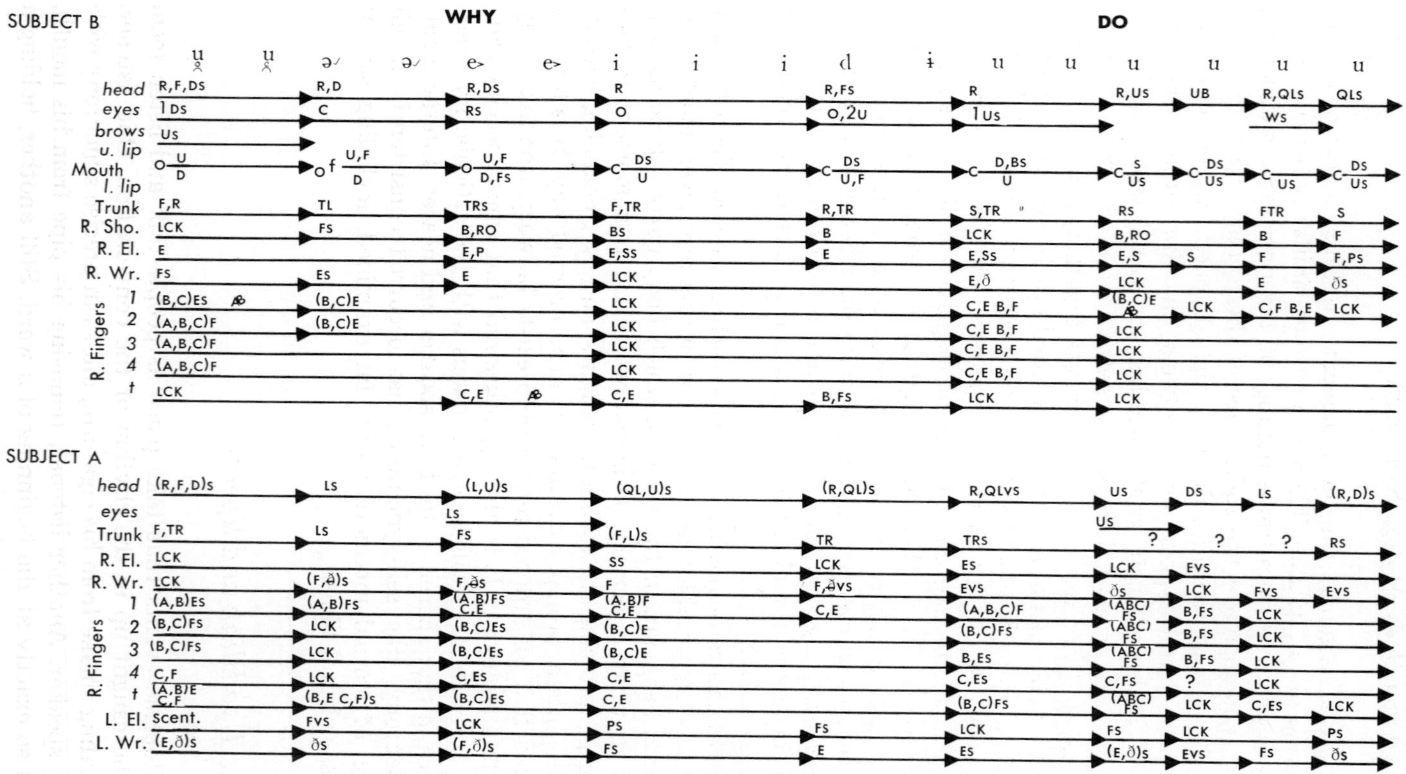

FIGURE 2. Interactional-synchrony between Subjects A and B.

160

as a total organism in the emergent, rhythmic cadence of the behavior of the speaker. There is a marked similarity between their change patterns from frame number 90 through frame number 94. Both tend to move the right sides of their bodies more than the left throughout the film. Both are right-handed. At certain points intricate "hand dances" occur between the two subjects. For example, both flex their wrists together across the same number of frames, then extend their arms together across the next series of frames, and finally extend their wrists together, again across the exact number of frames. This heightened synchrony has been noted in many films. It was observed to be a constant and marked characteristic of the interaction of mothers with their infants. (A mother chimpanzee and her infant displayed a similar langorous synchrony). In another film, a man and a woman sitting facing each other began to sweep toward each other at the same frame, get very close then straighten and raise their heads together, then sweep back together, and finally come forward slightly together. This occurs in the absence of speech and is presumably related to visual contact.

Self-synchrony and interactional-synchrony do not describe what will (as predictable) actually occur during any given moment of normal behavior, in the sense of which body parts will be moving and in what directions. Behavior will vary from moment to moment, expressing the feelings, thoughts, and ever changing pattern of the interaction, yet it will do so in an ordered way. It is hypothesized that an ordered relationship exists between whatever body parts are moving. It is also hypothesized that when speech occurs the body changes will be synchronous with the articulatory emergence of that speech — for both speaker and hearer. Interactional-synchrony, like self-synchrony, has occurred consistently in all films of normal interaction thus far examined, including several cross-cultural films.

The Eye Blink and Speech

Routine events that take place as people talk and listen seem to be caught up in the rhythm of the conversation. One listener, exhaling smoke from his cigarette, did so in precise synchrony with the speaker. Another listener, removing his pipe from his mouth, did so exactly at the beginning of a word. Still another, holding a piece of paper, moved it this way and that way with each change of direction occurring with the "syllables" of the speaker's words. These are only three of a great number of similar instances. We perceive, and almost while perceiving, it seems, respond to the speech of another; as if our behavior were orchestrated by the varying, but ordered, cadences of sound heard. The hypotheses of self-synchrony and interactional-synchrony implicate all aspects of normal behavior, including eye movements and eye blinks. As a consequence of this implication a large population of eye blinks were examined. The eye blinks, as relatively distinctive and observable behaviors, would, it was felt, provide further confirmation of self- and interactional-synchrony if they could be shown to occur isomorphically with the articulatory pattern of speech — for both hearer and speaker.

The eye blinks examined in this section were taken from three separate 24 f.p.s., 16 mm sound films.

Film One

This film has a young, female speech therapist and a young, male college graduate as subjects. They are sitting beside each other in separate chairs and both have scalp electrodes attached as part of another study. (They had not met prior to the filming). This 400 ft. film was initially examined without sound and all detectable eye blinks were recorded in the following fashion. The precise frame (1/24 of a second) at which the eye blink began, the form of change of the blink during its closure, the exact point of closure, the point at which opening began, the form of the opening and, finally, the exact frame at which opening was completed, were transcribed. This procedure of recording the eye blinks separate from the sound and then later segmenting the sound was adopted as a precautionary measure.

An eye blink, as a behavioral regularity, was tentatively identified as a relatively rapid closing and opening of the eyes. In some instances the eyes would remain closed for a brief period before opening again. The average blink tended to last six frames or $\frac{1}{4}$ of a second. They have a characteristic form which, however, will vary depending upon the changes occurring in the rest of the behavior. There is usually a rapid closure for two frames, then a slight hesitation for one frame (either remaining closed or opening very slightly) and, finally, a rapid opening for three frames, although not as rapidly as the initial closure. This seems related to the characteristic eye blink artifact seen on the polygraph. There is a short curved deflection downward, followed by an almost straight or slightly rising line, which is, in turn, followed by a relatively longer, curved deflection upwards. (This is illustrated later in Figure 4). A total of 376 eye blinks were micro-recorded in this film. While the order of occurrence of particular blinks was not examined, there appeared to be a tendency for an utterance to have at least one or more blinks. Eye blinks occurring during silences were recorded but were not examined in relation to what was occurring in their environments. A few blinks were probably not detected. There were times when the interactants had their heads lowered and the eyes were not visible. The male student wore glasses which occasionally obscured his eyes.

Following this procedure, the verbal material occurring with each eye blink was segmented to one frame; commensurate with the visually recorded blink. The eye blinks occurred in four locations in relation to speech. These four locations are referred to as Types A, B, C, and D for identification only and are not separate classes of blinks.

Type A: These are blinks that begin exactly at the beginning of words. This also includes blinks which begin with laughter and other paralinguistic vocalizations. In the present film, 198 blinks were found to occur in this position. "Exactly" means that the eyes begin to close in the same frame that the word begins.

Type B: In certain instances, the blink begins to close just prior to the beginning of a word. In this type of blink, the eyes close first, and it is the opening of the eyes that occurs exactly with the beginning of the word. 17 blinks of this type occurred. They appear to be a sub-class of Type A.

Type C: Here, the blink begins on the frame (1/24 of a second) immediately following the end of a word. 41 blinks occur in this position, including two that occur after laughter.

Type D: This type occurs in the middle of a word at an articulatory change point. 86 blinks occur in this position, including nine which occur at laughter pulse points.

The blinks during this film, to summarize, occurred in only four positions when they occurred with speech. No blinks were detected which violated these locations of occurrence. *Film One* has the following distribution.

		Type A	198	word beginning

Type A	198	word beginning
Type B	17	opening at beginning
Type C	41	word ending
Type D	86	internal to a word
Total	**342**	(plus 34 during silence)

Of the 34 blinks occurring during non-speech sequences, several seemed to occur synchronously with extraneous sounds and in several others, the total blink occurred just prior to speech onset.

Film Two

This was one of a series of demonstration films dealing with group behavior. Its primary subject matter was a presentation, using a real group in interaction, of how group dynamics might be analyzed. In dealing with a relatively minute item of behavior, such as the eye blink, close-up filming is required. The present film has a lengthy section with close-up views of individual members of the group. This section is selective but only insofar as the eye blinks could be clearly seen. The 142 eye blinks occurring in this section of the film have a distribution similar to those in *Film One*.

Type A	60	word beginning
Type B	20	opening at beginning
Type C	13	word ending
Type D	49	internal to a word
Total	**142**	

Film Three

This is a documentary film dealing with grade school children, particularly the difficulties of a child with a cleft palate who fights with her teacher. The scenes shift from close-ups of two teachers talking together about the child, to a small group of her classmates talking to the psychologist. The father of the child is also seen meeting in a group with the child's teacher, the school principal, and several others. The presence of excellent close-ups, again, led to the use of this film despite the scene shifts. Only a small portion, about ten blinks, could not be clearly detected, either because of inaudible speech or lack of visibility. There were 234 detectable blinks in the film and they also display the same distributional locations as those in the two preceeding films.

Type A	155	word beginning
Type B	16	opening at beginning
Type C	23	word ending
Type D	40	internal to a word
Total	234	

In the three films a total of 718 eye blinks were analyzed in relation to speech. All tended to occur in essentially three basic positions, if Type B is considered as a sub-class of Type A. The Type A and B blinks quite clearly occur, as defined, exactly at word beginnings. Type C occur precisely at the word terminal position. Type D, which occurs in word medial positions, is the most interesting and requires further examination. In the three films the number of blinks occurring at each position are as follows.

Type A	413
Type B	53
Type C	77
Type D	175
Total	718

The great majority of the blinks (543) can be said to occur in two major positions in relation to speech — at the beginning and end of words. Those occurring at the beginning, to emphasize, begin at the same frame (1/24 of a second) that the word begins. Those that occur at the end begin with the frame following the word and, obviously, when the word is followed by silence. These positions are, of course, the points of onset and arrest of major articulatory segments — the spoken words.

A specification of the 175 Type D blinks was more difficult. Although one of the authors has had some training in linguistics, the findings relating to blinks occurring within words must be considered as tentative and subject to revision. There does, however, appear to be a characteristic relationship between where the eye blink begins internal to a word and a certain clustering of articulatory changes at these points.

(1)   The breath control, is, relatively, either releasing or arresting the flow of air.

(2)   The tongue is changing direction of movement in contrast to its preceeding direction.

(3)   The lips are changing from opening to closing or closing to opening. (Or from a relatively held position to opening or closing.)

(4)   Onset of voicing or devoicing occurs concomitantly in many instances.

There appears to be a complex massing of articulatory change at the point of blink occurrence. These changes also occur constantly in the absence of blinks, but it seems that if a blink does occur internal to a word it will favor a point having these massing characteristics. Word onset and arrest also have similar articulatory massing characteristics so that it may become possible by distinctive feature analysis, to describe an articulatory structure that is common for all blinks during speech. These distributional patterns, observed in 718 blinks, hold for both speaker and hearer. One person listening to another person will blink, if and when he blinks, in the same positions in relation to speech that the speaker blinks. Figure 3 illustrates the type of location of eye blinks.

The eye blinks in Figure 3 were taken from the first film of the speech therapist and the student. Blink Types A, B, and D only, are emphasized, since a Type C occurrence appears in conjunction with the Type B blink.

The Type A blink is that of the speech therapist listening to the male student saying, "I.I.T.", referring to Illinois Institute of Technology. The therapist begins her blink exactly as the first "I" begins, and ends her blink at the conclusion of the second "I".

The Type B blink, where the opening of the eye begins at the beginning of the word, occurs as the speech therapist says "for . . . about" (This also illustrates the Type C blink, for closure begins at the end of "for" and occurs exactly across the slight pause). The therapist's eyes begin to open at the onset of "about", with opening lasting across the closure of her mouth to the /b/ position. The student's blink begins with the released /b'/ and the opening of the therapist's mouth for the second aspect of "about." It is a Type D blink occurring in the middle of the word and immediately follows the therapist's blink, ending at the end of the word.

In the Type D blink proper, the male student says, "I finally."

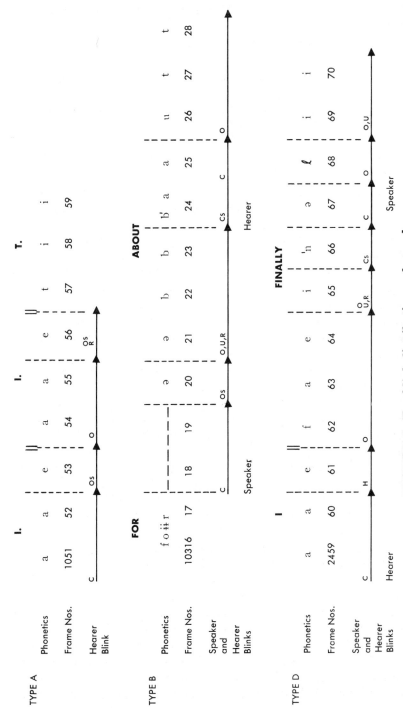

FIGURE 3. Eye blink distribution and speech.

167

His blink begins in the middle of the word "finally" where his mouth begins to close across the stressed, second part of the word. His blink ends exactly as the word ends. The therapist also blinks, her blink beginning with the word "I" and terminating at the end of the first part of "finally" just prior to the onset of the student's blink.

One can gain some sense of the relationship of eye blinks to speech by watching close-ups of speakers on television programs, particularly in news reports where the face is usually clearly visible.

The eye blink presents, as previously noted, artifact contour when seen in a polygraph. The following material, while peripheral, is included to illustrate other parameters which are relevant to the detection of eye blinks and are amenable to micro examination by the use of film. As indicated earlier, the therapist and the student each had five scalp electrodes attached from a standard 12-channel E.E.G. machine used as a polygraph. Two synchronous cameras, one on the subjects and one on the polygraph pen movements, were used. Sound was also recorded synchronously with the cameras. Figure 4 presents one of the eye blinks of the therapist and its accompanying polygraph pattern.

In the pen pattern section of Figure 4, the way the pens moved was analyzed in terms of three factors: direction of pen movement, speed of pen movement and manner in which the pens moved relative to each other. The symbols R and L refer to direction of pen movement. Due to camera positioning the upward deflections of the pen are seen in the film as left and the downward deflections as right. The curved lines indicate how the pens are moving in relation to each other and the small "s" indicates slow. The word "year" is articulated into two major segments, with closure across the first segment / i ɭ / and opening across / ɚ ɚ ɚ /. The pen patterns reveal forms of change which are isomorphic with the speech and blink patterns. There is an interesting reversal of pen direction between closing and opening which was characteristic of all blinks in *Film One* — for both therapist and student.

THE MICRO STRUCTURE OF THE EYE
BLINK AND SPEECH

Further examination of the 718 eye blinks indicated that the internal form of the blink varies directly with speech as it is occur-

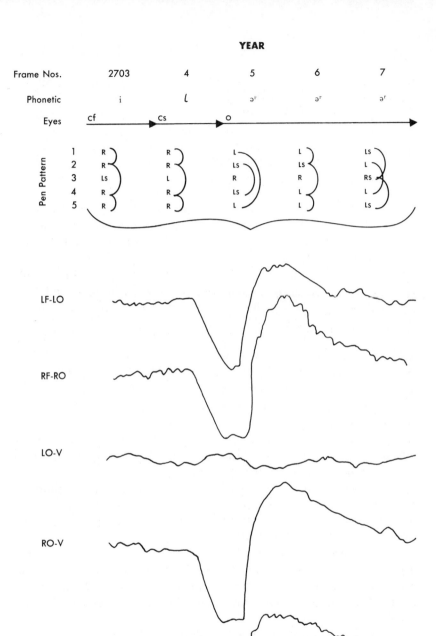

FIGURE 4. Eye blink, speech, and polygraph recording.

ring. Both the gross structure and the micro structure of an eye blink are isomorphic with the articulation of speech — for both speaker and hearer. The minute forms of change within the hearer's blink are synchronous with changes in the speaker's articulation. It seems that if a point of articulatory change occurs, the sub-structural change of the blink occurs with it. A Type A blink, for example, which begins exactly at the beginning of a word, will also have a sub-organization of change that is isomorphic with the further articulatory emergence of the word. It may close exactly across the first syllable of the word and open across the second, completing the opening exactly as the next word or syllable begins. In a great number of blinks the eyes close across the first word and open exactly across the second word. There seems to be some relationship to speed of articulation. If a word is expressed relatively slowly the blink will change with the internal structure of the word. If, however, several words occur very rapidly, the internal form of the blink will tend to coincide with the word boundaries. This is a tentative hypothesis and much further work is required before a more precise specification will be possible.

The six blinks in this figure were taken from the third film (the school situation) since the close-ups of the faces permitted accurate observation.

In the first blink the principal says, "something." The teacher's blink begins at the beginning of the word and follows the pattern of change in the word as it is articulated.

In the second blink the teacher rapidly says, "other children." Again, the blink begins at word onset, with closure and hold across "other" and opens across "children." The sub-structure of the blink follows the pattern of articulation.

Blink three is that of the school psychologist who listens as the principal tells the father of the child, "thank you very much for coming." The blink begins with and closes across the word "very," holds closed across "much for" and opens exactly across the first syllable of "coming."

In the fourth blink the teacher blinks as she says "work . . . she is having trouble." Eye closure begins exactly as "work" ends and occurs across the slight pause. Her eyes open slightly as she says, "she is;" then open across the first syllable of "having" and close slightly across the second syllable. The eyes open fast across the first aspect of trouble, ending the blink just prior to the terminal aspect / 1 1 /.

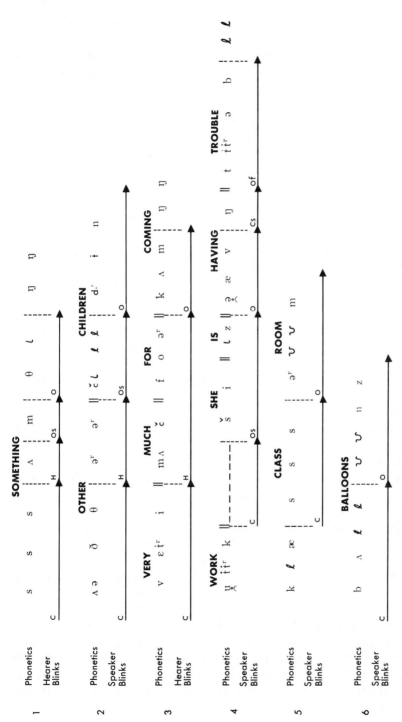

FIGURE 5. Sub-structure of eye blink and speech.

In blink five the teacher begins to blink in the middle of "class" as she says, "classroom." The blink begins as the mouth closes to form / s s s / and eye closure occurs across this segment, opening across "room."

Blink six is that of an eight or nine year old boy saying "balloons." His blink begins at the onset of the word, closing across the first aspect and opening across the second.

The blinks in Figures 1, 3, and 4 also reveal this microstructured synchrony with speech. All of the 718 eye blinks occur with the same exactness in relation to speech as those presented in the figures. If the reader will slowly speak the words in Figure 5, he may get some feeling for the articulatory changes that are occurring at the internal change points of the blinks.

SUMMARY

Several hypotheses concerning the nature of human behavior were presented, with emphasis upon the "units" of that behavior. A "process unit," so labelled to accentuate its configurational form of composition in contrast to more atomistic views, was characterized as ordered change within change. Behavior emerges as a sequential flow of changing "bundles of change" both during and in the absence of speech. The nature of these "bundles of change" was described and illustrated.

A person speaking exhibits a "self-synchrony" in which his body change patterns are isomorphic with the emergent, articulatory transformations of his speech, at many "levels." Further, a listener exhibits a form of "interactional-synchrony" in which his body change patterns are isomorphic with the speech and body motion change patterns of the speaker, primarily up to and including the word level only.

In further support of these hypotheses, 718 eye blinks of both hearer and speaker were examined for their pattern of occurrence in relation to speech. The beginning of an eye blink occurs in three distributional locations in relation to speech; (1) at the beginning of a word, (2) at an articulatory change point internal to a word, and (3) following the termination of a word. A hearer's eye blinks also tend to occur at these same locations.

The internal structure of the eye blinks was examined and also found to change synchronously with speech. Where a blink closes, opens, and terminates opening, including the minor changes within closure and opening, is related to articulatory variations at these points. This, again, was true for both speaker and hearer. The eye blink, although a distinguishable regularity, is not separate from the rest of behavior, but is integrated into the totality of on-going patterns.

One of the major tasks facing the behavioral sciences is the development of a descriptive basis for the analysis of behavioral processes which will reflect the nature of those processes. There is also a concomitant need to clarify the decisional criteria and the decisional logic for these descriptions as they develop. Retrospectively, the greatest impediments to the discovery of regularities were the assumptions of the observers concerning the nature of the universe under investigation. By insinuating themselves into the analysis as unexaminable prior commitments concerning the nature of behavior, they effectively prevented the observation of blatant regularities which were not compatible with their perspective. It was difficult to avoid a view of events as composed of discrete entities which are somehow put together to give rise, in some future moment, to organized behavior.

Self-synchrony and interactional-synchrony, if true, seem to imply a radical involvement of speech within the total behavior of the organism and between organisms, in a way that precludes a consideration of the source of speech apart from the evolution of the species.

REFERENCES

Condon, W. S., & Ogston, W. D. Sound film analysis of normal and pathological behavior patterns. *Journal of Nervous and Mental Disease*, 1966, **143**, 338-47.

Condon, W. S., & Ogston, W. D. A segmentation of behavior. *Journal of Psychiatric Research*, 1967, **5**, 221-35.

Lorenz, Konrad Z. *King Solomon's ring: New light on animal ways.* New York: Crowell, 1952.

Lorenz, Konrad Z. *On aggression.* New York: Harcourt, Brace and World, 1966.

Tinbergen, Nikolaas. *The herring gull's world: A study of the social behavior of birds.* (rev. ed.) New York: Basic Books, 1960.

Tinbergen, Nikolaas. *An objectivist study of the innate behavior of animals.* Leiden: Brill, 1942.

THE IMPORTANCE OF TEMPORAL FACTORS IN BEHAVIOR

ERIC H. LENNEBERG[1]

University of Michigan

The findings presented by Condon and Ogston are, in my opinion, very suggestive. It is this type of inquiry which may lead to new approaches to the relationship between brain mechanisms and behavior. The brain consists of elements that influence one another as they oscillate at varying frequency. With these capacities, limited as they seem at first glance, the complete universe of behavior — motor, perceptual, and cognitive skills — is elaborated. Until a generation or two ago, students of the brain tried to explain behavior primarily in terms of structural, topographical alterations and adjustments. Only gradually was the importance of variability of functions recognized; recently, theoretical constructs involving different parameters of activity have become more and more popular. Today, there are theoreticians who consider morphological features of the brain and their growth to be relatively unimportant for our understanding of brain-and-behavior interactions. This is, no doubt, too parochial an approach; however, there is much to be gained by further enriching our theories and models of the interaction of neurons. An important step in this

---

[1] Now at Cornell University.

direction is the identification of temporal aspects in both behavior and neuro-physiological events.

I do not wish to give the impression that this is an original thought. There is, in fact, a vast literature on temporal aspects of both behavior and brain functions, and the search for temporal quanta and rhythms has produced an embarrassing abundance of facts, some harmonious, some contradictory, some apparently totally unrelated, and some even militating against the notion of true time quanta or theoretically interesting rhythms (Barlow, 1959; Békésy, 1965, 1967; Meyers, 1965; Uttal, 1965; Uttal and Krissoff, 1966).

Since the data of Condon and Ogston also suggest discrete temporal entities within which "bundles of change" take place, I would like to summarize here why the discovery of rhythms and quanta is so attractive to many of us. Condon and Ogston have not explicitly mentioned rhythms, but it will be seen presently that temporal quanta actually imply rhythm. I will first review some logical considerations and then briefly point to neurophysiological and behavioral evidence in support of these notions.

LOGICAL CONSIDERATIONS

Motor coordination requires correct relative timing of a great many muscles in the body. This is accomplished largely by an assembly of reflex movements in which individual muscles are coordinated to certain others through fixed, inborn synergisms. (For example: the maintenance of equilibrium in stance and gait; the conjugation of the eyes and the interdependence between eye and head movements; swallowing mechanisms; the supplementarity between flexor and extensor muscles.) This suggests that the flow of movements that constitutes motor behavior consists of "chunks," each having a peculiar program of nervous integration. The musculature of different parts of the body, the head, the trunk, and the extremities, is controlled by a variety of synergisms. Distant anatomic parts must interact precisely for smooth motor coordination of complex activities such as running, food ingestion, reproductive activities, etc., so that the onset and cessation of each "behavioral chunk" also must be precisely timed with respect to each other. To accomplish this we may postulate that either (1) the timing of segments with respect to one another is a concatenation of irregularly spaced junctures, or (2) the length of every segment is a multiple of a given time-unit, so that the junctures are regularly spaced. The choice between these alternatives is contingent upon empirical verification, and much of the evidence points toward the latter alternative (Boynton, 1961; Marler, 1966, chapter 6). This is also what we would expect from logical considerations. The first alternative calls for an astronomically large memory, because it requires individual storage of long sequences of timing records — one record for every possible combination of muscle interactions. The other alternative suggests rhythmic changes, a central rhythm providing a mechanism whereby synchrony of distant parts in the body may be achieved with considerable economy of storage requirements.

There is another way of saying the same thing: motor integration of even the most primitive kind calls for a timing mechanism. The simplest and biologically most plausible clock is a rhythm of alternating states of facilitation and inhibition. With this conceptualization we have obviated the need to postulate a memory that stores information on the *exact lengths* of time-segments for every synergistic "behavioral chunk." However, we must still explain the capacity for adjusting a motor behavior pattern to fit a specific circumstance. Given the ability to throw, there must be instantaneous adjustment to the weight and shape of the missile and to the terrain in which the action is to take place, as well as to the peculiarities of the target.

It is important to realize that the "program" for the sequence of events is, essentially, a central phenomenon, fairly independent of the peripheral, muscular effectors. This assumption is necessary for two reasons. One, because a patterned motor sequence can be learned by one hand and then, without major loss in skill, be transferred at once to the other hand (or even the feet or the movements of the head); two, because in many instances the sequence-pattern may be executed in reverse. Neither of these would be possible if the muscles themselves emitted a cue that triggered the next event in the sequence. (These points were first made by Lashley (1951) who, incidentally, also postulated rhythms; some of the points in this paper support his view, although for different reasons.)

Wickelgren (1967) maintains that Lashley's argument does not necessarily invalidate an associative model of serial order learning. This may be achieved, Wickelgren argues, by postulating events entirely contained within the brain that are chained together by associative processes. However, this hypothesis still calls for memory capacities that appear unrealistic. The sequences of behavior in animals and man are, under normal conditions, extremely flexible. As the organism moves from situation to situation, the patterns of sequences are constantly readjusted to fit specific demands; the only common denominator that remains between one motor sequence, for example one episode of catching prey, and the next is a logical principle or, in other words, a generalized pattern. If individual associative chains of neuro-muscular events had to be stored one by one, it is difficult to see how and when the organism would have time to acquire the unique behavioral chains as they occur on one particular occasion, and how instantaneous transformations, which adjust behavior to the imperatives of the moment, could be performed without a new trial-and-error procedure.

Considerations of this sort lead to the suggestion that a hierarchy of programs exists, in which the highest program determines the type of motor behavior in its most general form and the lower ones are principles or patterns that more specifically regulate the sequence of events. Thus, a higher program determines the range of choices lower down, each choice being made from among a set of *principles* — not events — except for the final execution of muscular contractions.

German psychologists discussed this sort of thing under the heading *Aktualgenese*; the momentary genesis of action is a developmental history of states, i.e., differentiation of plans, to use Miller, Galanter, and Pribram terminology (1960). It is important that we do not equate it with a so-called left-to-right sequential associative model. In the latter case, one motor act (or its neuronal correlate) determines the next one. In the former, the sequence is not of acts but of plans for action that become more and more specific—better and better defined—until a final program which comprises a whole sequence of motor acts all at once is developed. When the last specificities emerge, the whole plan becomes clear; it is analogous to the development of a film: all of the details become clearly defined simultaneously. The final program contains the plan both for local synergisms and for the integration of these among one another. We may conceptualize the procedure by postulating two aspects: one consists of the development of the program — the working out of a function in which the parameters become specified; in the other, specific values are determined through the senses and presented to the computer, which can now give the exact positions of all limbs.

Our memory capacity for random sequences is extremely limited.

This is well illustrated by our short memory span for random digits, and the situation is no better for the acquisition of motor sequences randomly concatenated. Seven elements plus or minus two is about the limit in these chains. It is well known that this storage capacity can be improved if we can fit the elements into some pattern and thus recode the material.

It is the great variability in motor behavior that militates against any type of simple associative chain (no matter whether hypothesized to be entirely confined to the brain or whether we believe that peripheral structures are also involved). The same reason also induces us to look for pattern-generating principles and relations between them. Postulation of such principles simplifies our theories enormously.

It cannot be seriously questioned that all motor behavior consists of patterned sequences in contrast to random concatenation of muscle contractions. Even though there is, within limits, freedom to "shape" behavior, the synergisms or parcels of behavior cannot be further decomposed experimentally, and individual muscular contractions cannot be strung up arbitrarily. Furthermore, there are severe limitations to the arbitrary temporal reorganization of intact synergisms with respect to one another. We cannot train a horse to dance a waltz. Behavior consists of a limited set of generalized patterns (e.g., "... maintenance of equilibrium while ...") that impose conditions upon the more specific patterns (e.g. "... walking slowly ..."), which, in turn, contribute to the plan of execution (e.g., "... keeping within the vicinity of mother-mare who emits the following sensory cues ..."). Such might be a hierarchical arrangement of plans; it controls acceptance of incoming stimuli and channels them into an integrating mechanism — a computer programmed by that hierarchy of plans — which activates the motor events (cf. also Bullock, 1965). A hierarchy of this type is limited by species-specificities on all levels, though it is never uniquely or rigidly set. At its lower levels, and before the final execution stage, its proper functioning is dependent upon input from the environment.

We may now return to our *Leitmotif*: central rhythms. All behavior is a pattern in time; it cannot be random sequences because the observed versatility would require us to postulate memory capacities of a magnitude that is totally inconceivable. The only thing that distinguishes temporal *patterns* from temporal *randomness* is the existence of an underlying rhythm in the former case and its absence in the latter. This, then, is a further reason for expecting the existence of rhythms in behavior.

NEUROPHYSIOLOGICAL CONSIDERATIONS

The evidence for the existence of rhythms in the central nervous system is too well known to need any elaboration here. The material has been particularly well reviewed by Fessard (1959), Grey Walter (1959), and Brazier (1960). That the rhythms observed by electroencephalography are relevant to the timing of motor behavior has been suspected for well over a decade, though definitive proof is not yet available. A review of this material is not called for in the present context. I will, therefore, confine myself to a few hints on the possible relationship between the sequential programming of behavior and the modes of action of the brain.

The nature of the *response* in the nervous system is probably best thought of as a *change in the frequency of impulse generation* (cf. MacKay, 1968). Electrical recordings from single cells have shown that some units respond by a drop in their pre-stimulation frequency whereas others suddenly increase their frequency. Most normally functioning cells have a *range* of frequency with a minimum that never drops to zero and a maximum well below 100 cps. From this it follows that stimulus and response in the brain may be represented in the neural code as a complex modulation of ongoing activity.

This realization has far-reaching consequences for theory construction in the realm of perception which, unfortunately, we cannot pursue here. However, the same is true of theories on motor behavior. Neurons influence one another so that the activity of one always affects many others. From anatomical considerations we are led to believe that this influence spreads into different directions, so that not only are elements that are hooked up end-to-end (in series) as in a wiring system affected, but also elements that are parallel to one another. We have, therefore, whole fields of coupled oscillators. When the system is not disturbed they seem to beat in synchrony; but, with stimulation in a particular area of the field, some elements begin to change their frequency and, because it takes time for the disturbance to spread, the elements will oscillate out of phase (even if the change of frequency is eventually the same for many of the elements). A far-fetched analogy to a system of this kind (though much simpler) would be a row of elastically coupled pendula (Békésy, 1960). More complex but somewhat closer analogies could be constructed from coupled relaxation oscillators (Bremer, 1944, and Grey Walter, 1959). Because of the phase difference between the oscillations of individual elements, systems of this type generate travelling waves. If the elements have the capacity to change their frequencies — which is true of relaxation oscillators and of neurons but not of pendula — the travelling waves sweep through the system at varying speed; the propagation may change its sign, i.e., the wave may go "forwards and backwards" or it may stand still. It will always take time to build itself up, both in amplitude and in complexity (cf. also MacKay, 1961).

A system that functions in this fashion can, theoretically, account for a number of the phenomena observed in the sequential programming of behavior. For instance, the variability in motor rhythms (say, gait) could be hypothetically attributed to the capacity for generating travelling waves of different speed without changing the wave form; the automatic timing of muscular contractions in different parts of the body might be due to the different arrival time in various parts of, for example, the cortex, of a travelling wave. The hierarchical arrangements of action-programs, beginning with the most general "priming" and ending with specific activation of muscles, might be envisaged thus: let the action pattern be *pouncing on prey*. The system is disturbed from a particular locus and by a characteristic type of disturbance (smell of a rat) so that a peculiar travelling wave is set up, characteristic for its place of origin, its primary direction, its speed, its shape, its modifiability, or its form of decay. As the wave is built up and its general parameters are thus determined, other disturbances from elsewhere in the system (i.e., further information in the form of other stimuli of different modalities) influence it. Greater and greater specificity of the action program is produced and by the time the wave has reached some critical dimensions, parts of the brain are affected that can transduce the information and activate motor behavior.

We cannot further elaborate here on any of the attractive aspects of this type of speculation. Similar thoughts have been expressed by several students of brain function (for example, Fessard, 1961), most recently by John (1967). The reason for these transgressions was to show that research such as that presented by Condon and

Ogston has implications for very interesting and far-reaching problems. Their tangible results fit nicely into the panorama that I have sketched out. Their discovery of segments of behavior may be related to the generation of travelling waves and the synchrony observed to the resting or underlying frequency that is most natural to the undisturbed elements of the oscillating system.

FURTHER BEHAVIORAL CONSIDERATIONS

Quantal theories of behavior have not been restricted to motor aspects. Many studies of perception have resulted in similar suggestions, though the duration of the proposed quanta has varied. Figures that are reported again and again from a wide variety of experimental situations involving different sense modalities are ca. 30 msec., 60 msec., and 180 msec. A formal theory has been proposed by Bouman (1961) and some tentative conclusions based upon experiments in visual acuity have been contributed by Boynton (1961). Kahneman (unpublished) is preparing for publication a comprehensive survey of the literature on the subject.

In the realm of motor activities we find a large number of studies of rhythms based directly on observations of behavior as well as of function of nervous tissue (Bullock, 1961). The earliest investigator of note who studied behavior in this way was Bethe (1931), who was particularly interested in this phenomenon as it relates to the problem of cerebral reorganization and readjustment after surgical alterations. Subsequent studies by V. Holst on breathing and locomotory rhythms in fish are too well known to require special comment. A mathematical treatment of his physiological data may be found in V. Holst (1948). For more recent research see Gray (1953), Bullock (1956), Roeder, *et al.* (1960).

I would like to conclude this discussion by referring to further evidence of precisely the same phenomenon reported by Condon and Ogston, namely the perfect synchrony between change in bodily movements and changes in the configuration of oro-pharyngeal geometry during speech. If we ask a subject to beat out a rhythm with his finger and then engage him in conversation, it is possible to demonstrate that the taps will coincide closely with vocal motor readjustments, that is with syllable beginnings. This is well illustrated by the spectrogram shown in Figure 1. The subject in this instance was asked to tap the base of the microphone with a coin.

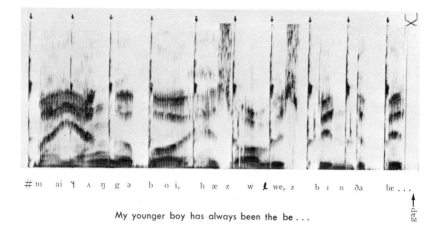

#m ai ˈɪ ʌ ŋ g ə b o iᵧ h æ z w ˈl weᵧ z b ɪ n ðə bɛ . . .

My younger boy has always been the be . . .

gap →

FIGURE 1. Subject tapping a microphone while speaking.

Taps (arrows) coincide with syllable boundaries.

No special indications about rate of rhythm were given except to "tap at a quick but comfortable speed." After about ten seconds he began to speak into the microphone. The sound /m/ marks the onset of his utterance; it is clear that he chose to speak at the moment of the beat.

In healthy individuals it does not matter much, as a rule, whether the subject is forced to tap with the right or with the left hand, the rhythm will be the same for either. However, it is the dominant hand that taps in most accurate synchrony with speech. In patients with lateralized lesions the rhythm of the two hands becomes markedly different in rate. Sometimes dysarthric speech continues to be synchronized with the dominant hand even though rhythms become abnormally slow and in many cases irregular.

I hope I have shown that Condon's and Ogston's investigations are relevant to many aspects of behavior. There are still a number of methodological problems in their work that have a bearing on interpretation of their data. Undoubtedly these can be dealt with in the general discussion.

REFERENCES

Barlow, J. S. Rhythmic activity induced by photic stimulation in relation to intrinsic alpha activity of the brain in man. *EEG Clinical Neurophysiology*, 1959, **12**, 317-26.

von Békésy, G. *Experiments in hearing.* New York: McGraw-Hill, 1960.

von Békésy, G. Inhibition and the time and spatial patterns of neural activity in sensory perception. *Annals of Otology, Rhinology, and Laryngology,* 1965, **74**, 1-18.

von Békésy, G. *Sensory inhibition.* Princeton, N.J.: Princeton University Press, 1967.

Bethe, A. Plastizität und zentrenlehre. *Handbook of Normal and Pathological Physiology,* 1931, **15**, 1175-1220.

Bouman, M. A. History and present status of quantum theory in vision. In W. A. Rosenblith (ed.), *Sensory communication.* Cambridge, Mass.: M.I.T. Press, 1961.

Boynton, R. M. Some temporal factors in vision. In W. A. Rosenblith (ed.), *Sensory communication.* Cambridge, Mass.: M.I.T. Press, 1961.

Brazier, M. A. B. Long-persisting electrical traces in the brain of man and their possible relationship to higher nervous activity. In H. H. Jasper and G. D. Smirnov (eds.), *EEG Journal, Supplement 13,* 1960.

Bremer, F. L'activité 'spontanée' des centres nerveux. *Bulletin de l'Academie Royale Medicale Belgique,* 1944, **9**, 148-73.

Bullock, T. H. The trigger concept in biology. In T. H. Bullock (ed.), *Physiological triggers and discontinuous rate processes.* Washington, D.C.: American Physiological Society, 1956.

Bullock, T. H. The origins of patterned nervous discharge. *Behaviour* 1961, **17**, 48-59.

Bullock, T. H. Integration and rhythmicity in neural systems. *American Zoologist,* 1962, **2**, 97-104.

Bullock, T. H. In search of principles in integrative biology. *American Zoologist,* 1965, **5**, 745-55.

Fessard, A. Brain potentials and rhythms. In J. Field, H. Magoun, and V. E. Hall (eds.), *Handbook of physiology. section 1: neurophysiology, volume 1.* Washington, D.C.: American Physiological Society, 1959.

Fessard, A. The role of neuronal networks in sensory communications within the brain. In W. A. Rosenblith (ed.), *Sensory communication.* Cambridge, Mass.: M.I.T. Press, 1961.

Gray, J. *How animals move.* Cambridge, England: Cambridge University Press, 1953.

Holst, E. V. Von de mathematik der nervoesen ordnungsleitung. *Experientia,* 1948, **4**, 374-81.

John, R. *The mechanism of memory.* New York: Academic Press, 1967.

Kahneman, D. *Temporal factors in vision.* (Unpublished.)

Lashley, K. The problem of serial order in behavior. In L. A. Jeffress (ed.), *Cerebral mechanisms in behavior.* New York: Wiley, 1951.

MacKay, D. M. Interactive processes in visual perception. In W. A. Rosenblith (ed.), *Sensory communication.* Cambridge, Mass.: M.I.T. Press, 1961.

MacKay, D. M. Neural communications: Experiment and theory. *Science*, 1968, **159**, 335-53.

Marler, P. Chain reflexes or endogenous control. In P. Marler (ed.), *Mechanisms of animal behavior.* New York: Wiley, 1966.

Meyers, O. E. Conversion from spectral to temporal pattern. *Nature*, 1965, **206**, 918-19.

Miller, G. A., Galanter, E. & Pribram, K. H. *Plans and the structure of behavior.* New York: Holt, 1960.

Roeder, K. D., Tozian, L., & Weiant, E. A. Endogenous nerve activity and behavior in the mantis and cockroach. *Journal of Insect Physiology*, 1960, **4**, 45-62.

Uttal, W. R. Do compound evoked potentials reflect psychological codes? *Psychological Bulletin*, 1965, **64**, 377-92.

Uttal, W. R., & Krissoff, M. Effect of stimulus pattern on temporal acuity in the somatosensory system. *Journal of Experimental Psychology*, 1966, **71**, 878-83.

Walter, G. W. Intrinsic rhythms of the brain. In J. Field, H. Magoun, and V. E. Hall (eds.), *Handbook of physiology. section 1: neurophysiology, volume 1.* Washington, D.C.: American Physiological Society, 1959.

Wickelgren, W. A. Context-sensitive coding, associative memory and serial order in (speech) behavior. (Unpublished, 1967.)

7

AN ANALYSIS OF
LATERALITY EFFECTS IN
SPEECH PERCEPTION[1]

DONALD SHANKWEILER[2]

Haskins Laboratories

It has been recognized since the time of Broca (1861) that one hemisphere of man's brain, usually the left, is specialized for speech functions. Fundamental though this fact is, it has remained somewhat isolated from the main body of knowledge about the brain, and only recently has it been subjected to experimental analysis. Many recent investigations have shown that the right hemisphere, the so-called minor hemisphere, has functions of its own which are not fully shared by the left hemisphere. Some recent studies of auditory perception, which I am about to review, point to the conclusion that the two brain hemispheres do have different functions not only in the perception of speech but also music and certain other complex sounds.

[1]This work was supported in part by a grant to Haskins Laboratories from the National Institute of Child Health and Human Development.
[2]Also at the University of Connecticut.

THE PHENOMENON

Through an application of Broadbent's dichotic listening experiment (1954), Doreen Kimura has opened a new approach to the investigation of the relative contribution of the two hemispheres to the perception of auditory patterns and speech (Kimura, 1961a, b; Milner, 1962). It was discovered by Dr. Kimura, while working in Brenda Milner's Laboratory at the Montreal Neurological Institute, that when groups of spoken digits are presented through earphones so that different digits arrive at approximately the same time at each ear, those presented to the right ear are more accurately reported than those presented to the left. On a typical test trial, a subject received three pairs of recorded digits, spaced one-half second apart. The task was to repeat all the numbers heard without regard to which ear they were delivered. Most subjects made fewer errors for the right ear than for the left. Although the ear difference was small, it was reasonably consistent from subject to subject — about 80 percent of the right-handed subjects were a little better with the right ear. This result seemed to suggest that the right ear has the better path to the speech processing areas of the left hemiphere. This suggestion was confirmed many times in subsequent experiments.

A number of animal studies had already indicated that each ear has greater representation in the opposite cerebral hemisphere. Rosenzweig (1951) had shown that for the cat the auditory projections have a stronger crossed component than uncrossed. His results were recently confirmed in the microelectrode studies of Hall and Goldstein (1968). Indications that this is true for man as well had been given by Bocca, Calearo, Cassinari and Migliavacca (1955), who discovered that the perception of speech presented to one ear alone is impaired when directed to the ear opposite a temporal-lobe lesion. Kimura's findings in perception of dichotically presented digits confirmed these earlier indications of the superiority of the crossed pathways and demonstrated, for the first time, an effect of cerebral dominance in a perceptual task performed by listeners with intact nervous systems. It was an important gain, because it meant we no longer had to rely solely on brain-damaged individuals as the only source of knowledge about the cerebral organization of auditory and speech functions.

Dichotic presentation is apparently a necessary condition for the occurrence of these lateral differences in perception. If the stimuli are presented for recognition monaurally, neither ear has an advantage, however unfavorable the signal-to-noise ratio (given ears of equal sensitivity and free of pathology). We know that each ear is represented by a somewhat larger population of cells in the opposite cerebral hemisphere. We do not know how great the inequality of representation is. Competition of inputs brought about by dichotic presentation may well result in a decided advantage to the input channel which has even slightly stronger representation in the hemisphere specialized for processing the type of material presented. Kimura (1964) has suggested a similar possibility based on Rosenzweig's (1951) demonstration in the cat that some cortical units serve both ears. The overlap may be such that the binaural interaction which results when both ears are stimulated simultaneously could enhance contralateral transmission in the system at the expense of ipsilateral transmission. Thus, some units which respond to both ears when each ear is stimulated alone may be driven selectively by the contralateral ear when both ears are stimulated in tandem.

We must still consider the possibility that the right ear can cope more effectively with competing speech than the left ear. A necessary control is the monaural presentation of the electrically-mixed output of two channels each containing different words. Experiments conducted at McGill University by Philip Corsi (1967) have shown decisively that competition does not bring about the ear effect unless the competition is interaural; that is, dichotically produced. This finding has been confirmed by Terry Halwes and myself in our Laboratories. Therefore, we may conclude that the ear effects in dichotic listening depend jointly on differences in function of the two cerebral hemispheres and a system arranged to favor contralateral transmission during simultaneous stimulation of the two ears.

DISSOCIATED LATERALITY EFFECTS FOR SPEECH AND NONSPEECH

The findings which link the ear advantage with cerebral lateralization of speech are remarkably clear-cut and encouraged further work with the dichotic technique. One question which seemed worth exploring was whether or not some non-verbal stimuli would give a left-ear advantage when presented dichotically, thereby reflecting specialization of structures in the right hemisphere for carrying out non-verbal perceptual processes. This possibility seemed likely in view of Milner's earlier finding (1962) that certain complex auditory discriminations are affected by right temporal lobectomy but not by left. Working with the Seashore Measures of Musical Talents, Milner has shown that tonal pattern perception and timbre discrimination are selectively impaired by right temporal lobectomy.

Kimura (1964) devised a dichotic melodies test in which pairs of different melody fragments are presented to the ears simultaneously. After each test trial consisting of a dichotically presented pair, a set of four melodies is presented, one at a time, posing an auditory multiple-choice problem. The subject had to indicate which two melodies had been presented dichotically. The task was one of recognition and did not involve naming. Kimura found that a significantly greater number of correct choices were made for melodies presented to the left ear. The same subjects were given the dichotic digits test and were more accurate on the right ear. The ear differences for digits and melodies presented dichotically go in opposite ways as she had predicted. It was recently reported by Curry (1967) that common environmental noises are also better recognized from the left ear. Kimura's melodies and digits tasks have been presented to patients with localized lesions of the left and right temporal lobes with the outcome of a significant double dissociation of deficits on the two tasks (Shankweiler, 1966; Kimura, 1967). That is to say, patients with left temporal-lobe lesion were impaired on the digits task but not on melodies, whereas patients with right temporal-lobe lesion were impaired on the melodies task but not on digits. Thus, it was the verbal or non-verbal nature of the task that seemed to be the deciding factor in determining whether a deficit occurred in cases of left or right temporal-lobe lesion. Both sets of data, those for patients and for normal subjects, agree with other indications that the minor hemisphere plays a greater role in processing some nonspeech sounds.

CEREBRAL ASYMMETRIES IN SPEECH PERCEPTION IN RELATION TO LEVELS OF LANGUAGE

These findings are clear in their indications of hemispheric differences in perception of verbal and nonverbal materials, but they are ambiguous in one respect. You will recall that Kimura originally used spoken digits as stimuli; that is to say, meaningful words were used. We did not know whether the meanings had to be perceived in order for the laterality effect to occur, or whether simply being perceived as speech was sufficient. The question has not often been asked whether all processes in the perception of language are lateralized. The answer has important implications. It bears on the general question of whether or not speech perception rests on mechanisms that are different from those that underlie the perception of other sound patterns. We know that the facts of hemispheric specialization point directly to the existence of specialized neural mechanisms that serve language in a broad sense. But let us consider speech in its narrowest sense, in the sense of the sounds of language and their perception as strings of phonemes. Speech this narrowly conceived is often not considered to be an integral part of the species-specific activity we call language. There are many reasons for believing, however, that the sounds of speech belong to the structure of language and are highly interconnected with other parts of the language hierarchy. If this is so, we would expect these interconnections to be evident in the neural foundations of language.

Much of the research with artificial sound alphabets has shown that not just any distinctive set of sounds can serve as an efficient vehicle for the transmission of language (Liberman, Cooper, Shankweiler, & Studdert-Kennedy, 1967). My colleagues at Haskins Laboratories were challenged to find out why the sounds we use naturally are so well suited to the task. We have turned to analysis of articulation in order to clarify certain unique properties of speech sounds. The motor activity of speech consists largely of gestures which overlap one another in time. As a consequence of this temporal overlap, the relationship between the acoustic characteristics of speech and the perceptual units (phonemes and their features) is highly complex. The distinctive features of the phonemes are emitted in parallel fashion, not in linear phoneme-sized bundles, so that at almost any instant during the articulation of a syllable, the acoustic cues convey information about more than one phoneme. Speech, then, becomes encoded or restructured in time in the process of transmission from the speaker to the hearer. The perceptual mechanism which recovers phonemes from the sound stream functions in some sense as a decoder.

We see then that special requirements are placed on the perceptual apparatus due to the encoded nature of the speaker's message. Because of this one might expect the perception of speech to differ from that of other sounds. It seemed that the type of experiment I have been describing offered a rather direct way to study some characteristics of the speech decoder.

When Dr. Michael Studdert-Kennedy and I began our experiments at Haskins Laboratories, the first question we explored was whether the specialized mechanisms of the dominant hemisphere are engaged in perceiving speech in the narrowest sense, or whether the same processors that operate in the recognition of other auditory patterns such as environmental sounds and music are used. The second question relates to the fact that in Kimura's task the digits were presented in groups. Since our interest was in perceptual mechanisms we wanted to avoid serial presentation, if possible. First, we had to determine whether lateral differences could be obtained with single pairs of stimuli. Since the laterality effect presumably depends upon some optimal level of competition, we hoped that by careful synchronization of the stimuli, we could limit a trial to a single pair of syllables.

We presented speech in the most elementary form, directing to each ear dichotically single consonant-vowel syllables, only one pair on each trial. In our first experiments (Shankweiler & Studdert-Kennedy, 1967b) we used synthetic speech generated by the Haskins Pattern Playback (Cooper, Liberman, & Borst, 1951), a device for converting simplified hand-painted speech spectrograms into sound. The stimulus pairs were made up of all combinations of the six stop consonants (/ b, d, g, p, t, k /) followed by the same vowel / a /. Each of the 15 possible syllable pairs such as / ka-da / was presented equally often, with / ka / going to the left ear and / da / to the right half the time and then in the reverse order.

Because we were working with single pairs of syllables which contrasted only in the beginning consonant portion lasting less than 50 msec., we had to solve the problem of synchronizing the onsets more precisely than had been done before. We eventually arrived at a satisfactory method for achieving the alignment. Copies of each syllable were made using a dual-channel tape recorder; some being dubbed on track 1, some on track 2. These stimuli were then spliced into tape loops, each loop containing a pair of syllables, such as / ba-da /. The next step was aligning the stimuli, by synchronizing the onsets of each syllable and equalizing peak intensity. This was done by playing back each loop on a tape deck which had been especially modified to permit the length of tape passing between two playback heads to be varied. This was adjusted until the two utterances coincided. The final step in the alignment procedure involved making an oscillographic record of the syllables using a Visicorder with a time marker as illustrated in Figure 1. The two upper tracings in the figure show synchronized syllables,

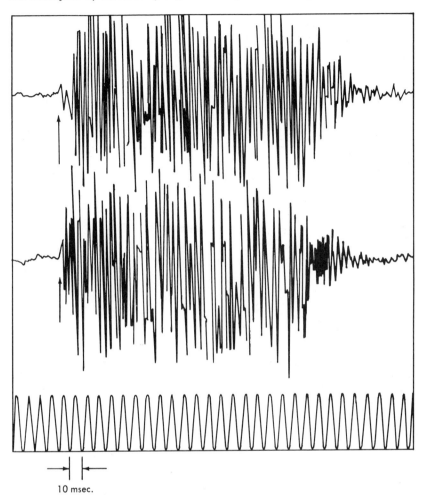

FIGURE 1. Oscillographic record displaying two syllables in temporal alignment.

The syllables shown here are real speech. The procedure was the same for aligning synthetically-produced syllables.

and the lower tracing is a time marker produced by a continuous 100 Hz. tone. We were thus able to align the stimuli within a few milliseconds.

The subjects were told that different syllables would always be presented to the two ears and that their task was to write down both in order of confidence. They were required to make two responses even if one or both had to be guesses. The set of syllables from which they were to make their choices was displayed at the top of the answer sheet. Each listener heard each test twice, and the earphones were reversed on the second run, so that no differences in the components of the playback system could contribute to the ear differences.

We found a substantial and highly significant advantage in the accuracy of identification of syllables presented to the right ear, with 14 out of 15 subjects receiving better scores on the right, and a mean right ear advantage of 16 percent. Since our stimuli consisted of nonsense syllables that contrasted in only one phone, we concluded that the specific language processing system of the dominant cerebral hemisphere is engaged at the level of the sound structure of the language; that speech perception in the narrow sense depends on the specialized machinery of the left hemisphere. Moreover, since the effect occurred with presentation of single pairs of syllables, we concluded, in agreement with Kimura (1962, 1967), Bryden (1967) and Satz (1968), that the effect has a genuinely perceptual basis, and is not due to memory.

Dr. Studdert-Kennedy and I made up a new test containing contrasting pairs of vowels alone. These were prolonged, monotone or steady-state vowels which in speech are formed with the vocal tract in a fixed, open-tube configuration. Therefore, we would expect them to be unencoded, or at least less encoded than the stops. It would follow that these vowels would not necessarily engage the processor specialized for speech. We found for this set of vowels a much smaller right ear advantage for the same group of subjects who had shown a decisive right ear advantage for stop consonants (Figure 2). This result suggested that these vowel stimuli were processed about equally well by either hemisphere of the brain. The vowel data did show a small net trend in favor of the right ear, however; and although this was not statistically significant, we wondered whether the difference might have been larger if the vowels had not been monotone or if they had been presented in syllabic context.

These experiments raised a number of further questions. In particular, the indication of a difference in the mode of processing consonants and vowels needed re-examination. We had used synthetic speech in these experiments because of the advantages it offers in achieving uniform and specifiable acoustic structure. But because of the particular synthesizer we used, these advantages

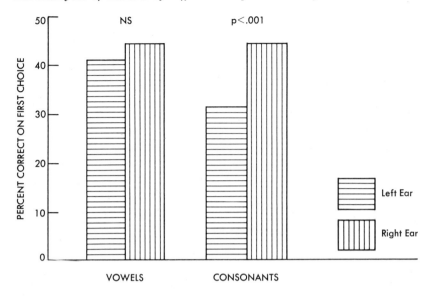

FIGURE 2. Ear differences for dichotically presented synthetic steady-state vowels and consonant-vowel syllables. Ten subjects.

were bought at the expense of natural quality. We wondered whether our results, particularly those for contrasting isolated vowels, might reflect characteristics of these particular synthetic stimuli.

IDENTIFICATION OF CONSONANTS AND VOWELS IN SYLLABLES

In order to clarify this result we performed a new experiment using real speech. In this experiment vowels as well as consonants occurred in syllabic context. The syllables were spoken by a phonetician experienced in making speech recordings. A spectrogram was made of each recorded syllable and the durations were measured. These ranged from 300 to 500 msec. For the consonant comparison, the stimuli consisted of consonant-vowel-consonant syllables formed by pairing the six stop consonants with each of six vowels (/ i, ɛ, æ, ɑ, ɔ, u /). All syllables were closed by the same consonant / p /. For every consonant, therefore, we obtained six separate estimates of the laterality effect. This required a much longer test, containing 360 trials as opposed to 120 trials for the previous experiments. Any given syllable pair differed only in the initial consonant as before, but in the test as a whole each consonant was followed equally often by each of six vowels. This test was appropriate for our purpose of obtaining a reliable estimate of the magnitude of the ear effect with different phonetic contrasts. The alignment procedure was the same as before as illustrated in Figure 1.

A second test consisted of pairs which contrasted in the vowel alone. This test was made up of different combinations of the same set of spoken consonant-vowel-consonant nonsense syllables, yielding a test of the same length as the consonant test.

We have given some thought to the problem of how best to estimate the magnitude of the ear advantage. This is an important problem since we would like to be able to make meaningful statements about the relative size of the ear difference with various classes of stimuli, not simply to say that a significant difference is present or not present. Our initial interest was in the first response the subject wrote. Analysis of our earlier data for Playback speech indicated that second responses contained little information, while the first response seemed to be a sensitive indicator of the laterality effect. We have abandoned this measure in describing the data of the present experiment because some subjects were more accurate on the second response than the first. Simple percent correct for each ear is also an unsatisfactory measure, since the size of the ear advantage may vary with the difficulty of the task. Indeed *a priori* limits are placed on the possible size of the ear advantage when the overall level of performance is high or low. There is an optimal range of difficulty levels over which the ear difference is not severely constrained.[3] An overall level of 50 percent correct is about ideal. At this level of performance the ear difference could in principal vary from 0 to 100 percent.

One way to achieve an optimal level of difficulty is to add noise to each channel. Noise, however, has the disadvantage of masking some acoustic features more than others. We have recently adopted the policy of scoring only those stimulus pairs on which one correct response and one error was made. Trials on which both responses are correct and both are wrong can contribute nothing to the ear difference. Discarding these trials also gives us the desirable 50 percent level of difficulty. We then express the score for each ear as a percentage of the total, $(L/L+R)100$ and $(R/L+R)100$, and the

---

[3] I am indebted to Terry Halwes of the University of Minnesota for pointing this out to me.

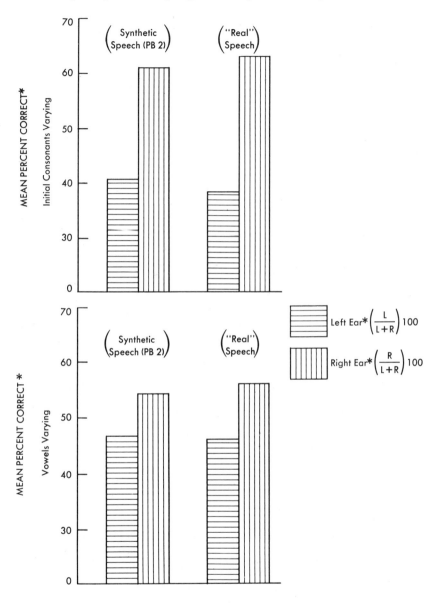

$$\frac{R-L}{R+L}$$

FIGURE 3. $\overline{\frac{R-L}{R+L}}$ **(100) as a measure of the ear difference for dichotically presented syllables, synthetic and real.**

This tabulation includes all trials on which one error occurred.

ear difference by $(L-R/L+R)100$, where L and R represent the frequencies of correct responses for presentations to the left ear and right ear.

Figure 3 shows this measure for the data from these experiments (Shankweiler and Studdert-Kennedy, 1967a). All 12 subjects were better on the right ear in the consonant test. The left portion of the Figure shows histograms for our earlier experiment with synthetic speech. The right half of the figure compares the results of the real speech consonant and vowel tests for the 11 subjects who took both tests. The two sets of data agree remarkably well although the subjects and the stimuli were different. The mean right ear advantage is greater by a factor of three for consonants than vowels in both experiments.

THE RIGHT EAR ADVANTAGE FOR INDIVIDUAL STOPS AND VOWELS

The indication that the left cerebral hemisphere participates more in the perception of stop consonants than vowels has important implications for understanding the nature of speech perception. Therefore, we would like to be sure that these differences are not the result of some artifact. We can immediately rule out the possibility that the differences in the size of the laterality effect for consonants and vowels are due to the greater difficulty of the consonants, because we have equated the difficulty of the tests by discarding trials on which both responses were correct and both were wrong. We can also rule out the possibility that the ear effects are attributable to a particular choice of stop-vowel combinations, since every stimulus was paired equally often with every other, and the whole test was presented a second time with channels and ears reversed.

We have noted that the ear effect for consonants was reliable from subject to subject and unreliable for vowels. We now examine for consistency the laterality effect for individual consonants and vowels. Figure 4 shows the ear advantages computed for each consonant and each vowel separately. The indices are arranged from left to right in order of decreasing magnitude. Consonants and vowels are perfectly segregated by this arrangement. All the consonant effects are signifiicant at $p<.001$. One vowel / i / was significant with $p<.01$. A still more stringent test of consistency was

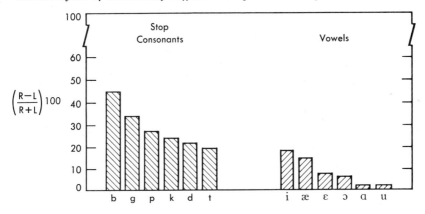

FIGURE 4. The right ear advantage for individual stop consonants and vowels.

The tabulation includes all trials on which one error occurred.

made by examining the ear effect for each of the 30 consonant pairs presented in the test. (Each subject received 12 presentations of each pair). A net right ear advantage was obtained for all but one of the 30 stimulus pairs. The vowel data are much more variable. Examination of all vowel pairs individually showed no ear difference or a *left* ear advantage on 13 out of 30 pairs. These analyses have demonstrated that the right ear advantage is present for the whole class of stop consonants, when joined in syllables with any of six vowels.[4]

When as in the earlier experiment, vowels were presented steady-state and in isolation, we were not surprised to find little advantage for the right ear because that set of vowels was relatively unlike speech. We find it remarkable that vowels embedded in CVC syllables should also fail to give a significant right-ear advantage. The result strongly supports our earlier suggestion that perception of stop consonants is highly dependent upon the dominant hemisphere function whereas vowels may or may not be processed in the dominant hemisphere. In view of the many indications that the perception of melodies and tonal patterns of complex structure de-

---

[4]A forthcoming paper by Studdert-Kennedy and Shankweiler will describe this experiment in detail and will present an analysis of the consonant data by feature.

pends more upon right hemisphere function than left (Milner, 1962; Kimura, 1964, 1967; Shankweiler, 1966; Curry, 1967) it appears that the vowels are processed neither like music and other nonspeech auditory patterns nor like what is most characteristic of speech. It is conceivable that the right ear advantage occurs mainly for speech cues of brief duration, such as the bursts and rapidly changing formant frequencies that characterize stop consonants but not vowels. We are doing experiments to examine this possibility, but we are doubtful that the laterality effect in perception of consonants can be tied to any particular acoustic characteristic. I think, rather, that these vowel-consonant differences demonstrate that the speech processing mechanism is particularly attuned to those phonetic properties of speech that are a consequence of encoding.

The degree of encoding should be a relative, not absolute difference between stops and vowels. Important changes in the articulation of vowels occur as the speaking rate varies. Vowels that occur in very rapid speech are not only much shorter than the vowel portion of syllables produced in isolated syllables, but they may fail to reach their "target" formant values altogether. These vowels are presumably encoded to a greater degree than the vowels contained in syllables produced in citation by paced reading from a list. We will be interested to learn whether or not these vowels behave more like stop consonants when presented dichotically than the vowels we have used.

I shall conclude by summarizing the questions examined in these experiments. The right ear advantage for contrasting consonants was relatively large and consistent when single pairs of syllables were presented, indicating that the ear advantage pertains to the recognition of the stimuli and not only to their retention. The left cerebral hemisphere has long been known to contain structures specialized for language functions. Our findings indicate that speech, in the narrowest sense, engages the specialized machinery of the left hemisphere. Perception, even of nonsense syllables, involves processes different than those involved in the perception of music and other nonspeech sound patterns. Finally, the ear effects are differentially sensitive to differences among speech sounds themselves. Syllables contrasting only in the vowel portion were identified almost equally well by either ear. We think this reflects differences between stop consonants and vowels in the degree of encoding — differences in the degree to which phonemes are restructured in time in the process of articulation.

REFERENCES

Bocca, E., Calearo, C., Cassinari, V., & Migliavacca, F. Testing "cortical" hearing in temporal lobe tumors. *Acta Oto-Laryngologica,* 1955, **45**, 289-304.

Broadbent, D. E. The role of auditory localization in attention and memory span. *Journal of Experimental Psychology,* 1954, **47**, 191-96.

Broca, P. Remarques sur le siège de la faculté du langage articulé suivies d'une observation d'aphémie. *Bulletin de la Societe Anatomique de Paris,* 1861, **36**, 330-57.

Bryden, M. P. An evaluation of some models of laterality effects in dichotic listening. *Acta Oto-Laryngologica,* 1967, **63**, 595-604.

Cooper, F. S., Liberman, A. M., & Borst, J. M. The interconversion of audible and visible patterns as a basis for research in the perception of speech. *Proceedings of the National Academy of Sciences,* 1951, **37**, 318-28.

Corsi, P. M. The effects of contralateral noise upon the perception and immediate recall of monaurally presented verbal material. Unpublished masters thesis, McGill University, Montreal, 1967.

Curry, F. K. W. A comparison of left-handed and right-handed subjects on verbal and nonverbal dichotic listening tasks. *Cortex,* 1967, **3**, 343-52.

Hall, J. L., & Goldstein, M. H. Representation of binaural stimuli by single units in primary auditory cortex of unanesthetized cats. *Journal of the Acoustical Society of America,* 1968, **3**, 456-61.

Kimura, D. Cerebral dominance and the perception of verbal stimuli. *Canadian Journal of Psychology,* 1961, **15**, 166-71. (a)

Kimura, D. Some effects of temporal-lobe damage on auditory perception. *Canadian Journal of Psychology,* 1961, **15**, 156-65. (b)

Kimura D. Perceptual and memory functions of the left temporal lobe: A reply to Dr. Inglis. *Canadian Journal of Psychology,* 1962, **16**, 18-22.

Kimura, D. Left-right differences in the perception of melodies. *Quarterly Journal of Experimental Psychology,* 1964, **14**, 355-58.

Kimura, D. Functional asymmetry of the brain in dichotic listening. *Cortex,* 1967, **3**, 163-78.

Liberman, A. M., Cooper, F. S., Shankweiler, D. P., & Studdert-Kennedy, M. Perception of the speech code. *Psychological Review,* 1967, **74**, 431-61.

Milner, B. Laterality effects in audition. In V. B. Mountcastle (ed.), *Interhemispheric relations and cerebral dominance.* Baltimore: Johns Hopkins Univ. Press, 1962. Pp. 177-95.

Rosenzweig, M. R. Representations of the two ears at the auditory cortex. *American Journal of Physiology,* 1951, **67,** 147-58.

Satz, P. Laterality effects in dichotic listening. *Nature,* 1968, **218,** 277-78.

Shankweiler, D. Effects of temporal-lobe damage on perception of dichotically presented melodies. *Journal of Comparative and Physiological Psychology,* 1966, **62,** 115-19.

Shankweiler, D. & Studdert-Kennedy, M. An analysis of perceptual confusions in identification of dichotically presented CVC syllables. *Journal of the Acoustical Society of America,* 1967, **41,** 1581 (A). (a)

Shankweiler D., & Studdert-Kennedy, M. Identification of consonants and vowels presented to left and right ears. *Quarterly Journal of Experimental Psychology,* 1967, **19,** 59-63. (b)

SOME PSYCHOLOGICAL ASPECTS OF THE PERCEPTION OF SPEECH-LIKE DATA

HERBERT RUBIN

University of Pittsburgh

This is an excellent paper, and it is a pleasure to react to it. Shankweiler has designed a careful series of studies logically grounded on the investigations of Milner (1958), Kimura (1961, 1964), and a group from Haskins Laboratories of which he was a member (Liberman *et al.*, 1967). It will be most interesting to follow his reports of the additional stimulus variables he is currently investigating, or plans to investigate, in the same experimental framework.

I want to select four points to qualify and to discuss a bit further. These deal with the neuroanatomic basis for differential processing of acoustic information; with the size of the acoustic unit to which the human observer reacts differentially, and at what level the reaction occurs; with the relative efficacy of the acoustic vs. the physiological model of speech perception; and finally with the psycholinguistic implications of this research and additional subjects to investigate.

With respect to the neural basis for the differential processing of acoustic input by the two ears, Shankweiler, as did Kimura, holds responsible the relatively greater contralateral representation rather than ipsilateral of the two ears at the auditory cortex. They are probably correct, at least in part. It is important to recognize, however, that we are dealing with relative, rather than absolute representation. This is not the picture of clearly crossed and unambiguous projection that we find in the occipital cortex for visual fields. Paul Kolers' comment is also appropriate here. Is the subject making a detailed analysis in one ear and a gross or more global analysis in the other? It certainly does not appear to be a case of on-off switching. The issue is further highlighted when both Kimura and Shankweiler report that the bilateral distinctions appear only under conditions of dichotic stimulation. When the stimuli are electronically mixed and fed to one ear, or when they are alternated between the ears, no hemispheric differences or advantages appear. In other words, we are observing a perceptual effect which can be elicited only when the two ears, or two hemispheres, depending upon where we localize the process, are pitted against each other with simultaneously competing stimuli. This is a dynamic situation, experimentally ingenious, but not representative of an ordinary listening task. It may involve a host of central mechanisms.

One of these mechanisms is inhibition. We have ample evidence of inhibitory activity throughout the auditory system (Galambos, 1966). Recently Boudreau and Tsuchitani (1967) have demonstrated this activity in the S segment of the superior olivary complex in cats resulting from contralateral acoustic stimulation. In other words, it is possible to inhibit activity on the side stimulated, at the level of a second order neuron, by the simultaneous stimulation of the contralateral ear. The inhibiting impulse can be traced back to the contralateral cochlear nucleus, indicating that the entire process takes place at a relatively peripheral level. The subjects are cats, as in the case of Rosenzweig's (1951) study, and the stimuli are pure tones. The inhibition is tonal specific, is most effective for identical, that is diotic, stimulation, and cannot be elicited from low characteristic frequency response units, but the application is feasible. The question to be raised here is: By what process and where does blocking take place for speech signals presented to the left ear and for non-speech signals presented to the right ear, when the presentation is dichotic? I think blocking is the appropriate term, since under conditions other than dichotic presentation, either ear transmits either kind of information equally well.

That question leads us to the second point for discussion, the nature and size of the acoustic unit, on the basis of which the observer, or some system within the observer, a "property detector" as Stevens (1960) calls it, decides whether this particular signal is speech-like or not. Liberman and associates have phrased the situation very nicely: "One seems either to be in the speech perception mode or out of it." (Liberman *et al.*, 1964). How does one decide whether he is in it or out of it? The trend of Shankweiler's investigations suggests that the decision is made automatically, at least subconsciously, on the basis of the acoustic characteristics of very small units, perhaps the duration of a stop consonant. The decision can be made at any level within the nervous system, from second order neurons in the superior olivary complex, as Boudreau and Tsuchitani have demonstrated, to the cortex itself. What he implies is that the decision is not a perceptual one in the sense that a judgment has been made. Perhaps *apperceptual* is the better term. The alternative to a property detector, of course, involves the subject taking a cortical look at the input and deciding, consciously or unconsciously, that the signal is of one form or the other. This is not very different from the procedure that McNeill described in the discussion of Eleanor Maccoby's paper, that is, the subject records the information and then operates upon it. Having recorded it, he can then initiate the appropriate channeling signals, facilitatory and inhibitory, and begin processing the data. The point is, on the basis of what kind and size of unit is he going to make this cortical decision? It would appear that the unit would not be one of decreasing magnitude, as Shankweiler proposes to investigate, but rather, one at least as large as the syllable, which the observer can scan comfortably. Certainly Kimura (1964) did this in the presentation of melodies, each of which lasted for four seconds. Perhaps the comparison of these data with responses to single phonemes or syllables is not even appropriate. One way to test for the size of the unit processed would be to present improbable consonant pairs like / pf /. If the subject identifies it as a more likely combination he is certainly reacting to larger units than one phoneme. However, if he reports the combination as presented, we are no closer to the answer than we were before. I would have to agree that in the absence of other cues the subject is going to work with the units he is given. But, what if we identify the nature of the message in advance? Here I am asking about the specific instructions presented to the subjects in this study. What differences, if any, would we get if the same signals were identified for some subjects as speech, and for other subjects as noise, or as music? A contrast of these cues should help to localize the level at which the channeling decision is made.

On the other hand, I must acknowledge that I, too, am puzzled by the fact that subjects process vowels dichotically presented in isolation no differently than the same vowels sandwiched between two invariant consonants. Apparently they ignore the consonants, which, after all, are not pitted against each other as the vowels are. Perhaps this means that Shankweiler is right, and that his subjects are not reacting to syllabic units or greater but are dissecting the acoustic input and reacting to the contrasted element, in the same way they do when that element is presented alone, unembedded. It is true the element here is a phoneme, but I am trying to characterize the direction of search for the unit, as well as its magnitude. This leads us to the third point, the relative efficacy of the acoustic vs. the physiological model of speech perception.

If we perceive speech as we tend to produce it, in a physiological or articulatory manner, as Liberman and associates (1964, 1967) say, then it will be to units such as the phoneme that we react, certainly not to smaller acoustic cues which are emitted in parallel rather than discretely. Indeed, how does the spectrographically unsophisticated observer identify the sounds of speech? He identifies them in the only way he knows, by applying the labels which his native language provides for these phonemes. Benjamin Lee Whorf might have suggested that the observer has little choice. He perceives this chunk of energy in the only way his language allows him to. It doesn't matter that the acoustic energy is not identical in pattern for a given phoneme in different contexts. As long as the contextual pattern is invariant, the speaker can learn, as a young child, what label to attach to a phoneme in that context. Eventually he will identify different patterns of acoustic energy as the same phoneme, but this does not matter as long as those patterns, in those contexts, are never identified as a different phoneme. What we seem to be learning with some pains, and perhaps some naivete, and perhaps the naivete is my own, is that the elementalism inherent in any alphabet, phonetic or otherwise, may not be the most efficient or most valid way of representing how we talk, but it certainly is the way we talk about the way we talk. Of course, it is reinforced by the visible and kinesthetic aspects of articulation. Logically, it would also be the way in which we perceive speech, and a minimal basis for identifying a signal as speech.

Now for the fourth and last point. If, on the other hand, Shankweiler is going in the right direction, if minimal units, not even phonemic, but of a phonetic nature characteristic of certain classes of phonemes, for example stop consonants vs. fricatives, are processed differentially by the receptive auditory mechanism, we have potential support, at least at the phonological level, for the Chomsky-McNeill hypothesis that the human organism is neurologically equipped to generate linguistic rules (McNeill, 1966). The support becomes powerful if the same processing skills can be demonstrated in children, and especially if they appear at the youngest ages testable. What about the facility, so remarkable when compared with adults, of young children to learn a foreign language? The same facility is demonstrated in the ability of children to echo faithfully a foreign utterance, including suprasegmental patterns, which they have never before heard or produced. One reason adults cannot echo so faithfully may be their lack of experience in production. What can we say about children? Either they do not function in the same manner, that is they do not require experience in production, or have had it in their early sound play, or are not as restricted as adults by the phonological system of their native language. In any case the child, or adult, can process as speech a meaningless or incomprehensible signal. If the child is using a physiological model for his perception and subsequent reproduction of a strange stimulus, he is reaching far back into his babbling repertoire for that physiological experience. This is, of course, the population who should also serve as subjects in dichotic perceptual studies. The data they provide could shed light on where in the nervous system the decision is made about the nature of the acoustic input, on whether or not this decision is made as well by children as by adults, and whether or not children appear to use the same model for the perception of speech as adults.

REFERENCES

Boudreau, J. C., & Tsuchitani, C. Binaural interaction in the cat superior olive S segment. Presentation at the 74th meeting, Acoustical Society of America, November, 1967.

Galambos, R. Neuroanatomy and physiology of the auditory system. Short course at the 42nd annual convention, American Speech & Hearing Association, November, 1966.

Kimura, D. Cerebral dominance and the perception of verbal stimuli. *Canadian Journal of Psychology*, 1961, 15, 166-71.

Kimura, D. Left-right differences in the perception of melodies. *Quarterly Journal of Experimental Psychology*, 1964, 14, 355-58.

Liberman, A. M., Cooper, F. S., Harris, K. S., MacNeilage, P. F., & Studdert-Kennedy, M. Some observations on a model for speech perception. *Proceedings of the AFCRL Symposium: Models for the Perception of Speech & Visual Form,* Boston, (November, 1964.)

Liberman, A. M., Cooper, F. S., Shankweiler, D. P., & Studdert-Kennedy, M. Perception of the speech code. *Psychological Review,* 1967, 74, 431-61.

McNeill, D. Developmental psycholinguistics. In Smith & Miller (ed.) *The genesis of language.* Cambridge, Mass.: MIT Press, 1966. Pp. 15-84.

Milner, B. Psychological defects produced by temporal lobe excision. *Publications of the Association of Research on Nervous and Mental Disease,* 1958, 36, 244-57.

Rosenzweig, M. R. Representations of the two ears at the auditory cortex. *American Journal of Physiology,* 1951, 62, 147-58.

Stevens, K. N. Toward a model for speech recognition. *Journal of the Acoustical Society of America,* 1960, 32, 47-55.

8

CHILDREN'S LANGUAGE DEVELOPMENT AND ARTICULATORY BREAKDOWN[1]

KATHERINE S. HARRIS

Haskins Laboratories

Since speech production and perception appear to be almost exclusively human capacities, we are somewhat limited in our ability to examine their several substrata experimentally. Consequently, it has been common practice to try to discover the function of various parts of the system by examining pathological cases. These studies can be divided into two rough classes which we might call disability-oriented and normal function-oriented. Some workers are interested in diagnosis, prognosis and treatment problems; others are interested in what the study of the abnormal can tell us about normal language function. For some reason, although

[1]The work I have discussed here has been generously supported by the National Institute of Dental Research. The experimental work has been done in collaboration with Donald Shankweiler and Dorothy Huntington, and has been much more completely reported in the papers cited.

there have been studies of general language function which fall into both classes, studies of pathological phoneme production are generally directed towards treatment. We might be able to gain considerable insight into the function of various parts of the nervous system in controlling articulation, if we used clinical material on damage at different levels and sites in the sensorimotor system. This would be a large undertaking; in this paper we will only discuss some preliminary results on a special population, in particular, disordered articulation in patients with cortical damage, and, for comparison, in a population of patients with profound sensori-neural hearing loss.

Let us begin by positing a simple hypothesis about the nature of the phonemic disintegration which occurs when there is injury to some part of the nervous system responsible for phoneme production. Jakobson (1962) suggested that there is a hierarchy of difficulty in the sounds of speech; they appear in a regular order in the developing speech of the child, and that trauma causes the sounds to disappear in an order opposite to the order in which they first appeared.

There are a number of difficulties with this hypothesis, not the least of which is that we know little about children's language development. Furthermore, the original statements of the hypothesis are rather unspecific about what stage of language development is being discussed.

The usual textbook accounts (see, for example, Miller, 1951) of children's language development discuss it as divided into several stages: an early "cry" stage, followed by a "babble" stage, in which the variety of speech sounds supposedly increases rapidly until the child runs through a repertoire in which "all" speech sounds supposedly occur. At about one year, this stage is followed by the painful acquisition of words with a more limited repertoire, until, finally, the child at age three, four or five "correctly" produces words containing all sounds.

The simple textbook account is extremely difficult to verify. It is easy enough to make some acoustic measure of the developing speech of the child, but it is not clear what correspondence, if any, this form of transcription has to a phoneme transcription. Even for adult speech, there is no simple three-way-correspondence between the speaker's generation of a phoneme, some brief acoustic event and the linguist's transcription of a phoneme. The lack of correspondence can be demonstrated by trying to synthesize speech through abutting acoustic segments. This experiment has been shown by Harris (1953) to produce an unintelligible output. More sophisticated attempts to synthesize speech by rule have not been entirely satisfactory either. Even though a trained linguist can listen to a speaker and transcribe a string of phonemes, it is not entirely clear how he does it. Many engineers assume that the problem has been solved; for example, J. R. Pierce (1963) has written a very humorous article on the incorporation of a high-quality synthetic talker into complex human engineering systems. The problem, as he realizes, is that we know that humans talk and people listen, but it is not clear what they listen to. We cannot turn to a more "objective" technique which will be the equivalent of transcription. To make matters worse, the observer of a child's speech lacks the two advantages that the transcriber of adult speech possesses. First, he is making inferences about the speech gestures made in a vocal tract which is not only much smaller than an adult's, but may differ significantly from it in characteristics such as the relative size of the pharyngeal cavity. Apes differ from adult humans in this way (Lieberman, 1968), and infants may well be more like apes than like adults (Lieberman, Harris, and Wolff, 1968).

These shape differences, of course, will affect the acoustic output for a given speech gesture and may, therefore, confuse the listener. A second problem is that the field linguist can persuade his older informants to repeat a phoneme string, and to produce a contrasting string. This procedure is difficult with older children, and impossible with babies. Various workers in the children's speech areas have attempted to solve the problems in different ways—in some cases by ignoring their existence. Some representative approaches are indicated below.

One possible indication of the fact that a child "knows" a sound is that specially-trained observers consistently transcribe it in listening to his speech. This approach can be illustrated by referring to the work of Irwin and his various co-workers. Irwin was able to train observers to do a reasonably reliable job of transcribing the sounds of speech (Irwin, 1945), in that two of his listeners would transcribe the same string as containing the same sounds. The technique can also be used before the child is producing "real" words. However, the phonemes extracted by this method do not necessarily represent the same articulatory maneuvers that an adult makes in producing the "same" sound. For example, let us consider the "vowels" transcribed by Irwin, at various points in the developmental sequence (Irwin, 1948). He shows that in infants up to 5-6 months, the vowels transcribed are overwhelmingly ɪ, ɛ, and æ. His generalization from this is that front vowels appear before back vowels. However, it is well known from general acoustic theory that the form and frequencies of the vowels will depend on the overall length of the vocal tract. (See, for example, Stevens and House, 1961). The listener may be transcribing as fronted vowels those which are in fact produced with the tongue in middle position, because his ear has not compensated adequately for the difference in tract size in infants. Obviously, this point can only be checked by instrumental means, coupled with some precise data on infant vocal tract size.

A second approach can be used only if the child will repetitively produce "real" words on an elicitation procedure of some sort, as in the work of Templin (1957) or Morley (1957). The elicitation may be by pictures, or by having the child repeat the word after a model. Since the observer "knows" the target word, he can transcribe the produced phoneme string as containing, or not containing, the required sequence. To return to vowels, the child would only be considered to have learned the extreme front vowel, / i /, if it occurred in those words for which it occurs in adults. This is a much more stringent criterion than Irwin's and will yield data which show phoneme appearances much later in development, and not necessarily in the same order.

A third approach is an intermediate approach between the previous two. The sounds of speech are considered to be bundles of features. A child is considered as having or not having, a feature contrast or series of contrasts. Albright and Albright (1958), for example, describe a one-year-old child as having a five-vowel system. This means that there are five vowels which are contrastively used in words, but these five vowels are not necessarily the same as those of adults, in that they are produced by the same shaping of the vocal tract.

It is clear that these three techniques, because of the changes in criterion, will yield different results when we ask at what age a child "knows" a given phoneme. Furthermore, techniques one and three do not yield data on errors, whereas a technique like that of Templin, in which a word is elicited that can be compared with an adult production, will allow a classification of errors. Let us assume, for the moment, that we will consider only elicitation data on speech development. Do the sounds of speech appear in a child's speech in the reverse order to their disappearance in adult pathology? The technique used in the two studies we know of, our own (Shankweiler and Harris, 1966) and Fry's (1959), both involve having the patient repeat a standard list of utterances, a technique closely analogous to the techniques of Templin and Morley.

A first problem is whether or not the elicitation procedure itself will yield repeatable, reliable data. The Morley and Templin studies used similar procedures and apparently similar child populations. In general, the children produced a standard series of words, and these words were analyzed for phonemic content. Phonemes could then be scored on the relative percent correct in the population as a whole. We would expect the relative percents correct for the series of phonemes to be highly positively correlated from the two studies. In fact, the correlation, for consonants only, for percent correct by phoneme is only $r = +.43$, a rather low value. Of course, there are a number of obvious differences between the two studies. The words used, and the detailed elicitation procedures were different. The Morley children were English, the Templin children, American. However, if we believe that the data reflect a basic biological capacity, we would expect it to be stable from group to group. Fortunately, the Templin data allow us an opportunity to see if two groups are closely comparable under her procedure. She administered her test to a group of 3.5-year-olds and a group of 4-year-olds. The correlation between scores is $r = +.95$. It is possible, then, to obtain stable data; the low correlation between Templin's and Morley's results must be due to factors other than fundamental instability. However, we obviously need some extremely painstaking work in this area to find out what are the relevant variables.

We come now to a comparison of the child and dysarthric data. Of course, the suspicions we have of the stability of data from elicitation studies affect any conclusions we might draw about the relationship between the child data and any other. However, if we forge ahead, we can correlate the Templin child data with data from an experiment in which the subjects were brain-damaged and, consequently, had dysarthric speech. The nature of the subject population and the experimental procedure have been previously reported in greater detail (Shankweiler and Harris, 1966). The correlation between the percent correct performance for various phonemes in the two groups is $r = +.70$ if we compare it with the Templin study, or $r = +.78$ if we compare it with the Morley study. These are extremely substantial values, especially in view of the possible instability of the basic data.

Apparently, then, there is some substantial basis for the notion that some consonant sounds are more difficult than others and consequently more likely to deteriorate when the production system is damaged. However, a more careful examination of the production problems of the child and adult dysarthric population suggests that things are not this simple. Templin does not give detailed data on error classification, but does remark (p. 55):

> Whenever a sound element was not produced correctly, the inaccuracy was classified into the following categories: Omissions, defective sounds, and substitutions... For the sample as a whole, substitutions were approximately 10 times as frequent as omissions, and about 4.5 times as frequent as the use of defective sounds.

In our own listening to the dysarthric speakers, we forced a transcription — that is, we did not allow the "defective" category. However, one interpretation of the difference between "defective" and "substituted" sounds is one of reliability of transcription. Templin's listeners had apparently no trouble classifying a substantial portion of the errors as another standard sound. In our experiment, we tended to transcribe errors as long, frequently non-English strings, but these transcriptions were not reliable from one observer to another. This might mean that the category, "defective sounds," is some substantial order of magnitude larger for dysarthrics than children. This impression is confirmed by listening to the production tapes. The same sounds seem to give trouble for the two groups, but the nature of the error is different — the dysarthrics just do not sound like children who can't quite articulate yet.

The category of voicing errors is worth special comment and has already been noted by Fry (1959). Voicing errors are rare among children, according to Morley. Menyuk (1968), in a recently published study, concludes that the voicing distinction develops quite early. Voicing errors are common in adult dysarthrics, as shown in both our study and Fry's. Again, this point argues against a simple disintegration hypothesis.

Thus far, we have been considering only consonant sounds. However, it is our feeling that we would not come to very different conclusions if we had included vowels. Children make fewer vowel errors, and so do dysarthrics. Our conclusion would have to be that simple error data give modest support to Jakobson's hypothesis, but that the nature of the errors suggests that the lack of coordination in the dysarthric is not simply primitive, but different in kind from that of a child. It is interesting to compare this data with that from a group of deaf speakers (Huntington and Harris, 1968). If we assume that certain sounds are inherently "harder" than others, then we might suppose that harder sounds would be

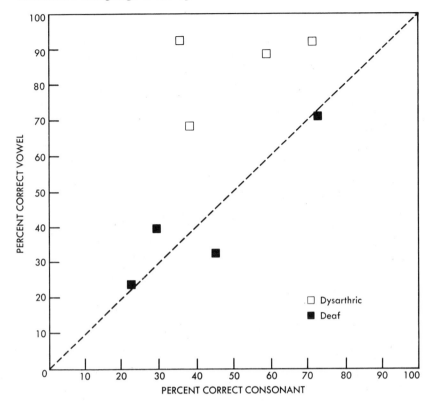

**FIGURE 1. Percentage of vowel and consonant errors in the deaf
and dysarthric groups.**

harder to teach and that, consequently, deaf speakers would have
trouble with the same sounds that are hard for children. Again,
we compared deaf speakers with Templin's and with Morley's
children. The correlations for order of difficulty of consonants are
+.58 and +.20, respectively, which are not as high as the child to
dysarthric correlation, but still suggest that some of the same problems are involved. However, again we find that the nature of the
errors is different. Voicing control is difficult for deaf speakers, as
has been known since the classic study of Hudgins and Numbers
(1942).

However, the most notable difference between deaf speakers
and the other groups is in the prevalence of vowel errors. Figure 1

shows the relative percentage of vowel and consonant errors in the deaf and dysarthric groups. It is easy to see that deaf speakers have markedly more trouble with vowels. "Hard" and "easy" sounds are different for the two groups. Again, this seems to argue against a simple one-factor primitivisation hypothesis for articulatory breakdown.

I would like to conclude by summarizing the points I have tried to make in this somewhat discursive presentation. First, we can gain some insight into the complex problem of articulation control and development by carefully examining the cases of articulatory insufficiency.

The highly inadequate data presently available suggest that different pathologies lead to rather specific patterns of deficit, and that these patterns cannot really be considered to be like those of a child who does not yet articulate correctly. Furthermore, our account of the development of articulation in normal children is itself in need of considerable further study.

REFERENCES

Albright, R. W., & Albright, J. B. Application of descriptive linguistics to child language. *Journal of Speech and Hearing Research*, 1958, **3**, 257-61.

Fry, D. B. Phonemic substitutions in an aphasic patient. *Language and Speech*, 1959, **2**, 52-61.

Harris, C. M. A study of the building blocks in speech. *Journal of the Acoustical Society of America*, 1953, **25**, 962-69.

Hudgins, C. V., & Numbers, F. C. An investigation of the intelligibility of the speech of the deaf. *Genetic Psychology Monographs*, 1942, **25**, 289-392.

Huntington, D. A., Harris, K. S., & Sholes, G. N. An electromyographic study of consonant articulation in hearing-impaired and normal speakers. *Journal of Speech and Hearing Research*, 1968, **11**, 147-58.

Irwin, O. C. Reliability of infant speech sound data. *Journal of Speech Disorders*, 1945, **10**, 227-35.

Irwin, O. C. Infant speech: development of vowel sounds. *Journal of Speech and Hearing Disorders*, 1948, **13**, 31-34.

Jakobson, R. Kindersprache. In *Selected writings*. Netherlands: Mouton, 1962, 328-401.

Lieberman, P. Primate vocalization and human linguistic ability. *Journal of the Acoustical Society of America*, 1968, 44, 1574-84.

Lieberman, P., Harris, K. S., & Wolff, P. Newborn infant cry in relation to nonhuman primate vocalizations. *Journal of the Acoustical Society of America*, 1968, 44, 365 (A). Manuscript in preparation.

Menyuk, P. The role of distinctive features in children's acquisition of phonology. *Journal of Speech and Hearing Research*, 1968, 11, 138-46.

Miller, G. A. *Language and communication*, New York: McGraw-Hill, 1951.

Morley, M. E. *The development and disorders of speech in childhood*. Edinburgh and London, 1957.

Pierce, John R. The paper dragon: a tale of the time. *Physics Today*, 1963, 16, 45-50.

Shankweiler, D., & Harris, K. S. An experimental approach to the problem of articulation in aphasia. *Cortex*, 1966, 2, 277-92.

Stevens, K. N., & House, A. S. An acoustical theory of vowel production. *Journal of Speech and Hearing Research*, 1961, 4, 303-20.

Templin. M. C. *Certain language skills of children*. Minneapolis: University of Minnesota Press, 1957.

9

PERCEPTION OF PHONETIC SEGMENTS: EVIDENCE FROM PHONOLOGY, ACOUSTICS AND PSYCHOACOUSTICS[1]

KENNETH N. STEVENS

Research Laboratory of Electronics and Department of Electrical Engineering
Massachusetts Institute of Technology

One of the fundamental properties of language is that there exists a code whose elements, called the distinctive features, form the smallest units of language and from which meaningful entities are constructed. The code underlying a given utterance is sometimes viewed as a sequence of units or segments, each of which consists of a set of distinctive features. Evidence for the nature of this code comes largely from the studies of linguists, who have observed that in any language there are constraints governing the

[1]This work was supported in part by the U. S. Air Force Cambridge Research Laboratories, Office of Aerospace Research, Contract No. AF19 (628)-5661 and in part by the National Institutes of Health (Grant NB-04332-06).

set of features that can occur together in a segment and the patterns of sequences of elements that are allowed. A set of distinctive features that form the elements of the code is considered optimal if it is, in some sense, a minimal set, and if the rules governing the patterns of elements that can occur in a language are as simple and as compact as possible.

The underlying code for an utterance, consisting of a matrix of these features, is actualized as sound through the appropriate manipulations of the articulatory mechanism. The distinctive features are considered to have well-defined correlates in the domains of articulation, acoustics and perception. This view has been set forth by Jakobson, Fant, and Halle (1963), who have proposed an inventory of distinctive features appropriate for describing a large number of languages and have suggested the tentative articulatory and acoustical correlates of these features.

This paper will review the evidence that may help to strengthen the basis for this view of the speech process and may suggest procedures for delineating the inventory of features that play a role in language. There are two kinds of evidence. First, an examination of the relationship between articulation and sound provides an indication of the kinds of articulatory activity that are likely candidates for actualizing distinctive features. Evidence will be presented to suggest that from an examination of articulation and its relation to sound, one can conclude that certain acoustic attributes are more likely to be selected than others. Secondly, experiments on the perception of speech and speech-like sounds provide evidence for the existence, in the auditory mechanism, of property detectors sensitive to stimuli with particular acoustic attributes.

THE QUANTAL NATURE OF SPEECH PRODUCTION

In the generation of speech there are a number of structures that can be controlled to assume a variety of configurations, positions and movements. It is natural to assume that there are continuous ranges of these configurations or movements and that particular values of parameters within these ranges are selected for generating the sounds in a given language. The sound output is, of course, determined by these parameters that describe the articulatory shapes and movements. The sound signal can be described in terms of a number of different properties or attributes of the sound, such as formant frequencies, locations of gross spectral energy concentrations, and particular types of time variation of spectral or periodic characteristics of the signal. (See, for example, Fant, 1960.) As the articulatory parameters are modified the acoustic properties change, and one expects to obtain a set of more-or-less monotonic relations between articulatory parameters and acoustic attributes.

There appear to be a number of situations, however, for which these relations are far from being linear and monotonic. There are certain articulatory conditions for which a small change in some parameter describing the articulation gives rise to an apparently large change in the acoustic characteristics of the output; there are other conditions for which substantial perturbation of certain aspects of the articulation produces negligible changes in the characteristics of the acoustic signal.

The nature of the relationship between articulation and sound can be visualized in the manner shown in Figure 1. We suppose that some acoustic measurement can be made to provide an indication of the magnitude of a particular attribute of the signal, and we plot this measurement on the ordinate. On the abscissa is plotted the value of a parameter that specifies one aspect of the articulation. The graph shows regions (labeled I) in which, for a range of articulations, the acoustic signal essentially does not possess the attribute in question. Adjacent to these regions, there are relatively narrow ranges of the articulatory parameter (regions II) within which the acoustic characteristics charge abruptly. In region III, there is a substantial range of values of the articulatory parameter for which the signal possesses the particular acoustic attribute.

The articulatory parameter that is represented on the abscissa in Figure 1 can refer to a variety of aspects of articulation. It may, for example, represent the position of some articulatory structure, such as tongue height for vowels or positions of tongue tip along the hard palate. In some cases, it may be more appropriate to think of the articulatory parameter as representing degree of muscle activity in some structure. If muscle action causes a given structure to be displaced to a point where it encounters a barrier (e.g., tongue tip making contact with the hard palate, or adduction of vocal cords to a closed position), then continuously changing muscle activity will give rise to a discontinuous displacement. This discontinuity in displacement could be responsible for discontinuities in the properties of the acoustic signal of the type shown in Figure 1.

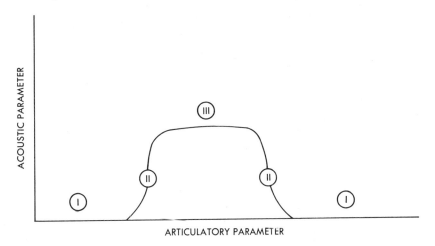

FIGURE 1. Schematized relation between an acoustic parameter of speech and a parameter describing some aspect of the articulation.

Regions I, II, and III are discussed in the text.

Support for this view of speech production stems in part from examination of the relationship between vocal-tract shapes and properties of the sound generated by these shapes. These relations can be derived using acoustical theories of sound generation and sound propagation in the vocal tract.

In order to illustrate these relations, let us consider the articulatory parameters corresponding to the place of articulation for vowels. Different vowels are, of course, produced by manipulating the tongue, lips and jaw to different positions, thus creating different shapes for the resonating air cavities between the vocal cords and the lips. Configurations corresponding to the vowels[2] /ɪɑu/, for example, are shown by the midsagittal tracings in Figure 2. The acoustic properties of these sounds can be calculated if the cross-sectional area at each point along the vocal tract between vocal cords and lips is known. In the case of the /ɑ/ configuration, for example, the midsagittal section shows that this cross-sectional area is narrow in the pharynx region and much wider in the region of the oral cavity. The vocal-tract shape can, in fact, be approximated by two uniform tubes connected together as shown in Fig-

---

[2]Examples of words that identify these vowel phonetic symbols are: / i / (beat), / a / (father), / u / (boot).

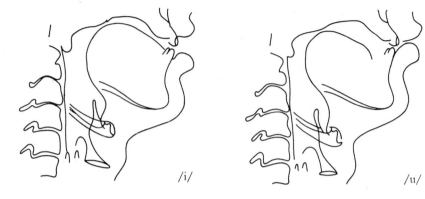

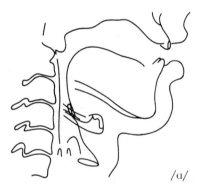

FIGURE 2. Tracings made from X-ray pictures of the vocal tract.
These tracings show the configuration of the vocal tract in the
midsagittal section for three vowels: /i/ upper left), /u/ (upper
right), and /a/ (lower left). The cervical vertebrae are at the left
of each picture, the lips are at the upper right, and the oval shape
at the lower end of the vocal tract indicates the position of the vocal
cords.

ure 3 — a narrow one, of cross-sectional area A_1, representing the
posterior portion of the vocal tract, and a wider one, of cross-
sectional area A_2, representing the anterior portion. Acoustical
theory shows that the resonant frequencies for this two-tube configuration are approximately equal to the resonances of each tube

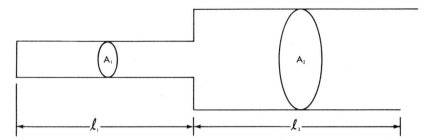

FIGURE 3. Two-tube approximation of vocal tract configuration for the vowel /a/.

separately, except that when the two individual resonant frequencies are about equal, the frequencies for the combined system are shifted slightly from these values. The lowest resonant frequency for a tube of length l cm, closed at one end and open at the other, is approximately the quarter-wavelength "organ-pipe" resonance, and is given by $f = 8500/l$ cps.

Consider now how the resonant frequencies of the two-tube resonator change as the lengths l_1 and l_2 are changed in such a way as to keep the total length $l_1 + l_2$ constant. Such a perturbation of the idealized configuration of Figure 3 would correspond roughly to a raising or lowering of the tongue body in the / a / configuration shown in Figure 2. The calculated frequencies F_1 and F_2 of the lowest two resonances, plotted as a function of the length l_1 of the posterior tube, are shown in Figure 4. A total length of about 17 cm., corresponding to the vocal-tract length of an average male talker, is assumed. We observe that there is a range of values for l_1 of about 2 cm., centered on 8.5 cm. (where $l_1 = l_2$), where F_1 reaches a maximum and F_2 a minimum, and within which the two frequencies do not change appreciably. Within this region the acoustic resonances are relatively insensitive to a perturbation of the length l_1 (and hence to a perturbation of tongue height in the actual / a / configuration). Outside of this region, the resonant frequencies become much more sensitive to perturbations in the vocal-tract shape.

Similar arguments can be used to show that the vocal-tract configurations corresponding to / i / and / u / in Figure 2 are also in regions where perturbations in tongue position give rise to relatively small changes in the resonances of the system and hence to small modifications of the properties of the sound output. These vowel

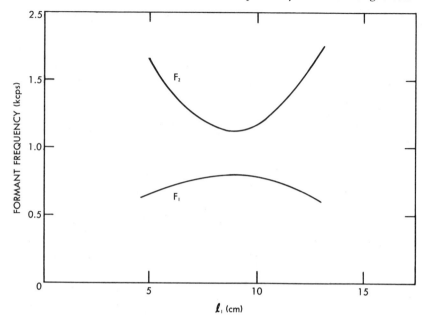

FIGURE 4. Example of relation between frequencies of first and second formants (F_1 and F_2) and the length, 1_1, of the back tube of the two tube resonator in Figure 3.

For this example, the areas A_1 and A_2 in Figure 3 are, respectively, 0.2 and 3.0 cm², and the overall length of the tube in 17 cm.

configurations are, therefore, optimal in some sense, since the requirements on the precision with which they need to be actualized are not severe. One would expect these configurations to occur frequently in the vowel systems of different languages, and, indeed, this is the case. Configurations corresponding to other vowels can also be shown to have characteristics of the type described above for / ɑ /, although the regions of minimum sensitivity to vocal-tract shape are not always so sharply defined.

The kind of analysis that has been described for vowels can also be used to examine a number of aspects of vocal-tract activity other than place of articulation for vowels. Some of these aspects have been discussed elsewhere (Stevens, 1969), and will only be reviewed briefly here.

One fairly obvious example of an articulatory parameter that gives rise to this discontinuous type of acoustic output is the degree of vocal-tract constriction in the oral cavity. At first sight this might appear to be a relatively continuous parameter with monotonically and smoothly changing acoustic correlates. As we change the degree of constriction, however, theoretical acoustical considerations suggest that there are at least four quantal steps corresponding to (1) low and mid vowels, (2) high vowels and sonorant consonants, (3) fricatives, and (4) stops. Each of these steps has its own distinctive acoustic characteristics.[3] Low and mid vowels are characterized by a relatively high first-formant frequency and by relatively more energy in the mid- or high-frequency range than other sonorants. The acoustic correlate of high vowels and sonorant consonants is a low first formant at a rather stable position. Fricative consonants have the distinguishing characteristic of continuous turbulence noise, whereas stop consonants exhibit a silent interval during closure. There appear to be sharp transitions from one of these regions to the next as the size of the vocal-tract constriction in the oral cavity is gradually decreased by raising the tongue.

Within each of these degrees of constriction there are, of course, parameters other than degree of constriction which can be manipulated to generate additional categories of phonetic segments. The possibility of categories within the class of low and mid vowels / ɑ / is a low vowel), and within the class of high vowels (/ i/ and / u /), has already been noted.

Various categories can also be observed for stop consonants, depending upon how the vocal cords are maneuvered. The vocal cords can be positioned closely together, in a configuration that is normally appropriate for voicing, or they can be positioned relatively far apart, the abducted configuration being a consequence of separation of the arytenoid cartilages and of the positive pressure in the glottis. Immediately following release of the closure in the vocal tract, the characteristics of the sound output will be quite different depending upon the vocal-cord configuration just prior to release. In the case of a voiced consonant, for which the vocal cords remain in an adducted position, the vocal cords begin vibrating immediately after release of the consonant, except for a brief interval of frication noise that may occur for some consonants. For a voiceless consonant, the adducting maneuver of the open vocal cords appears to be initiated immediately after release (possibly to changes in articulation. The existence of a relationship of this triggered by the pressure release in the glottis). During this

---

[3]These characteristics are discussed in more detail elsewhere. See, for example, Jakobson, Fant, and Halle (1963), and Stevens (1959).

relatively sluggish maneuver, there is an interval of aspiration noise. Thus, there are two distinctively different acoustic outputs corresponding to two extreme vocal-cord adjustments during stop consonants.[4]

As a final example of the inherent categorial nature of speech sounds, consider the articulatory parameters that govern the place of articulation for consonants. Consonants are, of course, generated with a narrow vocal-tract constriction. If a constriction is imagined to assume various positions along the vowel tract, one can predict, on a theoretical basis, quantal changes in the attributes of the sound output (Stevens, 1969). Acoustic analysis of different consonants verifies that this is the case.

A labial articulation, which corresponds to a constriction at the front of the vocal tract, gives rise to weak spectral energy at all frequencies. The transition from a labial consonant into the following vowel is characterized by energy peaks or formants that rise in frequency. Several centimeters back in the vocal tract there is a range of constriction positions which give rise to a major spectral energy concentration in the mid-frequency region. These are the velar consonants — / k / and / g / in English — which are made by raising the tongue body to the roof of the mouth. The mid-frequency energy burst for / k / and / g / splits into a pair of formants (the second and third) during the transition into the following vowel. A third class of consonants is made with a constriction between that for the labials and velars. The tongue tip or blade must be raised to form this constriction. The distinctive acoustic characteristic for this class of sounds is a high-frequency spectral energy concentration, followed by energy peaks that fall in frequency during the transitions into the following vowel. This place of articulation, as well as the velar place of articulation, gives rise to acoustic outputs whose major properties are not too sensitive to perturbations or inaccuracies in locating the constriction position during speech production.

These examples demonstrate that there are ranges of values of articulatory parameters for which the sound output has distinctive attributes that are relatively insensitive to perturbations in these parameters. These ranges are bounded by regions of articulation within which the properties of the sound output are sensitive type between articulation and sound output has certain implica-

---

[4]The categorial nature of these acoustic manifestations of stop consonants has been discussed in detail by Lisker and Abramson (1964).

tions for the inventory of articulatory and acoustic properties that are used as codes for signaling linguistic information. An acoustic property that is a suitable candidate for such a code is presumably one that can be generated by the articulatory apparatus without requiring precise positioning or maneuvering of the articulatory structures, as in region III of Figure 1. We would like to propose, as a working hypothesis, that many if not all of the features that form the smallest units of the language code have articulatory and acoustic correlates of this type. In fact, it is not unreasonable to suggest that a necessary condition for the existence of a distinctive feature in the phonological component of language is that the articulatory parameters involved in actualizing a segment with this feature and the attributes of the acoustic output are related in the way we have indicated.

PERCEPTION AT THE PHONOLOGICAL LEVEL

The hypothesis that distinctive features have their roots in quantal relations of the type discussed above cannot be based solely on properties of the speech production mechanism without reference to the auditory perception process. If an acoustic attribute is to have relevance as the acoustic correlate of a feature, then the auditory mechanism must respond to this attribute in a way that places it in an appropriate category distinct from the category associated with the auditory response to some other feature. We are suggesting, in effect, that the auditory mechanism must be endowed with "property detectors," each of which responds to an acoustic attribute corresponding to a feature of language. The characteristic of a property detector is that it yields a response when the acoustic signal has an appropriate attribute, but there is sharp reduction in response when the signal does not possess this attribute.

The attribute to which a property detector responds is not necessarily the absolute value of a simple physical entity such as the frequency of a spectral peak or the amplitude of some component of the signal. Rather, the attribute will generally correspond to a more complex pattern of events in time and frequency, such as a set of spectral peaks with the proper relative frequencies, a rising or falling spectral peak, or some other sequence of sounds with different spectral and temporal structure.

There is some evidence for the existence of such property detectors from psychoacoustic experiments and from data on electrophysiological responses measured in the auditory system. The evidence from electrophysiological experiments shows that there are units in the auditory cortex and in the inferior colliculus that respond to tones that are rising in frequency and other units that respond to falling tones (Whitfield and Evans, 1965; Nelson, Erulkar, and Bryan, 1966). It is a big step to connect these results of electrophysiology to the perception of acoustic properties relating to formant transitions and other spectral energy shifts in speech, but it is tempting to speculate that this connection may ultimately be found.

Psychoacoustic experiments provide data of a different kind in support of the hypothesis that there are "quantal" types of responses of the auditory mechanism to speech sounds. One type of psychoacoustic study examines the perception of stimulus items that constitute a series of speechlike sounds arranged along a physical continuum. Data from these experiments indicate that, for certain kinds of acoustic continua, there is not a monotonic relation between changes in the acoustic parameters of the sound and changes in the perception. (See, for example, the discussion in Liberman, Cooper, Shankweiler, and Studdert-Kennedy, 1967.) For these stimuli there are some ranges of the acoustic parameters in which perturbations in the stimuli are difficult to discriminate and the subjective distance between stimuli is small. There are other ranges in which small perturbations in the stimuli can be discriminated more readily, and adjacent items in the stimulus continuum are judged to be quite different.

In experiments designed to examine effects of this type, the stimuli are usually generated by means of a speech synthesizer, in which the characteristics of a given stimulus are determined by manipulating a number of parameters that control particular components within the synthesizer. A series of stimuli arranged along a continuum is assembled by producing synthesizer outputs corresponding to a sequence of values of one or more of the parameters. Some experiments have also been carried out by using real speech as the stimulus material and modifying or manipulating the recorded signal in various ways, usually through tape-splicing techniques or their equivalent.

One example of a stimulus series that has been examined in some detail is derived from a continuum obtained by manipulating the formant transitions at the onset of a vowel, such that each stimulus has the properties of a syllable consisting of a voiced stop consonant

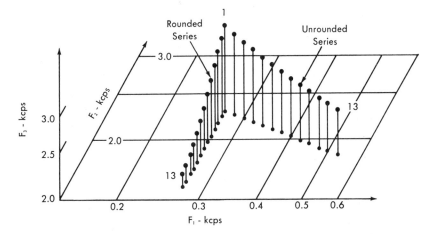

FIGURE 5. Arrangement of the stimuli in a rounded and unrounded vowel series used in a discrimination test.

The values of the first three formant frequencies are plotted on the three axes. Each point at the end of a vertical line indicates the first three formant frequencies for one of the stimulus items. The rounded series and the unrounded series each consists of 13 items; stimulus number 1 is the same in both series. (From Stevens, Liberman, Studdert-Kennedy, and Öhman, 1968).

followed by a vowel (Liberman, Harris, Hoffman and Griffith, 1957). If the stimuli in the series are arranged so that the starting point of the second-formant transition is at a relatively low frequency in the first stimulus and assumes gradually higher values in succeeding stimuli in the series, then listeners identify the initial consonant in the first few stimuli as / b/, the next few as / d /, and the ones with a high second-formant onset as / g /.[5] If stimuli in this series are arranged in the form of an ABX discrimination test, the resulting discrimination functions indicate that there are certain ranges of the stimulus in which discrimination between adjacent items in the series is poor, and these are bounded by regions where adjacent stimuli are discriminated fairly well. Identification experiments indicate that phonemes are placed in regions where discrimination is poor. Even casual listening to items in such a stimulus series indicates that there are large differences in the subjective distance between adjacent items depending upon where

---

[5]The formant starting frequencies corresponding to these consonants depend to some extent on the following vowel. The result described here would apply if the following vowel were a front vowel such as / ε / or / æ /.

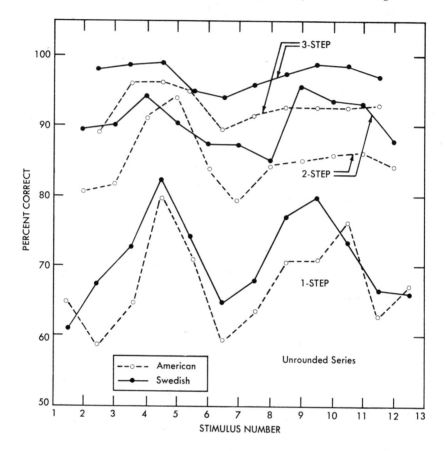

FIGURE 6. (a) Discrimination functions for the unrounded vowels for Swedish and American English listeners.

Each point represents the percent of items correct in an ABX discrimination test. Data are given for stimulus pairs spaced one, two

these items are located in the series. Within regions in which discrimination is poor and stimuli are identified as one phoneme, the subjective distance between stimuli is small. In the vicinity of phoneme boundaries, where discrimination is good, the subjective distance between adjacent items in the series is large. Whether these attributes of perception are a consequence of learning or whether they are part of a child's innately given perceptual apparatus is a question that has not yet been resolved.

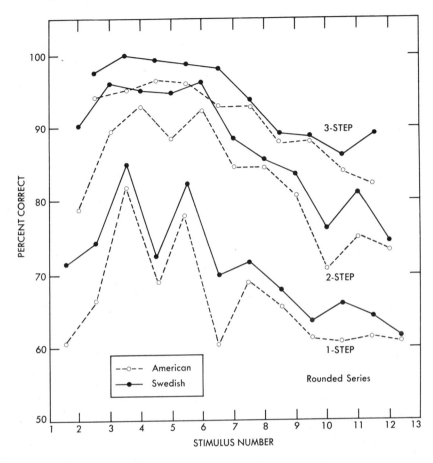

(b) Discrimination functions for the rounded vowels for the Swedish and American English listeners.

and three steps along the thirteen-point continua shown in Figure 5. (From Stevens, Liberman, Studdert-Kennedy, and Ohman, 1968.)

Similar but less pronounced effects have been observed in series of vowel stimuli constructed by interpolating between the formant frequencies corresponding to nominal values for standard vowels (Stevens, Liberman, Studdert-Kennedy and Öhman, 1968). Identification and discrimination functions were obtained for two series of synthetic vowels. One series consisted of a sequence of isolated unrounded vowels covering the range from / i / through / ɪ / to / ɛ /

in American English. The other series, consisting of isolated
rounded vowels, extend from / i / through / y / to / ʉ /. The last
two vowels are phonemic in Swedish and in some other languages
but not in English. Figure 5 shows the frequencies of the first three
formants for each of the stimuli in the two 13-item series of vowels.

Discrimination functions for these two sets of vowel stimuli for
listeners with two different language backgrounds were obtained by
using an ABX procedure. The results are shown in Figure 6. Data
were obtained for stimulus pairs that were spaced one, two and
three steps along the 13-point continuum. We observe, first, that
the curves for the two groups of listeners are similar in form (with
the possible exception of the two-step data for the unrounded
vowels), suggesting that the ability of listeners to discriminate
small changes in vowel quality is independent of their experience
in identifying the vowels. More relevant to this discussion is the
fact that there are peaks and valleys in the discrimination functions, indicating that discrimination is poorer in some vowel regions
than in others. In this case, the valleys in the discrimination functions correspond to centers of phoneme regions that have been
determined from identification experiments with the same stimuli.
Thus, for example, listeners were able to discriminate only poorly
between items 1 and 2 or between items 2 and 3 on the unrounded
series (63 percent of ABX responses were correct, on the average),
while discrimination between stimuli 4 and 5 was much better (81
percent correct). Listeners identified items 1 and 2 as the vowel
/ i /, whereas items 4 and 5 were in a region between two vowel
categories for both the Swedish listeners and the American listeners (although the precise location of the boundary was slightly
different for the two languages and for different speakers within a
language). Similarly, discrimination was poor between stimuli 1
and 2 on the rounded series but was much better between stimuli
3 and 4, for both the Swedish listeners who were familiar with
these vowels and the American listeners who presumably were not.
It is reasonable to suppose, then, that the subjective distance between some pairs of stimuli is less than between other pairs, even
though the physical distance between pairs of stimuli is equal in
some sense.

Discrimination functions have also been obtained for vowels syn-
thesized in a syllable frame (Stevens, 1968). The stimulus continuum in this case encompassed the vowels / i /, / ɪ / and / ɛ /,
and the initial and final consonants were / b / and / l /, respectively. Peaks and valleys in discrimination functions for these

stimuli were somewhat more pronounced than for vowels in iso-lation. Evidence toward the tendency for a series of vowel-like stimuli to be perceived in a non-continuous fashion has also been reported by Chistovich, Fant, de Serpa-Leitão and Tjernlund (1966).

These and other examples provide evidence that perception tends to be categorical for acoustic continua constructed by inter-polating between the acoustic characteristics of minimally sepa-rated pairs of phonetic items, particularly when the stimulus items are in a dynamic speech context. Within a given category, pertur-bations of the acoustic properties of the signal give rise to only small changes in the perception. When the stimulus is near the boundary between two categories, small perturbations of the stimulus characteristics cause large changes in the perception. We can conclude, therefore, that there is some evidence for the exis-tence, within the auditory system, of property detectors that pro-vide a response when the characteristics of a complex stimulus are within a certain range, but show a sharp reduction in response when the stimulus characteristics lie outside that range. The evi-dence would suggest that such property detectors are matched to the property-generating capabilities of the articulatory mechanism, and that the common acoustic properties correspond to features of language.

EFFECT OF CONTEXT ON SPEECH PRODUCTION AND PERCEPTION

The above discussion implies a rather idealized view of the speech production and perception processes. This view asserts that there are well-defined quantal acoustic attributes arising from specific ranges of articulatory configurations or maneuvers. An utterance consists of a sequence of units or segments, each of which is characterized by a bundle of these attributes or features. When a speech signal is received by a listener, the implication is that several property detectors are actuated, corresponding to the features comprising each segment, and the outputs of these prop-erty detectors provide a decoded version of the signal that is sub-jected to further processing at higher levels.

This model of the mechanisms of speech production and percep-tion may have some validity, but analysis of speech events at the articulatory and acoustic levels reveals that such a view is greatly oversimplified and cannot be interpreted literally. When a phonetic segment is generated in the context of a word or in a larger linguistic unit, the individual distinctive features are not necessarily actualized in the clear, unadulterated form implied by the above discussion. Certain acoustic attributes that underlie a given distinctive feature may be considerably distorted or even missing from the acoustic signal. In the place of these attributes there may be some vague acoustic marker that does not have the characteristics of the basic feature but which must, in some manner, be decoded or transformed by the listener in order to uncover the feature. The listener most certainly will be required to resort to higher-level information, such as constraints imposed by the phonological rules of the language, the lexicon, and syntactic and semantic rules, in order to decode the signal.

If the distinctive features have no clear-cut invariant correlates that are independent of context in running speech, what then is their role in language? They have the important function of providing a framework that underlies the production and perception of speech. They specify a set of ideal targets or goals which may not always be achieved during normal speech, but which govern the actualization of speech in the vocal mechanism and in terms of which speech is decoded by a listener. When a feature occurs in the context of other features, whether these features are in the same segment or in adjacent segments, the acoustic manifestation of the feature may be modified, particularly in rapid speech or speech that has been distorted in some way. The modifications presumably occur as a consequence of the dynamic properties of the speech-generating mechanism. The basic acoustic attribute that defines the feature is obscured, and there remain only some secondary characteristics which identify the feature, and which depend upon the particular context in which the feature appears. It might be expected that these secondary characteristics are not decoded by a listener through transformation by some property-detecting mechanism, but are interpreted by some process that requires the listener to learn the modifications that the speech mechanism imposes on the ideal acoustic attributes. One possible mechanism that has been suggested is an analysis-by-synthesis scheme (Halle and Stevens, 1962).

An example of a modification of a feature by context is the feature *voiced* as it occurs in the context of the feature *noncontinuant*, i.e., the acoustic manifestation of voicing in stop consonants. The underlying acoustic attribute of voicing is the existence of periodicities due to vocal-cord vibration. In the case of a stop consonant in English, however, vocal-cord vibration may not occur in the stop gap, and other secondary acoustic characteristics must be utilized by a listener in order to identify whether or not the segment is voiced. These characteristics are, of course, the presence of aspiration noise following the consonantal release, and the attendant delay in onset of voicing. Other examples include the modification of vowels by consonantal context (Lindblom and Studdert-Kennedy, 1967), and changes in temporal and spectral characteristics of consonants in post-stressed position.

SUMMARY

1. Examination of the relationships between articulatory configurations and the properties of the resulting acoustic signal suggest that there are, so to speak, preferred ranges of articulatory gestures. This range of articulation gives rise to acoustic outputs with attributes or properties that are distinctively different from the outputs for other articulatory gestures; within this range of articulation the acoustic properties are relatively insensitive to perturbations in articulation. It might be asserted that the human articulatory mechanism is endowed with a set of "property generators," i.e., has the capability of generating outputs with well-defined properties.

2. Experiments on the perception of speech and speechlike sounds indicate that the auditory mechanism responds selectively to acoustic stimuli that possess specific attributes. When a stimulus is perturbed in a way that moves it outside the region encompassed by a given attribute, there is a sharp change in the perception of the stimulus. These experimental findings suggest that the human auditory mechanism is endowed with a set of "property detectors."

3. An attribute that is matched to the property-generating capabilities of the articulatory mechanism and to the property-detecting capabilities of the auditory mechanism is, in some sense, optimal as a building block which forms an element of the language code. Such a building block is often called a distinctive feature of language.

4. During natural speech, in which a given distinctive feature may occur in various contexts, its ideal acoustic attributes may be modified, and a listener must utilize secondary cues and higher-level information to decode the signal in terms of the underlying features.

REFERENCES

Chistovich, L., Fant, G., De Serpa-Leitão, A., & Tjernlund, P. Mimicking of synthetic vowels. *Quarterly Progress and Status Report No. 2,* Speech Transmission Laboratory, Royal Institute of Technology, Stockholm, 1966, 1-18. Also Chistovich, L. Fant, G., & De Serpa-Leitão, A. Mimicking and perception of synthetic vowels, Part II. *Quarterly Progress and Status Report No. 3,* Speech Transmission Laboratory, Royal Institute of Technology, Stockholm, 1966, 1-3.

Fant, C. G. M. *Acoustic theory of speech production.* The Hague: Mouton, 1960.

Halle, M. & Stevens, K. N. Speech recognition: A model and a program for research. *IRE Trans. Info. Theory,* 1962, *IT-8,* 155-59. Also appears in J. A. Fodor and J. J. Katz (ed.), *The structure of language.* Englewood Cliffs, N.J.: Prentice-Hall, 1964, 604-12.

Jakobson, R., Fant, C. G. M., & Halle, M. *Preliminaries to speech analysis.* Cambridge, Mass.: M. I. T. Press, 1963.

Liberman, A. M., Cooper, F. S., Shankweiler, D. P., & Studdert-Kennedy, M. Perception of the speech code. *Psychological review,* 1967, **74,** 431-61.

Liberman, A. M., Harris, K. S., Hoffman, H. S., & Griffith, B. C. The discrimination of speech sounds within and across phoneme boundaries. *Journal of Experimental Psychology,* 1957, **54,** 358-68.

Lindblom, B. E. F. & Studdert-Kennedy, M. On the role of formant transitions in vowel recognition. *Journal of the Acoustical Society of America,* 1967, **42,** 830-43.

Lisker, L. & Abramson, A. S. A cross-language study of voicing in initial stops: acoustical measurement. *Word,* 1964, **20,** 384-422.

Nelson, P. G., Erulkar, S. D., & Bryan, J. S. Responses of units of the inferior colliculus to time-varying acoustic stimuli. *Journal of Neurophysiology,* 1966, **29,** 834-60.

Stevens, K. N. On the relations between speech movements and speech perception. *Zeitschrift fur Phonetik, Sprachwissenschaft und Kommunikationsforschung,* 1968, **21,** 102-06.

Stevens, K. N. The quantal nature of speech: Evidence from articulatory-acoustic data. In E. E. David, Jr. and P. B. Denes (ed.), *Human communication: a unified view.* New York: McGraw-Hill, 1969. (In press.)

Stevens, K. N., Liberman, A. M., Studdert-Kennedy, M., & Ohman, S. Crosslanguage study of vowel perception. *Language and Speech,* 1968, **12**, 1-23.

Whitfield, I. C. & Evans, E. F. Responses of auditory cortical neurons to stimuli of changing frequency. *Journal of Neurophysiology,* 1965, **28**, 655-72.

SOME COMMENTS ON THE DEVELOPMENTAL ASPECTS OF VOICING IN STOP CONSONANTS

MALCOLM S. PRESTON

The John F. Kennedy Institute for Habilitation of the Mentally and Physically Handicapped Child

I would like to raise two points in reference to the Stevens paper. The first point concerns the discussion of the way in which voicing may differentiate the stop consonants. The second concerns itself with the role of language development as it is related to the perception and production of phonetic segments. In this connection, I would like to discuss the results of some recent research we have conducted at The Johns Hopkins University and at Haskins Laboratories.

Stevens presents convincing evidence that there are ranges of values assumed by articulatory parameters within which the acoustic output has unique properties that are not present outside of the ranges. He suggests that these acoustic properties might be suitable candidates for signalling linguistic information by triggering "property detectors" within the auditory mechanism. It is Stevens' hypothesis that virtually all of the phonetic features of language have articulatory and acoustic correlates of this type.

Stevens goes on to point out that under certain conditions the basic acoustic attribute that triggers a "property detector" may not be present. In this case, a secondary characteristic may activate the detection mechanism. The example offered is the feature *voiced* as it occurs in stop consonants. The occurrence of periodicities in vocal cord vibrations is the underlying acoustic attribute. For stops in initial position, however, voicing may not occur during the period of occlusion and, in many cases, does not commence until after the consonantal release. In this case, the presence of aspiration noise following release and the attendant delay in the voicing may serve as secondary characteristics activating the voicing detector.

I would like to bring to your attention the work of researchers at Haskins Laboratories which provides a slightly different approach to this problem (Abramson & Lisker, 1965; Lisker & Abramson, 1964). In several studies involving both acoustic analysis of natural speech sounds and perceptual experiments with synthetic speech, these researchers found that the time interval between the release of air pressure and the onset of voicing is an effective measure for differentiating / b /, / d /, / g / from / p /, / t /, / k / when these phonemes occur in initial position. This time interval is called *voice onset time* or VOT. For the stops / b /, / d /, / g / voicing may start simultaneously with the release of air pressure (0 VOT) or may lag the release by as much as 30 msec. In some cases voicing may precede the release (referred to as voicing lead). On the other hand, for / p /, / t /, / k / voicing generally begins at least 35 msec after the release. Lags of 80 or 90 msec are not uncommon.

The results of this work, in my opinion, make clear the importance of a perceptual mechanism for timing two events. This mechanism apparently must be capable of sensing whether or not a given time interval exceeds a certain critical value. In any event, it must depend more on some internal criterion than on an invariant acoustic feature, since the acoustic patterns of the sounds it may differentiate probably do not differ grossly. For example, an apical stop with 20 msec voicing lag is not altogether different from an apical stop with 40 msec voicing lag. Yet, these two stops would clearly fall in different phonemic categories.

In summary, I am suggesting that voice onset time, rather than simple presence or absence of voicing, may be one of the more important cues distinguishing the voiced from the voiceless stops. In addition, I am suggesting that variations in an articulatory parameter such as timing in the onset of voicing in stop consonants, does not produce a radically different acoustic output when the delay in voicing is increased past the region of the phoneme boundary. I

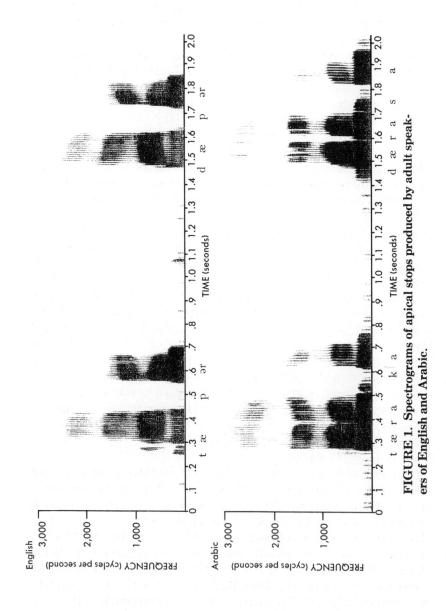

FIGURE 1. Spectrograms of apical stops produced by adult speakers of English and Arabic.

don't intend to suggest that the problems involved in the voiced-voiceless distinction are typical of the whole problem area of the perception of phonetic segments. Stevens' account makes a substantial effort toward linking some important aspects of articulation to perception.

My second point is not at all touched upon in the Stevens paper, but I think it raises an important issue. How does the young child acquire the ability to produce and perceive the basic sound units of language? Although some research has been done, this area has not been exhaustively investigated.

Our research has centered on the acquisition of the voiced-voiceless distinction in stop-consonants and has concentrated mainly on the productive aspects of this problem since the tools for its study were readily available. The work of Lisker and Abramson at Haskins has provided us with an effective acoustic measure (VOT) for differentiating / b / from / p /, / d / from / t /, and / g / from / k /. In a spectrographic study of the stop-consonants produced by speakers from eleven language communities, these researchers noted that three general ranges along the VOT continuum emerged when the frequency distributions for all eleven languages were combined: (i) 50-150 msec voicing preceding release of air pressure (lead); (ii) 0-30 msec voicing following release (short lag); and (iii) 50-110 msec voicing following release (long lag).

Figure 1 shows spectrograms of apical stops produced by adult speakers of English and Arabic and illustrates typical VOT values for the two languages. The VOT values for the two English words at the top are 50 msec voicing lag for "tapper" and 0 msec for "dapper." The two Arabic words at the bottom, "taraka" and "darasa", have VOT values of 15 msec voicing lag and 65 msec voicing lead respectively.

Figure 2 shows VOT distributions for speakers of English, from the work of Lisker and Abramson (1964). This figure, illustrating a point that I made earlier, shows that / b /, / d /, / g / fall mainly between 0 and 30 msec voicing lag while / p /, / t /, / k / fall between 40 and 100 msec voicing lag. Figure 3 shows distributions of data we have recently collected from adult speakers of Lebanese Arabic (Yeni-Komshian & Preston, 1967). This figure clearly indicates that incidence of voicing lead (30-150 msec) for / b /, / d /, and emphatic / d /. The other stops, / t /, emphatic / t /, / k /, and / q /, fall mainly between 0 and 50 msec voicing lag.

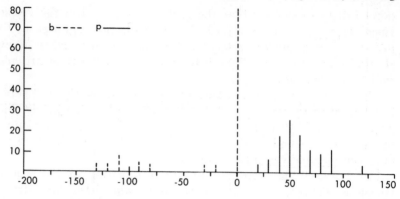

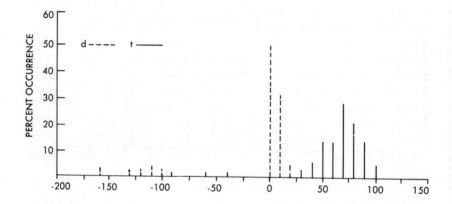

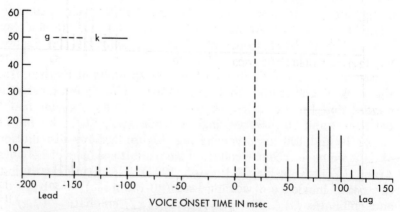

FIGURE 2. Words in isolation for adult speakers of English (from Lisker & Abramson, 1964, pp. 400-02).

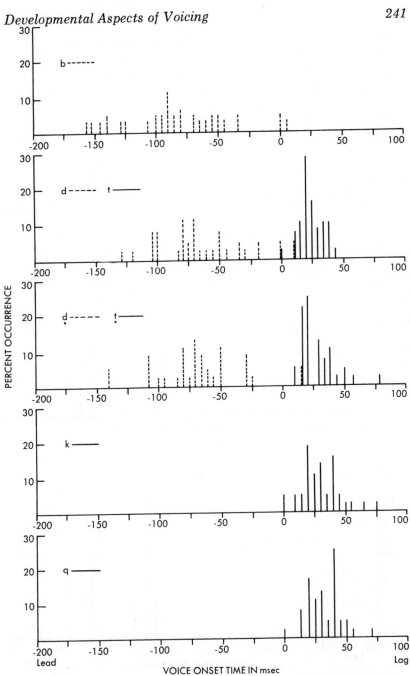

FIGURE 3. Words in isolation for adult speakers of Lebanese Arabic.

To summarize, in American English, the measurement of VOT can be used to distinguish / b / from / p /, / d / from / t /, and / g / from / k /. The voiced stops utilize the short lag position and to a lesser extent the lead position, while the voiceless stops utilize the long lag position. On the other hand, the Lebanese data demonstrate that Arabic makes use of the voicing lead and short voicing lag positions for distinguishing / d / from / t /, / d / utilizing voicing lead and / t / short voicing lag. The emphatic apicals, / d / and / t /, can be distinguished in the same fashion. In addition, Arabic / b / is generally produced with voicing lead, while the two back stops, / k / and / q /, utilize short voicing lag. Lebanese Arabic does not have / p / or / g /.

Since the language environment with respect to VOT differs for children from these two language communities, it seemed to us that a cross-language study of the stops occurring in the pre-linguistic vocalizations of these children might cast some light on this important feature of speech. We had several questions in mind:

1. When a child first produces enough stops in initial position to merit analysis, how will the stops distribute themselves along the continuum of voice onset time?
2. Will language environments which differ in the use of VOT produce correspondingly different VOT distributions in the pre-linguistic vocalizations of children raised in these environments?
3. If distributions characteristic of adult speakers are not found in the early vocalizations, when and in what fashion does the child approximate the adult model?

To answer these questions we have collected some longitudinal data from several Baltimore children covering roughly the chronological period between 52 and 104 weeks. In addition, we have collected some cross-sectional data from Lebanese Arabic children who were about twelve months old. The vocalizations of all these children were tape recorded over a period of about thirty minutes. The mother and sometimes an experimenter was present. The child was encouraged to vocalize as much as possible.

The procedure for analyzing this data involves a transcription of each session using a modified version of the *Peterson-Shoup* notation system. Following transcription, wide-band spectrograms are made of stops occurring in initial positions. A second experimenter then listens to all utterances for which measurable spectrograms

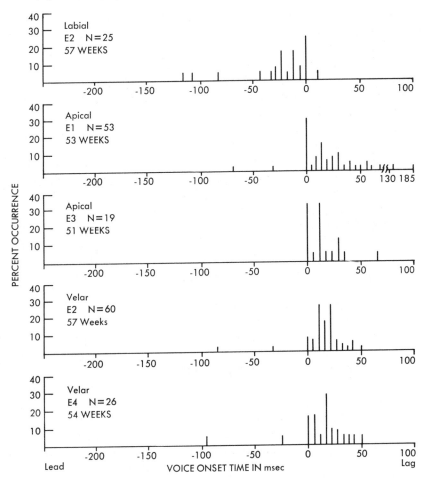

FIGURE 4. American children: normal hearing.

can be obtained and eliminates any questionable items. Thus, only the sounds which are classified as stops by both experimenters are included in the analysis. Measurements of VOT (to the nearest 5 msec) are taken by noting the time interval between the broadbanded vertical line representing release of air pressure and the first vertical striation representing glottal pulsation.

While the analysis of all these data is not yet completed, I would like to present some typical VOT distributions for the Baltimore and Lebanese children between 50 and 57 weeks of age and then

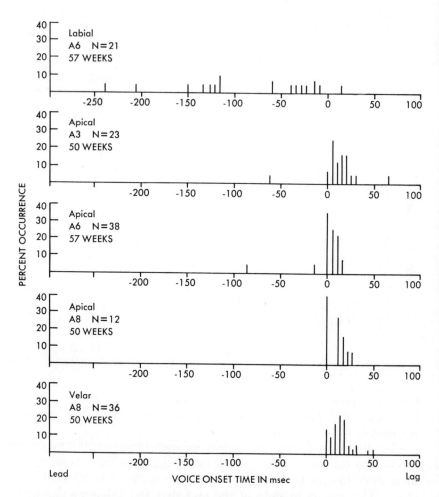

FIGURE 5. Lebanese children: normal hearing.

present some longitudinal data for one of the Baltimore children.
Figure 4 shows one labial, two apical, and two velar distributions
for the Baltimore children. In contrast to the bi-modal distributions seen for the adults, these distributions are generally uni-
modal. The distribution for labial stops shows a greater incidence
of voicing lead than that noted for adults. However, the distributions for the apical and velar stops closely match the adult models
for / d / and / g /.

Figure 5 shows one labial, three apical, and one velar VOT distribution for the Lebanese children. The velar distribution includes

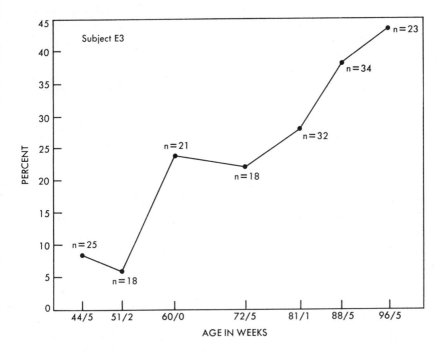

FIGURE 6. Percent apical stops with a lag of 30 msec or more.

both / k / and / q /. The distribution for labial stops shows voicing lead, while the distributions for apical and velar stops show voicing lag mainly between 0 and 30 msec.

The distributions for the Baltimore and Lebanese children are similar. In the apical stops which offers the most data, these children show uni-modal distributions falling in the 0 to 30 msec lag range. This occurs in spite of the fact that the Lebanese children had been exposed to apical stops with voicing lead while the Baltimore children had been exposed to apical stops with voicing lag between 40 and 100 msec or greater.

Figure 6 presents a graph of the percent increase of apical stops with a lag of 30 msec or more, i.e., the / t / range, as a function of age for one of the Baltimore children. Data has been analyzed for seven sessions spanning the period between 44 and 96 weeks of age. This figure suggests a gradual, perhaps linear, increase in the number of apicals with long lag as age increases. At 44 weeks very few long lag apicals occurred, but by 96 weeks almost half the apicals fell in this category. Of course, concomitant with the changes in Figure 6 is the general increase in communicative skills.

Thus, very few utterances at 44 weeks could be identified as words, but by 96 weeks speech and language development had progressed to recognizable words used in short sentences. Many of these words had initial stops that fell in the long lag range.

Our preliminary data suggest that productive capabilities are established for making the "voiced-voiceless distinction" between one and two years of age. At this point one might well ask how early in life a child can perceive a difference between / d / and / t /, utilizing, as adults do, the perceptually relevant cue VOT? In what way are perceptual capabilities related to productive capabilities? Does perception precede production? Can a child who produces only short lag stops perceive a difference between short lag and long lag stops? These are questions that we have begun to entertain as a result of our research on productive capabilities. Our plans for the coming year include some research that might help to answer these questions.

REFERENCES

Abramson, A. S. & Lisker, L. Voice onset time in stop consonants: Acoustic analysis and synthesis. *Proceedings of the 5th International Congress on Acoustics,* Liège, Belgium, 1965.

Lisker, L. & Abramson, A. S. A cross-language study of voicing in initial stops: Acoustical measurements. *Word,* 1964, **20**, 384-422.

Yeni-Komshian, Grace & Preston, M. S. A study of voicing in initial stop consonants: Lebanese Arabic. *Annual Report, Neurocommunications Laboratory,* Department of Psychiatry and Behavioral Sciences, The Johns Hopkins University School of Medicine, Baltimore, Maryland, 1967, 291-306.

10

GENERAL DISCUSSION OF THE CONFERENCE ON THE PERCEPTION OF LANGUAGE

JAMES DEESE

The Johns Hopkins University

Every conference has themes that are manifest and themes that are latent. The manifest themes are revealed in the title of the conference itself and in the titles of the individual papers. The latent themes are harder to detect but nonetheless real. I shall attempt to comment upon some of the latent themes I found in this conference, for I think that they reveal as much about the current state of the relationship between psychology and the linguistic sciences as the manifest themes. The latent themes I detected in this conference are (1) a lack of commitment to theory, (2) a reliance on particular specialized techniques as methods for defining particular scientific problems, (3) an emphasis upon language as a set of skills or competencies almost totally independent of other human skills and competencies. The general remarks that follow will comment upon each of these themes.

THE PLACE OF THEORY

The extraordinary absence of theoretical controversy is the most striking aspect of the whole conference. With the possible exception of some of the material in Fodor's paper, there were no signs of the abrasive confrontation of theories that has been the major feature of so many recent conferences in psycholinguistics. Fodor's paper, which stands almost alone in this conference because of its concern with testing the adequacy of a theory, has the melancholy effect of saying that the only well developed grammatical theory available does not seem to provide an empirically satisfying model for what occurs mentally when people interpret sentences. While Fodor is concerned with basic theoretical issues, his results are, in the main, rather discouraging.

The theoretical blandness of this conference can be attributed to several sources. It can be argued that the conflict we have come to expect in psycholinguistics is over, at least for a period of time. Nearly everyone in psycholinguistics accepts at least some of the important aspects of generative theory, particularly those aspects which have methodological consequences. Furthermore, this conference is about perception and not learning. The topic that was the central concern of many conferences in the past was learning. Students of perception, for reasons intrinsic to the subject matter and to the traditions of perceptual theory, find it easier to adjust to the nativistic, dogmatic, and rationalistic aspects of generative theory than students of learning.

Most of the papers presented at this conference were either almost totally neutral concerning theory or took the major outlines of linguistic theory of the past fifteen-years — both generative theory and distinctive feature theory — more or less for granted. It is to be noted, however, that the acceptance of either theory is seldom complete. Martin, for example, seems to accept the main outlines of generative theory in his interpretation of what happens in his investigations of pauses in speech, but he uses a grammatical analysis (basically, a division into function and content words) that did not arise in generative theory and applies that analysis in a way which ignores the sophisticated results of generative theory and contradicts its general methodological stance. His decision, I think, renders his experiments less incisive than they might have been.

The conference has a surprisingly practical bent. That bent was not so much revealed in the research reported, which was largely "pure" research, as in the origin of the problems under study.

Reading, compressed speech, and clinical disorders all provided problems for investigation. The research reported was not, in general, designed to test hypotheses derived from theory, but to test hypotheses about functions derived from practical considerations, hypotheses which often assumed but did not directly test, theoretical propositions. Perhaps Stevens's work on the perception of phonetic elements is an exception to this characteristic, though even his work can be regarded as a search for how it is possible for speech elements to be perceived, having assumed that speech consists of the application of some categorical structures to acoustic continua.

This de-emphasis of theory in the study of the perception of language and speech is healthy. We don't need tests of theoretical propositions in this area of psycholinguistics as much as we need studies aimed at telling us what the problems are. If I have any general criticism to direct against those studies that arise out of practical situations — such as the study of reading — it is that they are not clearly enough directed towards delineating the problems needing research. What is it we need to assume occurs in reading? Surely, some kind of interpretation is part of the task. Also, few doubt that there is recognition of and assimilation to discrete categories of the characters in written language. Can, therefore, the basic problem of reading be described as a problem of accounting for the detection of perceptual invariants of a certain kind of visually displayed material and the interpretation of the text in that material? Or, does the recognition of written characters transcend, as apparently the recognition of speech signals does, any invariants that might reasonably be said to exist in the pattern of stimuli? Is interpretation linguistic and linguistic alone, or does it call upon paralinguistic devices, perhaps something like images, in the sense that David Hume described images. While there were interesting problems of a particular kind under investigation in the various papers and discussions presented, I think that I was disappointed in the failure to face head on the more central issues, issues that do not arise out of theory or a tradition of empirical research but simply out of an attempt to characterize the nature of the problems in the perception of language.

TECHNIQUE VS. PROBLEM

Several of the papers presented at this conference were reports of the empirical exploration of techniques of investigation. Foulke's study of time compressed speech clearly belongs in this category as does Levin and Kaplan's study of the eye-voice span in reading aloud. Less obviously but surely in some aspects at least, Maccoby's study of selective listening in children and the Condon and Ogston study of speech and body motion synchrony fall into this category. There is a certain logic in the dogged exploration of the abilities of a tool. But this exploration is inevitably tangential to the essential psychological problem, which is the exploration of the abilities of people. Research designed to tell us what the Stanford-Binet test will predict is useful, but it will never lead us to characterize the nature of intelligence, nor, for that matter, to discover new and more powerful tests.

Foulke's basic practical problem is to find some way, if one exists, of mimicking the rapid processing of information possible with visual reading. To that end, he is exploring time-compressed speech. There is a certain sense to the exploration of that tool, but I think we know already that it cannot succeed in producing the full range of the temporal relations possible in visual reading. We know that it cannot succeed because there is only an incomplete analogy between the processing of information in the visual and auditory senses. Vision is essentially a spatial sense. Its temporal resolving powers are poor. The combination of its spatial representation and its poor temporal resolution makes possible scanning via saccadic movements. Hence, a vast amount of information can be stored in print, and can be scanned by the eye in a variety of ways and at a variety of rates. The ear has a high capacity to perform temporal resolutions, but it has acquired this ability at the expense of not being able to perform anything like the eye's scanning. Its spatial representation, as a matter of fact, has been converted to temporal resolution in the form of pitch discrimination.

A serious and systematic exploration of the abstract differences between the eye and the ear might suggest devices other than time-compressed speech for mimicking reading. If, for example, scanning is so important, perhaps a variable speed tape recorder, with all of its attendant nuisance of change in pitch, annoying transients, and difficulty of motor control, might provide a better analogy to reading than time compressed speech.

In a different way, I think that the work reported by Condon and Ogston is handicapped by their devotion to a single technique. In the discussion of this paper I detected a certain disinterest in speech and body motion synchrony on the part of many people at the conference. I want to record a vigorous dissent from this disinterest. Such synchrony, if it exists, is an important discovery that has a chance not only to illuminate certain aspects of the nature of speech but also to help us understand the psychophysiology of language and speech. However, the emphasis of Condon and Ogston upon the technique of analyzing slow sound motion picture recordings may lead us to miss the essential problem. The essential problem, as I think Lenneberg points out, is psychophysiological. The technique is only interesting insofar as it tells us something about the physiological processes responsible for the synchrony.

Furthermore, reliance of Condon and Ogston on the coding of sound and motion picture records produces an unconvincing case. They need to do a genuine experiment — that is to say, vary their technique. They should compare synchronous sound-visual records with non-synchronous records. They need to show us that the synchrony is actually there. They need to place some stress tests upon their subjects, tests aimed at deliberately disrupting synchrony. Finally, they need to introduce some carefully controlled variations into their fascinating social interaction situations. One could imagine, for example, that a dynamogenic effect of anxiety and tension might reveal itself. Only in this way will they manage to convince many people, not only of the genuineness of their phenomenon, but of its relevance for speech and other problems.

Levin and Kaplan's study of the eye-voice span suffers from much the same limitation. That is to say, a skeptic can doubt its validity. The measurement of the eye-voice span demands a kind of reading that, as Kolers points out, is distinctly not "normal." Levin and Kaplan want to find out, among other things, what kind of linguistic chunks can be processed in a single psychological unit in reading. (I deliberately avoided using the term fixation, since I think the problem is more complicated than that of a simple fixation limitation.) Levin and Kaplan have excellent tools for linguistic analysis at their disposal, and I think that their essential strategy has been to pit these against their experimental measurement of the eye voice span. Despite the fact that these investigations fit into a broad spectrum of work being done on reading at Cornell University, I think that they suffer from a narrow experimental analysis. We are reaching the point in research on reading at which we need to ask really serious questions. What is reading for? What is the end product of reading? We often try to judge the efficiency of reading by comprehension tests of various sorts, but we are aware that these tests are among the least sophisticated in the repertory of tests. The reason the tests are so unsatisfactory is that we really do not know what reading accomplishes.

Here we return to my first theme, the absence of theory. What we need is an explicit theory of the psychological processes that occur in understanding and interpretation. We assume that something we label as "understanding" occurs in reading, and it ought to be terribly important to research on reading to know what understanding is, to be able to characterize it. We know that the end of reading is not an analysis of the surface structure of the sentences we read. In fact, Koler's cases of extremely rapid reading suggest that at least some of the time, it is impossible for any analysis of the surface structure to occur. I am skeptical about what information is processed in extremely rapid reading (rates in the thousands of words per minute), but there is no doubt that there is understanding and interpretation at these rates. If paralinguistic processes are not involved in understanding at extremely rapid rates, at least the ordinary linguistic processes must be modified in some way (as, indeed, they seem to be in many psychological processes — free association, for example). These are all matters that are central to the investigation of meaning, and they must enter into the evaluation of the success of any particular technique — such as the eye-voice-span — as a tool of investigation.

LINGUISTIC AND NONLINGUISTIC SKILLS

The one feature of this conference about which there seemed to be high agreement and which I found to be truly disturbing was the repeated, usually latent, implication that the structure of linguistic skills is unrelated to other cognitive skills. The notion is implicit in almost all of the papers, but it takes a particularly important form in the papers by Fodor and Shankweiler. Fodor comes the closest of any of the participants in the conference to making an explicit statement that linguistic and nonlinguistic skills are independent, though the implications of Shankweiler's empirical data appear, at least on the surface, to urge us in that direction more strongly than any other. I shall comment on Fodor's position first and then turn to an account of the implications of Shankweiler's data and some of the puzzles they produce.

I have always considered the greatest psychological significance of generative theory to be its provision of an explicit and consistent characterization of the kinds of things for which any theory of linguistic competence must account. Considerably less important, I have always thought, is generative theory as a theory about the processing device in the head. In fact, I had always thought that we took generative theory seriously in this situation only because of the absence of a serious competitor. There seem to be too many important facts (to use "facts" in a sense favored by generative theorists) that are inconsistent with the direct psychological application of generative theory in its particular sense. There is, for example, the intuitively compelling countercase made by the place of adjectives in the theory. Adjectives require a complicated derivation from some underlying structures in generative theory, and yet their use in test sentences does not seem to reveal such a derivation. Furthermore, adjectives seem to have a kind of fundamental psychological simplicity about them (at least English adjectives do) that makes one unhappy about their derived status in generative theory.

From the beginning, there have been empirical examinations of the adequacy of generative theory as a model of intellectual linguistic processes. There is, of course, nothing inherently wrong with such a use of generative theory; it is only, as Fodor points out, that there does not seem to be any strong evidence that the mind works this way. In short, there doesn't seem to be anything really compelling about the conclusions one arrives at by applying transformation theory to tests which examine how people operate upon the grammatical structure of sentences. That is not what I am concerned about here, however. I am disturbed by the use of generative theory as a psychological theory, because linguistic operations always seem to call upon, in their specific examples, other operations. Various propositional algebras are required to specify the logical patterns of inferences which must constitute in some sense the underlying (deep) structure of extended discourse in a language. Answers to questions, paraphrasing, selecting alternatives for ambiguous constructions, all require the application of various complicated logical operations. Furthermore, my colleague, DeSoto, has published a long and I think important series of studies demonstrating that people refer many reasoning problems to a kind of spatial computing model for generating logical (or, as DeSoto prefers) paralogical relations among terms. There is no point in regarding arithmetic or any other formal algebra as a model of what goes on in people's heads when they are required to solve particular problems, though they clearly provide models of competencies of various sorts, competencies, which like linguistic ones, are possessed by different people in varying degrees.

An even more serious problem in separating linguistic from nonlinguistic competence is encountered at the opposite end of the linguistic continuum, and it is here that Shankweiler's paper is relevant. It is now well established that phonemic categorization depends upon the appreciation of the contextual (in some respects, at least, specifically grammatical) characteristics of the speech message. In short, phonemic categorization cannot depend exclusively upon the acoustic signal. The perceptual recognition and production of certain phonemes, as these phonemes are judged to occur in the flow of speech, depend upon their acoustic environments. The assimilation of the initial sound in "cow" and "key" to / k / depends upon linguistic features at some level higher than the phonetic sequence. The recognition of this fact has led to the general methodological reforms that have been instituted in the attempts to arrive at the morphophonemic rules for particular languages. We have abandoned the assumption that phonemes are bundles of acoustic characteristics, some of which remain invariant from occasion to occasion.

However, a disturbing consideration in the attempt to divorce linguistic and nonlinguistic competence is that the same problem applies in other cases, some of which are reactions to acoustic signals and none of which is strictly linguistic. I think, for example, that I can recognize the various noises my dog makes upon the arrival of visitors. These, which I generally characterize as barking, vary enormously from time to time in their acoustic characteristics and temporal distribution. I think that it would be very difficult to find invariants in any segment of the acoustic signals provided by my dog. Yet those signals are clearly recognizable for what they are, and, furthermore, they are rather clearly segmented. Of course, in some sense they are meaningful — they require me to get up and go to the door. But, by no fancy of the imagination can they properly be called linguistic.

It seems reasonable to me to suppose that my recognition of these nonlinguistic acoustic signals is determined by the application of a set of rules to a signal which ascribes to that signal its interpreted characteristics (the familiar bark of my dog). Whether or not this particular example is a good one, I think it is easy to argue that many cases of detection of something that is not represented by any invariant in the perceptual field, may be found in visual and auditory perception. In these cases, the detection of some objects of phenomenal experience requires the application of some set of rules, probably in large measure innate, to an incoming signal or signals. Therefore, in this respect at least, it is difficult to see how language is unique.

The separation of the perceptual aspects of the linguistic signal and of other kinds of acoustic signals is the puzzle provided by the data reviewed for us by Shankweiler. His paper reviewed a set of empirical findings that are astounding to me. That is because these data seem to imply that the devices for processing linguistic and nonlinguistic signals are quite distinct. Therefore, I should like to examine them in some greater detail.

Shankweiler's experiments and the earlier experiments upon which they are built are designed because of the general belief that in man, unlike all the other mammals, there is a laterality of function in the cortex. Speech and language are, in some way not clearly understood, assigned to the left hemisphere (though, of course, the situation is complicated by individual differences and apparent shifts in lateralization of function). In accordance with this laterality (indeed, as evidence for it), is a lot of evidence showing that the right ear (which has a more direct connections with the left hemisphere), can cope more effectively than the left ear with competing speech in dichotic listening. Possibly the reverse effect occurs with melodic acoustic signals, and at the very least the effect of right ear dominance disappears with melodies. Building upon these results, in an elegant series of studies, Shankweiler shows us that right ear dominance fails for vowel sounds but remains for stop consonants, when these acoustic signals are removed from general linguistic contexts. Stop consonants are essentially noisy sounds while vowels are musical. Both of these signals, in isolation, are linguistic only in the most elementary sense. It is not certain, I think, that they would be assimilated to any class of speech sounds when heard outside of the context of the laboratory.

In short, it is not clear whether the right-left ear difference is one of linguistic vs. nonlinguistic signals or one of noisy vs. musical signals. In short, would one find a laterality for some segment of the acoustic signal provided by the bark of a dog? These fascinating experiments on laterality in dichotic stimulation lack some critical comparisons, comparisons which must be performed before they are completely convincing on the points for which they are evidently intended. As things stand now, I think that these observations provide deep puzzles about the borderline between linguistic and nonlinguistic events. This is a borderline which invites investigation both at the perceptual and at the conceptual (cognitive) level.

CONCLUDING REMARKS

We have evidently reached the point in the development of psycholinguistics during which relatively quiet gathering of empirical data in the light of generative theory and distinctive feature theory will be the prevailing mode. Certain rumblings, faint though they may be, disturb the calm. I think that there is no place at which the premonitions of impending difficulties are stronger than on the borderline between linguistic and nonlinguistic events. It is the discovery of disturbing, unassimilable facts that is most important in this respect. That is why the data provided by Fodor and by Shankweiler, in their different contexts, are so important and interesting. Condon and Ogston provide us with an intriguing problem, and it is conceivable that this problem could also have a bearing upon the problem of resolving the linguistic-nonlinguistic relation. Perhaps, in the investigation of reading, placing studies of visual perception of linguistic material in the broader context of the study of visual perception generally, may have a similar bearing. These are all things which forecast the greatest importance for the issues at stake in the various papers presented at this conference.

AUTHOR INDEX

SUBJECT INDEX